Choosing the Better Part?

Women in the Gospel of Luke

Barbara E. Reid

A Michael Glazier Book
THE LITURGICAL PRESS
Collegeville, Minnesota

A Michael Glazier Book published by The Liturgical Press.

Cover design by David Manahan, O.S.B. Jan Vermeer, "Christ in the House of Martha and Mary," c. 1654–1656. National Gallery of Scotland, Edinburgh, Scotland. Courtesy of: Bridgeman/Art Resource, NY.

6   7   8

Library of Congress Cataloging-in-Publication Data

Reid, Barbara E.
    Choosing the better part? : women in the Gospel of Luke / Barbara E. Reid.
        p.   cm.
    Includes bibliographical references and indexes.
    ISBN 0-8146-5494-0
    1. Women in the Bible. 2. Bible. N.T. Luke—Criticism, interpretation, etc.   I. Title.
    BS2595.6.W65   1996
    226.4'083054—dc20   95-47162
                                                          CIP

To
Feminist Christian Women and Men
Committed to Building a Church
of Equal Disciples

Contents

Abbreviations

AAR	American Academy of Religion
AB	Anchor Bible
ANEP	*Ancient Near East in Pictures*
BA	*Biblical Archaeologist*
BAGD	W. Bauer, W. F. Arndt, F. W. Gingrich, and F. W. Danker, *Greek-English Lexicon of the NT*
BAR	*Biblical Archaeology Review*
B.C.E.	Before the Christian Era
BETL	Bibliotheca ephemeridum theologicarum lovaniensium
Bib	*Biblica*
BibRev	*Bible Review*
BibSac	*Bibliotheca Sacra*
BTB	*Biblical Theology Bulletin*
C.E.	Christian Era
CurTM	*Currents in Theology and Mission*
CBQ	*Catholic Biblical Quarterly*
ConcJ	*Concordia Journal*
DRev	*Downside Review*
EspVie	*Esprit et Vie*
ETL	*Ephimerides theologicae lovanienses*
EvQ	*Evangelical Quarterly*
ExpTim	*Expository Times*
FoiVie	*Foi et Vie*
HeyJ	*Heythrop Journal*
HTR	*Harvard Theological Review*
HTS	*Harvard Theological Studies*
IBS	*Irish Biblical Studies*

ICC	International Critical Commentary
IDB	*Interpreter's Dictionary of the Bible*
Int	*Interpretation*
JBL	*Journal of Biblical Literature*
JFSR	*Journal of Feminist Studies in Religion*
JNES	*Journal of Near Eastern Studies*
JSNT	*Journal for the Study of the New Testament*
JSNTSup	JSNT—Supplement Series
JSOT	*Journal for the Study of the Old Testament*
JTS	*Journal of Theological Studies*
LQ	*Lutheran Quarterly*
LumVie	*Lumière et vie*
LXX	Septuagint (Greek translation of the Hebrew OT)
MillStud	*Milltown Studies*
NAB	*New American Bible*
NIGTC	New International Greek Testament Commentary
NJB	*New Jerusalem Bible*
NJBC	*New Jerome Biblical Commentary*
	(Ed. R. E. Brown et al.)
NovT	*Novum Testamentum*
NRSV	*New Revised Standard Version*
NT	New Testament
NTMS	New Testament Message Series
NTR	*New Theology Review*
NTS	*New Testament Studies*
NTTS	New Testament Tools and Studies
OT	Old Testament
RB	*Revue Biblique*
Rel & Int Life	*Religion and Intellectual Life*
RSRev	*Religious Studies Review*
RTL	*Revue théologique de Louvain*
SBL	Society of Biblical Literature
SBLDS	Society of Biblical Literature Dissertation Series
SBLMS	Society of Biblical Literature Monograph Series
SJT	*Scottish Journal of Theology*
SLJT	*Saint Luke Journal of Theology*
SNTSMS	Society for New Testament Studies Monograph Series
SpToday	*Spirituality Today*
TBT	*The Bible Today*
TD	*Theology Digest*

TDNT	*Theological Dictionary of the New Testament*
THKNT	Theologischer Handkommentar zum Neuen Testament
TS	*Theological Studies*
TToday	*Theology Today*
TynB	*Tyndale Bulletin*
USQR	*Union Seminary Quarterly Review*
VT	*Vetus Testamentum*
ZNW	*Zeitschrift für die neutestamentliche Wissenschaft*

Preface

My own journey in coming to feminist consciousness and committing myself to work toward building a Church of equal disciples began over twenty years ago. It has been a painful process, at times, when sexism is so deeply ingrained in our culture and Church. It has also been a process of great joy and hope, as women and men become increasingly aware of the sinful effects of patriarchy and become committed to constructing communities that more fully embody Christ's inclusivity.

There have been countless persons who have led and accompanied me on this journey. I would particularly like to thank my Grand Rapids Dominican Sisters, whose commitment to equality for women in Church and society has inspired and sustained me over the last two decades. I am also grateful to those with whom I first ministered in the Diocese of Saginaw: Fr. Don Christensen, Fr. Jim Heller, Fr. Bert Gohm, Sr. Maryellen McDonald, O.P., Sr. Margaret Hillary, O.P., and Sr. Carmelita Switzer, O.P. They were the first to model collaborative ministry for me and continue to be a mainstay of support for me.

I am grateful as well to my colleagues at Catholic Theological Union in Chicago who work tirelessly to educate ministers for the global Church who are committed to equality and inclusivity in all ways. I am especially indebted to my colleagues in the Department of Biblical Languages and Literature: Dianne Bergant, C.S.A.; Barbara Bowe, R.S.C.J.; Leslie Hoppe, O.F.M.; Timothy Lenchak, S.V.D.; Carolyn Osiek, R.S.C.J.; Rabbi Hayim Perelmuter; Marianne Race, C.S.J.; Donald Senior, C.P.; and Carroll Stuhlmueller, C.P. (R.I.P.). I am most grateful to my colleague Steve Bevans, S.V.D., who team-taught with me a seminar on Feminist Hermeneutics in Bible and Theology in the winter of 1995. Steve's insights from the perspective of Systematic Theology and his commitment to collaboration helped to put flesh and bones on this feminist endeavor.

I would also like to thank the students who explored Women in the Gospel of Luke with me in several seminars from 1994–1995. Their insights and experiences helped refine many of the interpretations in this book. I am especially grateful to Laurie Brink, O.P., for her secretarial and research assistance.

I want to express my gratitude to the administration of Catholic Theological Union for granting me a one quarter study leave in 1993 to begin research for this book. I am indebted to The Helen and Omar Osiek Faculty Development Fund and to the Catholic Biblical Association of America Young Scholars Fellowship Program, which provided the financial resources that made this study leave possible.

It is my hope that these reflections on the women in the Gospel of Luke will be of help, particularly to preachers, teachers, religious educators, students of the Bible, and all who ponder the Word. By considering both the pitfalls and the liberative possibilities of these stories from a feminist perspective, my aim is to assist the reader in knowing how to "choose the better part" toward equality and inclusivity.

Chapter 1

Choosing the Better Part:
Methodological Choices

CHOOSING THE BETTER PART

In the well-known story of Jesus' visit to the home of Martha and her sister Mary (Luke 10:38-42), the concluding declaration of Jesus would seem to settle once and for all the ideal stance for women disciples. Martha, who serves, is chided, whereas Mary, who sits at Jesus' feet listening to him speak, "has chosen the better part and it will not be taken from her" (10:42). In many ways the conflicts among the characters in this story epitomize the struggles that continue in today's Church over the roles of women. In a world where gender roles have changed drastically from those of first-century Palestine, does the reply found on Jesus' lips still apply? Can it be read in a more liberative way?

This book aims to show that there is more than one way to read the biblical tradition and that it matters vitally *how* one reads. It will examine a number of possible approaches to the texts, and strive to uncover their presuppositions and their consequences. Biblical interpretation and its relation to life involves making choices. It is my hope that this book will help both women and men, particularly those who preach and teach the Scriptures, to do so in a way that will promote a Church of equal disciples, where gender differences would no longer determine ministerial roles. This would be today's way of "choosing the better part."

1

LUKE AND WOMEN

This study focuses on stories from the Gospel of Luke in which women characters figure. One reason for concentrating on the Third Gospel is that it contains more stories about women than any other. Only in Luke do we find the stories of Elizabeth (1:5-7, 24-25, 39-45, 57-66); Mary (1:26-56; 2:1-52; Acts 1:14); Anna (2:36-38); the widow of Nain (7:11-17); the woman who showed great love (7:36-50); Mary Magdalene, Joanna, Susanna, and the other Galilean women who minister (8:1-3); Martha serving and Mary listening (10:38-42); the woman bent double (13:10-17); the woman who searches for a lost coin (15:8-10); the widow demanding justice (18:1-8); and the women of Jerusalem lamenting Jesus on the way of the cross (23:26-32). In addition Luke shares with Mark and Matthew the stories featuring: Simon's mother-in-law (4:38-39); Jairus' daughter and the woman with a hemorrhage (8:40-56); a woman baking bread (13:20-21); a widow who gives her all (Luke 21:1-4); the Galilean women who witness Jesus' death and burial (23:49, 55-56) and who discover the empty tomb (24:1-12).

Only Luke, in his second volume, gives us the traditions about the women disciples in the upper room (Acts 1:14); Sapphira (5:1-11); the slave girl of Philippi (16:16-24); Tabitha (9:36-43); Lydia (16:13-15, 40); Damaris (17:34); Priscilla (18:2, 18, 26); and Philip's four daughters who were prophets (21:8-11).

It is the abundance of stories involving women that has led commentators such as Alfred Plummer to remark, "the Third Gospel is in an especial sense the Gospel for *women* . . . all through this Gospel they are allowed a prominent place, and many types of womanhood are placed before us."[1] In addition, Luke's construction of parallel pairs of stories of men and women has created the popular notion that Luke regards women and men as equals. Robert O'Toole, for example, asserts, "Men and women receive the same salvific benefits. God, Christ, and the disciples act in their lives in similar fashion. Women and men have similar ex-

---

[1] Alfred Plummer, *The Gospel According to S. Luke,* 5th ed. ICC. (Edinburgh: T. & T. Clark, 1981) xlii–xliii. See Robert J. Karris, "Women and Discipleship in Luke," *CBQ* 56 (1994) 2, n. 4, for a list of scholars who hold that Luke had a favorable view of women.

periences and fulfill similar functions. They believe and proclaim the gospel message."[2]

Recent feminist interpreters have noted, however, that Luke's portrait of women is ambiguous[3] at best, and dangerous at worst.[4] Elisabeth Schüssler Fiorenza was one of the first to show that although Luke knows of women prophets, leaders, and missionaries, he does not portray them as such in his narratives.[5] Mary Rose D'Angelo has examined the prophetic ministry in Luke and has found his purpose is to restrict and control women: beyond the infancy narratives, where "women prophets belong to the exotic biblical past,"[6] no woman speaks except to be corrected by Jesus.[7] Women are beneficiaries of Jesus' ministry and engage in charitable works, but are seen to have "chosen the better part" when they remain silent and receptive (10:42). Jane Schaberg demonstrates that in Luke "women are included in Jesus' entourage and table community, but not as the equals of men."[8] Luke "shows only the men empowered to speak and act and bear responsibility within the movement."[9]

These scholars rightly alert the modern reader to the danger of too simply exalting Luke as a "friend of women." Although it is indisputable that there are women disciples in Luke and Acts, a closer study reveals that they do not participate in the mission of Jesus in the same way that the men disciples do. If we are looking to Luke's narrative to show that women and men shared equally in Jesus' mission in the first century, we will be disap-

---

[2]Robert F. O'Toole, *The Unity of Luke's Theology: An Analysis of Luke-Acts,* Good News Studies, vol. 9 (Wilmington: Glazier, 1984) 120. See p. 119 for his list of paired stories in Luke and Acts.

[3]Mary Rose D'Angelo, "Women in Luke-Acts: A Redactional View," *JBL* 109/3 (1990) 441–461; Turid Karlsen Seim, *The Double Message: Patterns of Gender in Luke-Acts* (Nashville: Abingdon, 1994).

[4]Jane Schaberg, "Luke," *The Women's Bible Commentary,* ed. Carol A. Newsom and Sharon H. Ringe (Louisville: Westminster/John Knox, 1992) 275–292.

[5]Elisabeth Schüssler Fiorenza, *In Memory of Her: A Feminist Theological Reconstruction of Christian Origins* (New York: Crossroad, 1983) 50.

[6]D'Angelo, "Women in Luke-Acts," 460.

[7]Ibid., 452. See Luke 10:41-42; 11:27-28; 23:28.

[8]Schaberg, "Luke," 291.

[9]Ibid., 281.

pointed. In order for this gospel to reveal God's liberating word to a Church of equal disciples, a process of recontextualization and reinterpretation is needed that engages the following tools of modern biblical criticism.[10]

HISTORICAL CRITICISM

The underlying principle of historical criticism is that an ancient text must first be understood in its original context before it can be engaged as a dialogue partner for our own day. This entails textual criticism: an analysis of the variants in the Greek manuscripts so as to determine which reading is most likely to have been the original.[11] It also involves a study of the sources used by the author, how these have been redacted, what has been composed, added, deleted, and changed. From this type of analysis scholars attempt to understand the author's purpose and theology.

Historical criticism also tries to separate "what really happened" from the accretions of decades of oral tradition and the redactional alterations of the evangelist. It recognizes that the text we now have has gone through a long process of formation. It attends to how the text has been shaped by the preaching of the early Church and filtered through the lenses of those who passed on the traditions.

SOCIAL STUDY

A related method that has developed in recent years is social study of the New Testament.[12] This area of study engages bibli-

---

[10]For further detail see Daniel J. Harrington, *Interpreting the New Testament: A Practical Guide,* NTMS, vol. 1 (Wilmington: Glazier, 1979); Terrence Keegan, *Interpreting the Bible: A Popular Introduction to Biblical Hermeneutics* (New York: Paulist Press, 1985).

[11]We do not have the original manuscripts of any of the books of the New Testament. The oldest text of Luke is a portion of the gospel preserved on a papyrus manuscript, P[75], which dates to the beginning of the third century C.E. The earliest complete text of the Gospel dates to the fourth century C.E.

[12]See Carolyn Osiek, *What Are They Saying About the Social Setting of the New Testament?,* 2d ed. (New York: Paulist Press, 1992) and "The Social Sciences and the Second Testament: Problems and Challenges," *BTB* 22

cal scholars, experts in social science, classicists, and ancient historians, who collaborate to reconstruct the history and the economic, social, and political life of Greek and Roman civilizations of the first centuries before and after Christ. They use art, contemporary literature, inscriptions, coins, and the findings of archaeological excavations to gain knowledge of the institutions, social dynamics, and horizons of consciousness of people who lived at the time of the beginning of the Jesus movement.

LITERARY CRITICISM

Literary criticism attends to such questions as the literary form and function of a passage. It considers the context and structure of individual literary units as well as that of the overall work. It analyzes words, images, symbols, and their range of meanings. It looks to parallels in contemporary literature for further clues to meaning.

NARRATIVE CRITICISM

A relatively new branch of literary criticism is narrative study of the Gospels.[13] This method focuses on the form of the text as we have it, not on its process of composition or the layers of tra-

---

(1992) 88–95; Bruce J. Malina and Richard L. Rohrbaugh, *Social-Science Commentary on the Synoptic Gospels* (Minneapolis: Fortress Press, 1992). An important work that applies the method to Luke and Acts is Jerome H. Neyrey, ed., *The Social World of Luke-Acts: Models for Interpretation* (Peabody, Mass.: Hendrickson, 1991).

[13]See Mark A. Powell, *What is Narrative Criticism?*, Guides to Biblical Scholarship (Philadelphia: Fortress Press, 1990). Works that use this approach with the Third Gospel include: Mark Coleridge, *The Birth of the Lukan Narrative: Narrative as Christology in Luke 1-2*, JSNTSup 88 (Sheffield: JSOT, 1993); John A. Darr, *On Character Building: The Reader and the Rhetoric of Characterization in Luke-Acts*, Literary Currents in Biblical Interpretation (Louisville: Westminster/John Knox, 1992); James M. Dawsey, *The Lukan Voice: Confusion and Irony in the Gospel of Luke* (Macon: Mercer University Press, 1986); Jack Dean Kingsbury, *Conflict in Luke: Jesus, Authorities, Disciples* (Minneapolis: Fortress Press, 1991); William S. Kurz, *Reading Luke-Acts: Dynamics of Biblical Narrative* (Louisville: Westminster/John Knox, 1993); Steven M. Sheeley, *Narrative Asides in Luke-Acts,*

dition. Its goal is to understand how the story is told in terms of its plot, character development, point of view, narrative patterns, events, and settings. Narrative criticism alerts the reader to how the text communicates and the ways in which the author shapes the auditor's reaction to the discourse.

Narrative criticism attends to how the reader's response is conditioned by one's cultural context. Our own reactions, like those of the reader in antiquity, are determined by factors like gender, class, social setting, education, age, vocation, and ideological orientation.[14] Reaction to a narrative is further colored by one's individual experience within the wider culture.

In recent years attention has been paid to how the gender of the author and that of the reader affect the manner in which the message is conveyed and received.[15] It is important to be aware that men and women may read the same text differently. As applied to Luke, this method reminds us that the third evangelist writes from a male perspective and that his text has power to structure our experience. Today's readers of Luke must ask whether it will be necessary to consciously read against the evangelist's intent rather than be persuaded to adopt his perspective. When Luke's rhetoric eclipses women and reinforces silent, passive roles, then ''choosing the better part'' is to read the text against the grain.[16]

JSNTSup 72 (Sheffield: JSOT, 1992); Charles H. Talbert, *Literary Patterns, Theological Themes and the Genre of Luke-Acts,* SBLMS 20 (Missoula: Scholars Press, 1974); *Reading Luke: A Literary and Theological Commentary on the Third Gospel* (New York: Crossroad, 1982); Robert C. Tannehill, *The Narrative Unity of Luke-Acts: A Literary Interpretation,* 2 vols. (Foundations and Facets: New Testament; Philadelphia: Fortress Press, 1986, 1990).

[14]Darr, *On Character Building,* 25.

[15]See Elizabeth A. Flynn and Patrocinio P. Schweickart, eds., *Gender and Reading: Essays on Readers, Texts, and Contexts* (Baltimore and London: Johns Hopkins University Press, 1986).

[16]Schaberg, "Luke," 281; Elisabeth Schüssler Fiorenza, *But She Said: Feminist Practices of Biblical Interpretation* (Boston: Beacon, 1992) 35–37, 215. See also Patrocinio Schweickart, "Reading Ourselves: Toward a Feminist Theory of Reading," *Gender and Reading* (Baltimore: Johns Hopkins University Press, 1986) 31–62; Judith Fetterley, *The Resisting Reader: A Feminist Approach to American Fiction* (Bloomington & London: Indiana University Press, 1978).

FEMINIST BIBLICAL INTERPRETATION

Feminist methods of biblical interpretation have arisen from the experiences of women who have come to realize that the Bible has not always been used to bring them fullness of life. There has been a dawning awareness that the Scriptures have been used to legitimate patriarchy and violence toward women. Before describing feminist methods of biblical interpretation, a definition of terms is needed.

Patriarchy is "any system, organization, or institution in which the men own, administer, shape, or control a major portion of all the facets of society."[17] The world of Jesus was a patriarchal world, as is our own, although that is beginning to change. Feminism, as a response to patriarchy, is "a commitment to the humanity, dignity, and equality of all persons to such a degree that one is willing to work for changes in structures and in relationship patterns so that these occur to the equal good of all."[18] By this definition, feminism does not advocate replacing male domination with female domination. Rather, it works for the liberation of all. Feminism does not deny the differences between the sexes; but differences are recognized precisely as differences, not as indicators of inferiority or superiority.

As applied to the faith community, feminism advocates a community of equals that provides full opportunity for all the members, women and men alike, to use their God-given gifts to the benefit of all. Christian feminists are women and men committed to eliminating sexism in their relations with one another and in the structures of their faith communities and in society. They see this as a work of justice that is truly faithful to the teaching and life of Jesus.

---

[17] Joan Chittister, "Yesterday's Dangerous Vision: Christian Feminism in the Catholic Church," *Sojourners* (July 1987) 18. Elisabeth Schüssler Fiorenza (*But She Said,* 8; *Jesus. Miriam's Child, Sophia's Prophet* [New York: Continuum, 1994, 14] redefines patriarchy, recognizing that it involves not only the rule of men over women, but "a complex social pyramid of graduated dominations and subordinations" (*Miriam's Child,* 14). She uses "Kyriarchy" to express the rule of the emperor/master/lord/father/husband over his subordinates, which include not only women but disadvantaged men.

[18] Chittister, "Dangerous Vision," 18.

New methods of feminist interpretation have developed in the last decades.[19] The approaches are diverse and yield varying results. One approach is to reject the biblical tradition as so thoroughly sexist that it is irredeemable for women. At the opposite end of the spectrum is the stance that Scripture cannot be oppressive; if it is perceived to be so, the fault is with the interpretation, not the text. From this point of view, the task of feminist interpretation is simply to find the interpretation that will be liberative. Another approach is to focus on feminine symbols in the Bible and to exalt these over those that are masculine. Still another method is to try to separate out the underlying liberating message of the Bible from its patriarchal context.

A LIBERATIONIST APPROACH

I consider a liberationist approach to be the most helpful. This method begins with the conviction that the central message of the Bible is that God sides with the poor and oppressed and liberates them, not only in the hereafter, but incipiently here and now. From a feminist liberation perspective, whatever "denies, diminishes, or distorts the full humanity of women" is not of God; "what does promote the full humanity of women is of the holy."[20] For liberationists, the task is not simply to reinterpret biblical texts within their patriarchal framework, but to dismantle the patriarchal structure itself and replace it with an alternate vision.[21] This involves conversion[22] of individuals and communities as well as the transformation of social, political, economic, and ecclesial structures.

[19]For surveys of various approaches to feminist hermeneutics see Elizabeth Johnson, "Feminist Hermeneutics," *Chicago Studies* 27 (1988) 123–135; Carolyn Osiek, "The Feminist and the Bible: Hermeneutical Alternatives," *Feminist Perspectives on Biblical Scholarship* (Chico, Calif.: Scholars Press, 1985) 93–105; Schüssler Fiorenza, *But She Said,* 20–50.

[20]Rosemary Radford Ruether, *Sexism and God-Talk: Toward a Feminist Theology* (Boston: Beacon, 1983) 18–19.

[21]Letty Russell (*Human Liberation in a Feminist Perspective* [Philadelphia: Fortress Press, 1974]) is one of the earliest to articulate this perspective.

[22]See Carolyn Osiek, *Beyond Anger: On Being a Feminist in the Church* (New York: Paulist Press, 1986).

An advantage of this method is that it addresses the root cause of women's oppression: patriarchy. But in doing so it avoids the dualism of some approaches that pit women and men against one another. Furthermore, it does not reject the biblical tradition, but neither does it allow for its too easy rehabilitation. It recognizes that the Bible has been both the source of oppression and the source of power for women,[23] and gives the means for it to be the latter.

A HERMENEUTICS OF SUSPICION

Elisabeth Schüssler Fiorenza offers a four-fold procedure for a feminist liberationist method.[24] The first step is to apply to the text a Hermeneutics of Suspicion. The term "hermeneutics" refers to the study of the methodological principles of interpretation. A hermeneutics of suspicion recognizes that the biblical texts and their interpretations through the centuries have been written, for the most part, by men, for men, and about men, and that they serve the interests of patriarchy. One who reads with a hermeneutics of suspicion is wary that the text can be oppressive for women. This does not deny the inspiration of Scripture, but recognizes the limitations of the human authors who set forth God's word.

A HERMENEUTICS OF PROCLAMATION

The second movement is a Hermeneutics of Proclamation. This aspect draws attention to the fact that the biblical writings do not tell us what Jesus really did and said, but rather record how the tradition was understood by the men who shaped it, both in the decades of early Christian preaching and in the formation of the written traditions. A hermeneutics of proclamation assesses the

[23]Schüssler Fiorenza, *In Memory of Her*, 35.

[24]See her groundbreaking works *In Memory of Her*; *Bread Not Stone: The Challenge of Feminist Biblical Interpretation* (Boston: Beacon, 1984); and the recent two-volume work edited by her that provides a feminist introduction and commentary: *Searching the Scriptures*, 2 vols. (New York: Crossroad, 1993, 1994).

Bible's power to continue to shape the faith community and advocates that texts that promote sexism or patriarchy no longer be proclaimed in the worship assembly.[25]

A HERMENEUTICS OF REMEMBRANCE

A Hermeneutics of Remembrance reclaims the struggles of women of past decades and attempts to reconstruct their history. It is conscious that the canonical Scriptures relate only part of the experience of the early Church. It searches for clues and allusions that indicate the reality of women's experience about which the text is silent. Retrieving this subversive memory places women in the center of the biblical community and the theological endeavor, not as appendages to men's religious history. Thus women's history can be integrated into the mainstream of biblical history, both past and future.

A HERMENEUTICS OF RITUALIZATION AND CELEBRATION

Finally, a Hermeneutics of Ritualization and Celebration recognizes the importance of creative expression of the active part women play in the ongoing biblical story. It engages in literary originality in retelling the biblical stories from a feminist perspective. It calls for the artistic use of music, dance, and all the creative arts to liberate the imagination from the confines of a patriarchal worldview. It celebrates a new vision of women and men equally created in God's image, equally redeemed by Christ, equally called to be disciples, equally entrusted with Christ's mission, and equally endowed with the Spirit.[26]

---

[25]Alternatively, if texts that are abusive toward women are proclaimed, it is in *memoria passionis,* and with the resolve that such will never again be promulgated as God's will. See Phyllis Trible, *Texts of Terror* (Philadelphia: Fortress Press, 1984).

[26]See also the ten strategies outlined in chapter one of Schüssler Fiorenza, *But She Said,* 20–50.

LIMITS

Each of the methods described above will be engaged to some degree in this book. Each provides a different key to the meaning of the biblical text. None by itself gives the full picture, and each has its limitations. Historical methods are limited by the nature of the sources. Our sources are partial and incomplete. For example, ancient literature and inscriptions often preserve what is exceptional, not typical. Archaeological excavations tend to focus on monumental remains, which do not unearth as much information about daily life of ordinary people.

In addition, biblical texts were written for the purpose of building up the faith of believing communities. They did not intend to report history (in the modern sense of the word), nor did they aim to leave a record of the social, economic, and political life of the time. So when we make conclusions about these aspects, they are based on clues in the text and partial evidence from other sources.

Another limitation involves drawing inferences about an author's intent when analyzing the author's redactional choices. Such conclusions are necessarily tentative, based on probability, not certainty.[27] With regard to analyses of intricate literary patterns, there is the risk of attributing to the ancient author concerns that are more likely those of the modern interpreter. As for trying to determine how Luke's original audience reacted to his narrative, we must admit that many of the factors that would give us this information are lost to us.

Another caution is that some of the methods (e.g., social science theories and narrative analyses) are modern constructions, not devised specifically for biblical study. There is the question of how well such methods can be applied to ancient texts and societies.

A limitation of this book is that in choosing to analyze only the stories with women characters in Luke, there is not an adequate treatment of the silences and absences of women from the whole of the narrative. Nor is there attention to the sayings, such

---

[27]See, for example, Luke T. Johnson ("On Finding the Lukan Community: A Cautious Cautionary Essay," *SBL Seminar 1979 Papers*, vol. 1 [Missoula: Scholars Press, 1979] 87–100) who illustrates six different possibilities for interpreting Luke's theme of prayer.

as that of the woman who utters a blessing (11:27-28) or Jesus' words to the women of Jerusalem (23:28-31), or to feminine imagery (e.g., 13:34-35) that occurs elsewhere in the Gospel.

In taking a feminist approach, one pitfall can be the tendency to universalize the experience of "women," forgetting that race, class, education, age, and social location are also influential factors. This is true for both ancient and modern women. The treatment of women in antiquity was not uniform; nor is the experience of modern women. I am aware that I write as a white, middle class woman from the U.S.A., born in the early 1950s, a city-dweller, a Roman Catholic vowed woman religious, with advanced education, and a number of experiences of living in other cultures. It is important for each person to identify their own particular social location and experiences that shape the lenses with which they approach the text.

A final caution is that Christian feminists must be wary of fomenting anti-Judaism. In their attempts to show Jesus as a great liberator of women, some Christians wrongly see his treatment of women as totally different from that of other Jews of his day. Jesus was a Jew, and his attitudes toward women should be understood to represent a possibility *within* emerging Judaism, not in total contrast to it.[28]

OLD TEXTS ON NEW QUESTIONS

Modern believers desire to find in the Gospels their preferred response to contemporary questions. But to expect either the earthly Jesus or the evangelist to address new issues directly is to forget the nature of the biblical text. It must also be remembered that the overall intent of the evangelist was to convey the good news of Jesus. His focus was first and foremost on Jesus, not on the women characters. With regard to the question of

[28]See Judith Plaskow, "Feminist Anti-Judaism and the Christian God," *JFSR* 7 (1991) 95–134; "Christian Feminism and Anti-Judaism," *Crosscurrents* 28 (1978) 306–309; "Blaming the Jews for the Birth of Patriarchy," *Nice Jewish Girls,* E. Torton Beck, ed. (Watertown, Mass.: Persephone, 1982) 250–254; Katharina von Kellenbach, *Anti-Judaism in Feminist Religious Writings,* AAR Cultural Criticism Series 1 (Atlanta: Scholars Press, 1994).

women's roles in the Church today, to look to Jesus or Luke to be a feminist,[29] in the modern sense of the word, is anachronistic. This means that when we employ the Gospels in our search for what would be true to Jesus' words and deeds in our own day, we must engage in a process of recontextualization and reinterpretation that involves three key elements.

First, it demands that believers be attuned to the signs of the times, both in their individual experience, as well as in that of the wider Church and society. With such a global consciousness believers are ready to let their horizons expand beyond the way things have always been. A second necessary element is reliance on Scripture and tradition. One must be aware, however, that both of these are subject to interpretation. One of the aims of this book is to explore possible new interpretations of portions of the Lukan text. Finally, we look to the Spirit for guidance throughout the process. What is truly the leading of the Spirit will be confirmed by the prevalence of peace, joy, and fullness of life for all God's people.

An example of this process at work can be found in one of Luke's own writings. In Acts 15 is one version of how the early Church came to resolve new questions surrounding the admission of Gentiles. Some held the position that unless Gentiles were circumcised according to the Mosaic practice, they could not be saved (Acts 15:1). Others, like Paul and Barnabas, disagreed and there was "no little dissension" (Acts 15:2). When the apostles and presbyters met in Jerusalem to resolve the issue, they first listened to testimony from Peter, Paul, and Barnabas, who "described the signs and wonders God had worked among the Gentiles through them" (Acts 15:12). Then James invokes Scripture, quoting Amos 9:11-12 and reinterpreting the prophet's words in a messianic sense (Acts 15:16-18). The outcome, namely, that the Gentiles need not be circumcised, but that they observe some Jewish dietary regulations, is presented as "the decision of the holy Spirit and of us" (Acts 15:28).

And so, I invite the reader to use this book not as the definitive interpretation of the Lukan stories of women, but as an aid in critical biblical study, coupled with reflection on experiences

---

[29]E.g., Leonard Swidler, "Jesus Was a Feminist," *The Catholic World* 212 (1971) 177–183.

of the global community and reliance on the Spirit to "choose the better part" to bring fullness of life for all.

In the following chapters I will first investigate the Lukan portrayal of discipleship and mission. I will show that the Gospel of Luke and Acts of the Apostles depict women's participation in the mission very differently from that of male disciples. Then I will analyze each of the passages of the third Gospel in which women figure. I hope to offer a direction for engaging the liberating potential of the Gospel to move us toward a more inclusive praxis for transformation of Church and society.

Chapter 2

Luke, His Audience and Purpose

Before investigating Luke's portrait of disciples and their mission, a brief sketch of the identity of the evangelist, his audience, sources, genre, and purpose follows.[1]

THE AUTHOR

The evangelist, like many ancient authors, nowhere identifies himself. He discloses that he was not an eyewitness to the events he recounts, while insisting on the care with which he has investigated the tradition that he passes on (Luke 1:2-3). Most scholars believe he was not a native of Palestine; our oldest traditions associate him with Antioch. He appears to be a Gentile Christian writing for a predominantly Gentile community. The third evangelist was well-educated: his Greek is polished and he uses well-known Greco-Roman literary forms.

Whether the author of the third gospel was "Luke the beloved physician" mentioned in Colossians 4:14, is debatable. It is true that the third evangelist expands some descriptions of illnesses in his healing stories[2] and some manuscripts of Luke 8:43 lack

---

[1] See further Joseph A. Fitzmyer, *The Gospel According to Luke I-IX*, AB 28 (Garden City, N.Y.: Doubleday, 1981) 3-283; Earl Richard, ed., *New Views on Luke and Acts* (Collegeville, Minn.: The Liturgical Press, 1990) 15-63; Mark Allan Powell, *What Are They Saying About Luke?* (New York/Mahwah: Paulist Press, 1989).

[2] See Luke 4:38; cf. Mark 1:30; Luke 5:12; cf. Mark 1:40.

the derogatory remark about doctors (cf. Mark 5:26). However, all the supposed medical vocabulary of Luke can be found in the works of other ancient Greek authors who were not physicians.[3]

A co-worker of Paul named Luke is also mentioned in Philemon 24 and 2 Timothy 4:11. In addition, sections of Paul's sea voyages in Acts[4] are told in the first person plural, suggesting that the author of Luke and Acts accompanied the apostle on these journeys. There are difficulties with the assertion that the third evangelist was this same close co-worker of Paul. Luke's portrayal of Paul in Acts differs greatly from what the apostle says about himself in his own letters. Moreover, the author of Acts seems to have had no acquaintance with Paul's letters, and does not attribute to Paul the same theological concerns found in his letters. As for the first person accounts in Acts, such is known to have been a common literary device in recounting sea voyages in antiquity, and does not necessarily mean that the author actually accompanied Paul.[5] Alternatively, the third evangelist could have been acquainted personally with Paul, but only as a "sometime companion."[6]

Because the third evangelist includes more stories about women in his gospel, some postulate that the author was a woman.[7] However, in Luke 1:3 the verb *parēkolouthēkoti*, "investigating," is a masculine participle. In other words, the author has assumed the persona of a man.[8] It is entirely possible, though, that some

[3]H. J. Cadbury, *The Style and Literary Method of Luke,* HTS 6/1 (Cambridge, Mass.: Harvard University Press, 1920).

[4]Acts 16:10-17; 20:5-15; 21:1-18; 27:1–28:16.

[5]See S. M. Praeder, "Acts 17:1–28:16: Sea Voyages in Ancient Literature and the Theology of Luke-Acts," *CBQ* 46 (1984) 683–706; Vernon K. Robbins, "By Land and Sea: The We-Passages and Ancient Sea Voyages," *Perspectives on Luke-Acts,* ed. C. H. Talbert (Danville, Va.: Association of Baptist Professors of Religion, 1978) 215–242.

[6]Joseph A. Fitzmyer, "The Authorship of Luke-Acts Reconsidered," *Luke the Theologian: Aspects of His Teaching* (New York/Mahwah: Paulist Press, 1989) 1–26.

[7]E.g., E. Jane Via, "Women in the Gospel of Luke," *Women in the World's Religions: Past and Present,* ed. Ursula King (New York: Paragon House, 1987) 49–50, nn. 37–40.

[8]Mary Rose D'Angelo, "Women in Luke-Acts: A Redactional View," *JBL* 109/3 (1990) 443.

of the traditions that came to Luke were preserved in circles of women disciples.[9]

In sum, the third evangelist is an anonymous man, a Greek-speaking Gentile Christian, well-educated, a city-dweller, who may have been a companion of Paul for a time.

THE LUKAN AUDIENCE

Luke addresses both the Gospel and Acts to a certain Theophilus (Luke 1:3; Acts 1:1), who is otherwise unknown, perhaps a catechumen. "Theophilus" may also encompass anyone "beloved of God" or "loving God," thus good news for a wider audience than "His Excellency" (1:4).

From internal evidence, we can surmise that Luke's audience was Greek-speaking, predominantly Gentile, sophisticated, and at home in a Hellenistic urban environment. The Lukan communities most likely were born of a mission to Antioch, and of missions from that city. They, in turn, had a keen sense of their own participation in the mission.[10]

SOURCES

Because more than half of Luke's material has a counterpart in the Gospel of Mark and is told in the same sequence and often

---

[9]See Dennis MacDonald ("Virgins, Widows, and Paul in Second Century Asia Minor," *SBL 1979 Seminar Papers* [Missoula: Scholars Press, 1979] 169–184), who provides evidence for women as ecclesiastical storytellers. See also Ross S. Kraemer, "Women's Authorship of Jewish and Christian Literature in the Greco-Roman Period," *"Women Like This": New Perspectives on Jewish Women in the Greco-Roman World,* ed. Amy-Jill Levine, SBL Early Judaism and Its Literature 1 (Atlanta: Scholars Press, 1991) 221–242.

[10]See Fitzmyer, *Luke the Theologian,* 57–59; Luke T. Johnson, "On Finding the Lukan Community: A Cautionary Essay," *SBL Seminar 1979 Papers,* vol. 1 (Missoula: Scholars Press, 1979) 87–100; Robert J. Karris, "Missionary Communities: A New Paradigm for the Study of Luke-Acts," *CBQ* 41 (1979) 80–97; Eugene LaVerdiere, *Luke,* NTMS 5 (Wilmington: Glazier, 1980) xiv–xv; Marion L. Soards, "The Historical and Cultural Setting of Luke-Acts," *New Views on Luke and Acts,* ed. Earl Richard (Collegeville, Minn.: The Liturgical Press, 1990) 33–47.

the same wording, most scholars believe that Luke relied on Mark as one of his primary sources.[11] In addition, there are some 230 sayings common to Luke and Matthew, but absent from Mark. Much of the wording is identical, and the sayings occur in the same order in the two Gospels, although not always in the same context. Most scholars believe that Luke and Matthew have used a hypothetical written source, that has been dubbed "Q" (from the German *Quelle,* meaning "source").[12] Finally, Luke also had recourse to sources unique to him, generally referred to as "L." Some postulate that the unique stories of women in Luke came to him from sources preserved by women believers.

There is a small number of scholars who resolve the source question differently. They believe that Luke relied on Matthew as a source and that Mark is an abridgement of Luke and Matthew.[13] This theory eliminates the need for "Q," but, ultimately, creates more difficulties than it resolves.

It is also important to realize that the third evangelist himself had an important role in shaping the gospel. He did not merely paste together material from his sources, but rather composed sections himself and shaped the material overall so as to convey the good news in a manner that would address the particular pastoral concerns of his communities.

[11]See Joseph A. Fitzmyer, "The Priority of Mark and the Q Source," *To Advance the Gospel: New Testament Studies* (New York: Crossroad, 1981) 3–40; Powell, *What Are They Saying About Luke?* 16–41.

[12]See John Kloppenborg, *The Formation of Q: Trajectories in Ancient Wisdom Collections,* Studies in Antiquity and Christianity (Philadelphia: Fortress Press, 1987); Richard Edwards, *A Theology of Q. Eschatology, Prophecy and Wisdom* (Philadelphia: Fortress Press, 1976).

[13]This hypothesis was first proposed by the eighteenth-century scholar Johann Griesbach. William R. Farmer (*The Synoptic Problem: A Critical Analysis* [New York: Macmillan, 1964]) has spearheaded the revival of "The Two-Gospel Hypothesis" in recent decades. A separate group of scholars, led by M. D. Goulder (*Luke: A New Paradigm,* JSNTSup 20 [Sheffield: JSOT, 1989]) and John Drury (*Tradition and Design in Luke's Gospel: A Study of Early Christian Historiography* [London: Darton, Longman, and Todd, 1976]) also deny the existence of Q and hold for direct dependence of Luke on Matthew.

GENRE

There is at present no consensus on the literary genre of Luke and Acts. Scholars see similarities to Hellenistic biographies, monographs, histories, antiquities, apologies, historical novels, and accounts of philosophical succession. Both Lukan books are a mixture of popular first-century Greco-Roman literary types. In addition they are suffused with language, imagery, settings, and character types from the Septuagint, the Greek translation of the Hebrew Scriptures. This points to an audience that is both highly Hellenized and familiar with Jewish biblical tradition.[14]

PURPOSE

Luke's stated purpose is to "compile a narrative of the events that have been fulfilled among us." After "investigating everything accurately anew," he has decided to "write it down in an orderly sequence" for Theophilus so that he "may realize the certainty of the teachings" he has received (1:1-4). Luke is a pastoral theologian, narrating the story of Jesus and his first followers in such a way as to console, guide, and challenge his faith communities. The communities' concerns and struggles are revealed in the themes that recur: prayer, Jesus' boundary-breaking practices, table companionship, material possessions, the Spirit, endurance under persecution, continuity and discontinuity between Israel and the Church, the fulfillment of God's promises, and the delay of the parousia, to name a few.

Within Luke's general purpose, then, is his intent to offer guidance to his communities on new questions that arise. One of their disputed questions concerns the exercise of ministry by women

[14]See David Aune, *The New Testament in its Literary Environment*, Library of Early Christianity (Philadelphia: Westminster, 1987) 77-157; John A. Darr, *On Character Building: The Reader and the Rhetoric of Characterization in Luke-Acts*, Literary Currents in Biblical Interpretation (Louisville: Westminster/John Knox, 1992) 27-28, 48-49; Mikeal C. Parsons and Richard I. Pervo, *Rethinking the Unity of Luke and Acts* (Minneapolis: Fortress Press, 1993) 20-44; Richard Pervo, *Profit With Delight: The Literary Genre of the Acts of the Apostles* (Philadelphia: Fortress Press, 1987); Charles H. Talbert, *Literary Patterns, Theological Themes and the Genre of Luke-Acts*, SBLMS 20 (Missoula: Scholars Press, 1974).

believers. But it is anachronistic to imagine that the questions in Luke's communities were the same that we bring. Nor can we say with utter certitude what, precisely, Luke's stance was. It has long been observed that Luke may consistently bring up a particular topic, but he does not speak about it consistently. G.W.H. Lampe describes Luke's style as holding "a large number of threads in his hand at once, introducing first one and then another into a somewhat untidy and ill-defined pattern, without allowing any one of them so to predominate over the rest as to give unity and coherence to the whole."[15] Thus, we will not be surprised if Luke presents more than one message about women and their roles in the Church.[16]

With these presuppositions we now examine the dynamics of discipleship and mission in the Gospel of Luke and the Acts of the Apostles.

---

[15]"The Lucan Portrait of Christ," *NTS* 2 (1955/56) 160.
[16]See Turid Karlsen Seim, *The Double Message: Patterns of Gender in Luke-Acts* (Nashville: Abingdon, 1994).

Chapter 3

Women's Participation in Discipleship and Mission in Luke and Acts[1]

DISCIPLESHIP

The third evangelist does not give a definition of discipleship, *per se*. Nonetheless, it is possible to identify what Luke regards as exemplary responses to the Christian kerygma by examining the instructions of the Lukan Jesus to his disciples. In addition, by looking at what Jesus does, we see what disciples are to do, since Luke presents Jesus' actions as providing the pattern for those of his disciples.[2]

---

[1]An earlier form of this chapter, entitled, "Luke: The Gospel for Women?" appeared in *Currents in Theology and Mission* 21/6 (1994) 405–414.

[2]Robert O'Toole (*The Unity of Luke's Theology: An Analysis of Luke-Acts,* Good News Studies 9 [Wilmington: Glazier, 1984] 62–94) has outlined the ways in which the Lukan disciples continue the work of Jesus. He delineates the parallels between Jesus and Stephen; between Jesus and Paul; and parallel actions performed or endured by Jesus and his followers. He shows that disciples frequent the same places as Jesus (e.g., Jerusalem, the Temple, synagogues); that the same words describe Jesus' and his followers' preaching and message; and that Luke provides the same description of Jesus and his followers. In the abundant references given by O'Toole the only examples of women are Philip's four daughters (Acts 21:9) who are described as prophets, as was Jesus (Luke 4:24-27; 7:6, 39; 9:7, 9, 19; 13:33-34; 24:19;

HEARING, SEEING, AND OBEYING THE WORD

That discipleship begins by hearing the word of God[3] is high-lighted by Luke in the way he has redacted the Markan source to present Jesus teaching (4:15, 31; 5:3) and preaching (4:44) before any disciples follow him. The Lukan Jesus repeatedly exhorts people to hear and obey the word of God. In the Sermon on the Plain he adjures his listeners to hear his words and do them (6:27, 47). In his explanation of the seed parable Jesus holds up as exemplary those who, "when they have heard the word, embrace it with a generous and good heart, and bear fruit through perseverance" (8:15). Jesus declares that whoever hears the word of God and does it is family to him (8:21).[4] He proclaims blessed those who hear the word of God and obey it (11:28). Jesus uses the example of the queen of the South, who listened to the wisdom of Solomon, to emphasize how important it is to listen to him, for he is "greater than Solomon" (11:31). The command of the voice from the cloud at the transfiguration, "listen to him" (9:35), and the summons, "Whoever has ears to hear ought to hear" (8:8 and 14:35), epitomize the initial step of discipleship.

Seeing is another metaphor for perceiving the word of God.[5] The shepherds, after seeing the newborn Jesus, "returned, glorifying and praising God for all they had heard and seen" (2:20). Simeon declares, "my eyes have seen your salvation, which you prepared in sight of all the peoples" (2:30-31). Jesus' mission in-

---

Acts 3:22-23), and two generic references to women and men being "handed over" (*paradidōmi*, Acts 8:3; 22:4) as was Jesus (Luke 9:44; 18:32; 20:20; 22:4, 6, 48; 23:25; 24:7).

[3] The "word of God" *(ho logos tou theou)* refers to Jesus' own preaching in the Gospel: Luke 5:1; 8:11, 21; 11:28; and to that of the apostles in Acts: 4:29, 31; 6:2, 7; 8:14; 11:1; 12:24; 13:5, 7, 44, 46, 48; 16:32; 17:13; 18:11. The phrase *ho logos tou theou* appears only once in each of the other Gospels: Matt 15:6; Mark 7:13; John 10:36.

[4] Here Lukan redaction shows Luke's stress on hearing and doing. Mark 3:35 does not have "hearing," but simply, "whoever does the will of God" is family to Jesus.

[5] See Alan Culpepper, "Seeing the Kingdom of God: The Metaphor of Sight in the Gospel of Luke," *CurTM* 21 (1994) 434–443; Dennis Hamm, "What the Samaritan Leper Sees: The Narrative Christology of Luke 17:11-19," *CBQ* 56 (1994) 273–287.

cludes bringing "recovery of sight to the blind" (4:18; 7:21). After the healing of the man who was paralyzed, all were seized with astonishment and glorified God saying, "We have seen incredible things today" (5:26). Stories of Jesus healing people who were blind are more than accounts of physical healings. The ability to see is equated with the capacity to perceive and respond properly to Jesus. Of the ten lepers healed, only the Samaritan "saw" that he was healed and returned to Jesus, glorifying God (17:15-16).[6] When the man in Jericho who had been blind received his sight, he responded as a disciple: he followed Jesus and gave glory to God (18:35-43). When the centurion sees Jesus' death, he too glorifies God and declares Jesus upright (23:47). The post-resurrection understanding of the disciples en route to Emmaus is described as "their eyes were opened" (24:31).

When the messengers from John the Baptist ask Jesus if he is the one who is to come, he replies, "Go and tell John what you have seen and heard" (7:22). Visual and oral perception should lead one to recognition of Jesus and proper response to him. Jesus, using the words of the prophet Isaiah, warns his disciples about looking but not seeing, and hearing but not understanding (8:10). He later says to his disciples, "Blessed are the eyes that see what you see. For I say to you, many prophets and kings desired to see what you see, but did not see it, and to hear what you hear, but did not hear it" (10:23-24).

THE RESPONSE OF A DISCIPLE

The parable of the sower (Luke 8:4-8) and its explanation (Luke 8:11-15) illustrate the variety of ways in which people respond to what is heard: some hear, but then "the devil comes and takes away the word from their hearts that they may not believe and be saved" (8:12); others "believe only for a time and fall away in time of trial" (8:13); still others hear, "but as they go along, they are choked by the anxieties and riches and pleasures of life, and they fail to produce mature fruit" (8:14). The ideal response is to hear "the word, embrace it with a generous and good heart, and bear fruit through perseverance" (8:15).

[6]Hamm, "Samaritan Leper," 283.

Just as there is a variety of responses to what is heard, so also to what is seen. This is illustrated in the parable of the Good Samaritan. When the priest and the Levite each saw the man who had been robbed, they passed by on the opposite side (10:31, 32). But the Samaritan traveler "was moved with compassion at the sight" (10:33). There are those who only want to "see" Jesus out of curiosity, like Herod (9:9), or who watch him like the scribes and the Pharisees so as to find fault with him (6:7). A disciple, however, sees with faith, perceiving Jesus' true identity and acting on it.[7] The themes of proper hearing and seeing also frame Luke's second volume (Acts 2:33; 28:26-27).

Other Lukan terms that express the initial positive response of a disciple include: receiving *(dechomai)* the word, believing *(pisteuō)*, repenting and converting *(metanoeō, epistrephō)*, and being baptized *(baptizō)*. Ongoing demands of Christian life involve: following *(akoloutheō)* Jesus; proclaiming *(kēryssō, katangellō, anangellō, apangellō, diangellō, euangelizomai, katangellō)* or witnessing *(martyromai)* to what one has heard; praying *(proseuchomai)*; communal living *(koinōnia)*, including sharing of material possessions. A disciple participates in the mission of Jesus by doing what he did: preaching, teaching, healing, exorcising, forgiving, serving, and enduring conflicts and persecution. This is possible when disciples are commissioned and filled with the holy Spirit.[8] We will examine each occurrence of these responses in Luke and Acts to determine whether or not the third evangelist portrays women disciples responding in these ways.

---

[7] Dennis Hamm, "Sight to the Blind: Vision as Metaphor in Luke," *Bib* 67 (1986) 457-477.

[8] See Joseph Fitzmyer, *The Gospel According to Luke*, AB 28 (Garden City, N.Y.: Doubleday, 1981, 1985) 235-257; O'Toole, *Unity*, 191-224; Dennis M. Sweetland, "Following Jesus: Discipleship in Luke-Acts," in *New Views on Luke and Acts*, ed. Earl Richard (Collegeville, Minn.: The Liturgical Press, 1990) 109-123; *Our Journey With Jesus: Discipleship According to Luke-Acts*, Good News Studies 30 (Collegeville, Minn.: The Liturgical Press, 1990); Charles H. Talbert, "Discipleship in Luke-Acts," *Discipleship in the New Testament*, ed. Fernando F. Segovia (Philadelphia: Fortress Press, 1985) 62-75.

INITIAL POSITIVE RESPONSES

Receiving *(dechomai)* the Word

Receiving is a favorite Lukan way to express acceptance of the word.[9] Simeon receives the child Jesus (2:28), but the people of Samaria will not receive Jesus when his face is set toward Jerusalem (9:53). Jesus advocates receiving the word with joy (8:13) and receiving the reign of God like a child (18:17). Jesus' instructions to his disciples who are being sent out to proclaim the word alert them that at times they will be received (10:8) but at others they will not (9:5; 10:10). Receiving a child in Jesus' name is receiving him as well as the one who sent him (9:48).

In Acts 8:14 Luke relates that Samaria "had accepted *[dedektai]* the word of God," having heard and seen what Philip had done (8:6). Gentiles also "accepted *[edexanto]* the word of God" (Acts 11:1). The Jews in Beroea were more receptive than those in Thessalonica, "for they received *[edexanto]* the word with all willingness and examined the scriptures daily to determine whether these things were so" (Acts 17:11). In Jerusalem, however, Paul is told by Jesus in a trance to leave the city "because they will not accept *[paradexontai]* your testimony about me" (Acts 22:18).

In each of these instances, no reference is made to the gender of those who receive the word.

Believing *(pisteuō)*

The first person to hear and believe is Mary (1:45). In contrast to Zechariah who did not believe Gabriel's words (1:20), Mary is declared blessed by Elizabeth for believing what was spoken to her by the Lord. Mary prefigures the ideal response of a disciple, but she does not appear among the disciples in the Gospel. She is a transition figure from the era of Judaism. She is first

---

[9]In Luke *dechomai* occurs thirteen times in the Gospel (2:28; 8:13; 9:5, 48, 53; 10:8, 10; 16:4, 6, 7, 9; 18:17; 22:17) and eight times in Acts (3:21; 7:38, 59; 8:14; 11:1; 17:11; 22:5; 28:21) in contrast to Matthew, where it occurs only six times (10:14, 40, 41 [2x]; 11:14; 18:5); Mark, where it appears three times (6:11; 9:37; 10:15); and John, where it is found only once (4:45). Luke also employs *paradechomai* twice: Acts 15:4; 22:18.

portrayed as a prophet, in line with Deborah (Judges 4–5), Huldah (2 Kgs 22:14; 2 Chr 34:22), and Miriam (Exodus 15), as she sings of justice (1:46-52). After Jesus' birth, her role shifts to that of mother (2:6-7), law-observer (2:22-24, 42), anxious parent (2:48), and silent theologian (2:19, 51). While Luke 8:19-21 (contrary to Mark 3:31-35) leaves open the possibility that Jesus' mother and siblings may join his family of disciples, it is only in Acts 1:14 that Mary is found among Jesus' followers, gathered in the upper room in Jerusalem, awaiting the coming of the Spirit. Luke provides no further information as to what role Jesus' mother, who first heard and believed the word, plays in the post-resurrection community of disciples.

Others in the Gospel who are said to have faith *(pistis)* are: the friends of the man who was paralyzed (5:20); the centurion whose slave was ill (7:9); the woman who had been forgiven much (7:50); the woman suffering from a hemorrhage (8:48); the Samaritan man with leprosy (17:19); the man who was blind and begging near Jericho (18:42). It is implied that Jairus, the synagogue official, has faith (8:50). Jesus' disciples have faith, but it falters. After the storm on the lake, Jesus asks them, "Where is your faith?" (8:25). During the journey to Jerusalem the apostles ask Jesus to increase their faith (17:5). That Peter has faith is implied in 22:32 where Jesus confides to him that he has prayed for him that his faith may not fail. Jesus rebukes Cleopas and his companion for being "slow of heart to believe all that the prophets spoke" (24:25).

In Acts Jesus' followers are often called "those who believed" or "believers."[10] There are frequent references to large numbers who come to believe.[11] The Samaritans believed (8:12), as did Simon the magician (8:13), the proconsul Sergius Paulus (13:12), the Gentiles (14:27; 15:7, 9; 21:25), Timothy's mother (16:1), Lydia (16:15), the jailer and his household at Philippi (16:34), Dionysius the Areopagite, Damaris, and others (17:34), and Crispus and his household (18:8). The man at the Beautiful Gate was healed by faith in Christ's name (3:16), as also the man at

---

[10]Acts 2:44; 4:32; 10:45; 18:27; 19:2; 22:19.
[11]Acts 4:4; 5:14; 6:7; 9:42; 11:21; 13:48; 14:1; 16:5; 17:12; 18:8; 19:18; 21:20.

Lystra (14:9). Stephen was "a man filled with faith" (6:5), as was Barnabas (11:24).

In sum, women as well as men are specifically said to believe in Acts 5:14; 8:12; 17:12. Individual women who have faith are Mary (Luke 1:45), the woman who loved greatly (Luke 7:50), the woman healed of a hemorrhage (Luke 8:48), Timothy's mother (Acts 16:1), Lydia (Acts 16:15), and Damaris (Acts 17:34).

Repenting and Converting *(metanoeō, epistrephō)*

Calls to repentance are found on the lips of Jesus a number of times in the Gospel.[12] Jesus declares that "there will be more joy in heaven over one sinner who repents than over ninety-nine righteous persons who need no repentance" (15:7, 10). He also warns his followers that if another disciple repents of an offense, they must forgive, even if this happens seven times a day (17:3-4). That "repentance and forgiveness of sins" is to be preached in his name to all nations is part of Jesus' message to his disciples at his resurrection appearance to them in Jerusalem (24:47). In Acts Peter takes up this same call to repentance in his preaching, as do Philip and Paul.[13]

In Acts a major theme is that Gentiles have been granted "life-giving repentance" (*metanoia*, 11:18) and conversion (*epistrophē*, 15:3). Many of them turned (*epistrephousin*) to God (15:19). All the inhabitants of Lydda and Sharon "turned [*epestrepsan*] to the Lord" when they saw that Peter healed Aeneas (Acts 9:35). In Antioch "a great number who believed turned [*epestrepsen*] to the Lord" (11:21).

No individual woman is said to repent in Luke or Acts, although they are undoubtedly to be understood as part of the groups of Gentiles and residents of Lydda and Sharon and Antioch who turned to the Lord. Only the male disciples Peter, Philip, and Paul preach repentance.

---

[12]Luke 5:32; 10:13; 11:32; 13:3, 5. John the Baptist also preached repentance in Luke 3:3, 8. This is also mentioned in Acts 13:24; 19:4.

[13]Peter preaches repentance in Acts 2:38; 3:19; 5:31; Philip does so in Acts 8:22; as does Paul in Acts 14:15; 17:30; 20:21; 26:18, 20; 28:27.

Being Baptized *(baptizō)*

Closely linked to repentance and conversion is baptism. Jesus' baptism by John prefigures the means by which people who respond positively to the Christian kerygma would be initiated into the community of believers. John baptizes crowds, including tax collectors (Luke 3:7, 12, 29), and Jesus (3:21) with water; Jesus will baptize with the holy Spirit and fire (Luke 3:16; Acts 1:5; 11:16).[14] No baptism of Jesus' followers is related in the Gospel. It is in Acts that baptism becomes constitutive of discipleship.

In his Pentecost speech in Acts 2:38 Peter adjures his listeners, "Repent and be baptized, every one of you, in the name of Jesus Christ for the forgiveness of your sins." Those who did numbered three thousand persons (*psychai*, 2:41). In Samaria "both men and women" (cf. 8:12) and even Simon the magician (8:13) were baptized in response to Philip's preaching. Philip's encounter with the Ethiopian eunuch ended in his baptism (8:38). Paul's experience on the road to Damascus leads to his baptism (9:18). In Caesarea the holy Spirit fell on Cornelius and his relatives and close friends (10:24) after listening to Peter's speech. Peter then "ordered them to be baptized in the name of Jesus Christ" (10:48).

Lydia, a dealer in purple cloth and a worshiper of God, listened to Paul and "the Lord opened her heart" to what he was saying (16:14). She, along with her household, were baptized (16:15). The jailer in Philippi and all his family were baptized (16:33) after the earthquake shook open the doors of the prison where Paul and Silas were held. In Corinth, Crispus the synagogue official and all his household, and many of the Corinthians who heard Paul, became believers and were baptized (18:8). Twelve Ephesian men, who were baptized with John's baptism, came to be "baptized in the name of the Lord Jesus" (19:5) when Paul visited Ephesus.

In sum, Acts relates stories of individual men who accepted baptism: Simon the magician, the Ethiopian eunuch, Paul, Cornelius, the jailer in Philippi, and Crispus. There is one story of a woman who is baptized: Lydia. There are also statements that groups (2:41; 8:12; 18:8), families, and households (10:24; 16:33) were

---

[14] In Luke 12:50 Jesus speaks metaphorically of his passion as a baptism.

baptized; these presumably include women. Acts 8:12 explicitly says that "both men and women" were baptized.

ONGOING DEMANDS OF DISCIPLESHIP

Following *(akoloutheō)*

That following Jesus is constitutive of discipleship is clear from the first stories about disciples in Luke. In some instances Jesus specifically invites a person to follow him; in others the request to follow Jesus comes from the potential disciple. There are also episodes in which a person responds to Jesus' words or deeds by following him, although there is no invitation or request to do so. The latter is the case with Simon Peter and his partners James and John, who leave everything to follow Jesus (5:11).[15] So too, the man healed of blindness near Jericho spontaneously followed Jesus (18:43).

In the story of Levi, the tax collector, Jesus invites him to follow (5:27) and he does (5:28). Jesus issues an invitation to all, "If anyone wishes to come after me, he must deny himself and take up his cross daily and follow me" (9:23).

In 9:57-62 Jesus speaks to three potential disciples about the rigors of following him. The first character takes the initiative, saying to Jesus, "I will follow you wherever you go" (9:57). In response Jesus speaks about having no place to lay his head. With the second character, Jesus issues the invitation, "Follow me" (9:59). The person responds with a request to be allowed to bury their father, to which Jesus replies, "Let the dead bury their dead; But you, go and proclaim the kingdom of God" (9:60). The third person offers to follow Jesus after bidding farewell to family. Jesus speaks about not looking back, once having set a hand to the plow (9:62). In this episode the characters are anonymous and it remains unclear whether or not they actually end by following Jesus.

In another instance Jesus invites a rich official to sell all he owns, distribute the money to the poor, and to follow him. But the official became sad on hearing this (18:18-23). Luke does not

[15]The direct invitation from Jesus to follow is omitted in the Lukan version. Cf. Mark 1:17 and Matt 4:19.

relate whether or not the rich official overcame his sadness and became a follower. In the Markan account (10:17-22) it is clearer that he did not. Peter and his companions, however, are assured an abundant return for having given up their possessions to follow Jesus (Luke 18:28-30). That Luke has in mind only male followers becomes clear when Jesus assures Peter, "there is no one who has given up house or wife or brothers or parents or children for the sake of the kingdom of God who will not receive [back] an overabundant return in this present age, and eternal life in the age to come" (18:29-30).

There are several instances in which a crowd follows Jesus. In Luke 7:9 the crowd provides the backdrop for the healing of the centurion's slave. There is no clue here whether their following indicates anything more than curiosity. A crowd of five thousand men (*andres,* v. 14) follows (v. 11) Jesus to Bethsaida, where he receives, heals, and feeds them. All ate and were satisfied (9:17), but no more is known of their response. Since the crowd is distinguished from the disciples (vv. 13-14), it is unlikely that their following is to be given the significance that following has in the individual call stories. On the way of the cross, "a large crowd of people followed Jesus, including many women who mourned and lamented him" (23:27). With Jesus' ensuing admonition to these "daughters of Jerusalem" (vv. 28-31) the women appear not to be disciples. The only other reference in the Third Gospel to women following Jesus is at the death of Jesus, where "all his acquaintances stood at a distance, including the women who had followed him from Galilee" (23:49).

To summarize, the broad invitation in 9:23 issued to "all" may be interpreted to include women. The gender of the three potential followers in 9:57-62 is not specified. But in 18:29-30 followers are clearly thought to be male. There is no story of a woman called by Jesus to follow him, and only one clear instance in which women are said to have done so.

Proclaiming
(kēryssō, anangellō, apangellō, diangellō, katangellō)

In Jesus' inaugural preaching at the synagogue in Nazareth he declares that his mission entails proclaiming *(kēryxai)* release to captives and a year of God's favor (4:18-19). He continues proclaiming *(kēryssōn)* the message in the synagogues of Judea (4:44), and throughout towns and villages in Galilee (8:1). Before him, John the Baptist had proclaimed *(kēryssō)* a baptism of repentance (Luke 3:3; Acts 10:37). The man healed of demon possession in the territory of the Gerasenes is sent home by Jesus and told to "recount what God has done for you." So he went off and "proclaimed *[kēryssōn]* throughout the whole town what Jesus had done for him" (8:39). Part of the mission entrusted to the Twelve is to proclaim *(kēryssein)* the reign of God (9:2).[16] In his parting words to the disciples gathered in Jerusalem after the resurrection Jesus says that repentance and forgiveness of sins is to be proclaimed *(kērychthēnai)* in his name to all nations (24:47).

In Acts 8:5 Philip "proclaimed *[ekēryssen]* the Messiah" to the Samaritans. Peter tells Cornelius and his relatives and friends that the risen Christ commissioned those who were chosen by God as witnesses, and who ate and drank with him after he rose from the dead to preach *(kēryssein)* and testify about him (10:41-42). Paul proclaims *(ekēryssen)* Jesus in the synagogues of Damascus immediately after his conversion (9:20). In Acts 19:13 some Jewish exorcists "tried to invoke the name of the Lord Jesus over those with evil spirits, saying, 'I adjure you by the Jesus whom Paul preaches *[kēryssei]*.' " Paul speaks of his having "preached *[kēryssōn]* the kingdom" to the Ephesians (20:25). The last verse of Acts (28:31) tells of how Paul "proclaimed *[kēryssōn]* the kingdom of God and taught about the Lord Jesus Christ" with all boldness and without hindrance during his Roman imprisonment.

In Acts, then, those who proclaim *(kēryssō)* are Peter, Philip, and Paul. The audience for the commission in Luke 24:47 is ambiguous.

The above examples all relate to the verb *kēryssō*. Words deriving from the root *angel-* are also used for Christian proclamation. Foremost is the verb *euangelizomai,* "to proclaim good news." The angel Gabriel brings good news (Luke 1:19), as does the angel that announces Jesus' birth to the shepherds (2:10). John

---

[16]In sending out the further seventy(-two) Jesus tells them to say *(legete)* to whoever welcomes them, "the kingdom of God is at hand for you" (10:9); he does not use the verb *kēryssein*.

the Baptist "preached good news to the people" (3:18). Jesus was anointed "to bring glad tidings to the poor" (4:18). Jesus explains why he leaves Capernaum, "To the other towns also I must proclaim the good news of the kingdom of God" (4:43). When John's disciples inquire whether Jesus is the "one who is to come" Jesus recounts what he has done, including "the poor have the good news proclaimed to them" (7:22). Jesus continues to travel through cities and villages "preaching and proclaiming the good news" (8:1). When the Twelve are sent on mission, they likewise "went from village to village proclaiming the good news" (9:6). In 16:16 Jesus refers again to his ministry in which "the good news of the kingdom of God is proclaimed." In Jerusalem Jesus was teaching people in the temple "and proclaiming the good news" (20:1).

In Acts "the apostles" continue "proclaiming the Messiah, Jesus" every day in the Temple and at home (5:42). Those who were scattered from Jerusalem after the death of Stephen "went about preaching the word" (8:4). Philip "preached the good news" in Samaria (8:12), on the road from Jerusalem to Gaza to the Ethiopian eunuch (8:35), and to all the towns from Azotus to Caesarea (8:40). Acts 21:8 refers to him as "Philip the evangelist *[tou euangelistou]*." Peter and John "preached the good news to many Samaritan villages" (8:25). In his speech to Cornelius Peter tells of how God "proclaimed peace through Jesus Christ" (10:36). Peter also speaks to the apostles and presbyters in Jerusalem about God's choice that he should be the one through whom the Gentiles "would hear the word of the gospel and believe" (15:7). In Antioch some men of Cyprus and Cyrene were proclaiming the Lord Jesus to the Hellenists (11:20). Paul and Barnabas proclaim the good news at Antioch in Pisidia (13:32), Lystra, Derbe, and the surrounding countryside (14:7, 15, 21), and Antioch (15:35). Paul was convinced in a vision that he was called to proclaim the good news in Macedonia (16:10). Paul preached about Jesus and the resurrection in Athens (17:18). In his farewell to the elders at Ephesus Paul hopes that he may finish his course and the ministry that he received from the Lord Jesus, "to bear witness to the gospel of God's grace" (20:24).

In sum, angels and John the Baptist foreshadow Jesus' mission of "bringing good news" *(euangelizomai)*. Disciples who continue this mission are all male: the Twelve, the apostles (whom

Luke equates with the Twelve), Philip, Peter, John, Barnabas, and Paul.

The same is true of other verbs from the root *angel-*. In Luke 9:60 Jesus instructs a potential disciple to "go and proclaim *[diangelle]* the kingdom of God." In his speech at Solomon's portico Peter asserts, "all the prophets who spoke, from Samuel and those afterwards, also announced *[katēngeilan]* these days (Acts 3:24). In Jerusalem Peter and John created a disturbance because they were proclaiming *(katangellein)* that in Jesus there is the resurrection of the dead (Acts 4:2). Barnabas and Saul proclaimed *(katēngellon)* the word in the synagogues at Salamis (Acts 13:5). In his address at Antioch in Pisidia (Acts 13:38) Paul affirms that through Jesus "forgiveness of sins is being proclaimed *(katangelletai)*. In both Antioch and Jerusalem Paul and Barnabas proclaimed *(anēngellon)* all that God had done with them (Acts 14:27; 15:4). In Acts 15:36 Paul proposes to Barnabas that they make a return visit to every city where they "proclaimed *[katēngeilamen]* the word of the Lord." The slave girl in Philippi cried out after Paul and his companions, "These people are slaves of the Most High God, who proclaim *[katangellousin]* to you a way of salvation" (16:17). In Thessalonica Paul proclaims *(katangellō)* Jesus as the Messiah who suffered and rose from the dead (17:3). He proclaimed *(katēngelē)* the word of God in Beroea as well (17:13). To the Athenians Paul asserts, "What therefore you unknowingly worship, I proclaim *[katangellō]* to you" (17:23). In his farewell speech to the Ephesian elders Paul speaks of his proclaiming *(anangeilai)* the message (Acts 20:20) and his declaring *(anangeilai)* the whole purpose of God (20:27). To King Agrippa Paul states that his message agrees with that of the prophets and Moses: "that the Messiah must suffer and that, as the first to rise from the dead, he would proclaim *[katangellein]* light both to our people and to the Gentiles" (26:23).

In conclusion, all those who proclaim (expressed with verbs from the root *angel-*) are male: Peter, John, Barnabas, and Paul. One time *katangellō* is used of the predictions of the prophets; once the subject is the Messiah.

One instance is found in which women are the subject of the verb *apangellō*. In Luke 24:9 the women returning from the tomb "announced" *[apēngeilan]* all these things to the eleven and to all the others." The following verse identifies them: "The women were Mary Magdalene, Joanna, and Mary the mother of James; the others who accompanied them also told this to the apostles." But these did not believe them (24:10).

Witnessing *(martyromai)*

In his instructions about the coming persecution, Jesus tells his disciples that this will give them an opportunity to testify (*eis martyrion,* 21:13). And in their commissioning in 24:48 he asserts, "You are witnesses *[martyres]* of these things." This is echoed in Acts 1:8 where Jesus, about to ascend, tells the disciples, "you will be my witnesses in Jerusalem, throughout Judea and Samaria, and to the ends of the earth."

The theme of witnessing recurs throughout Acts. Judas' successor is to become a witness with the apostles to Christ's resurrection (1:22). In his Pentecost speech Peter asserts, "God raised this Jesus; of this we are all witnesses" (2:32). It appears that the "all" Luke has in mind are Peter and the Eleven (2:14). In addressing the "Israelites" in his speech at Solomon's portico, Peter says, "The author of life you put to death, but God raised him from the dead; of this we are witnesses" (3:15). Presumably he and John (v. 11) are the "we" who are witnesses. Before the Sanhedrin Peter and the apostles (5:29) assert, "we are witnesses of these things" (5:32). To Cornelius Peter says, "we are witnesses of all that he did both in the country of the Jews and [in] Jerusalem" (10:39). He continues, saying that after he rose, Jesus appeared "not to all the people, but to us, the witnesses chosen by God in advance, who ate and drank with him after he rose from the dead" (10:41).

Similar words are spoken by Paul in Antioch of Pisidia, "for many days he appeared to those who had come up with him from Galilee to Jerusalem. These are [now] his witnesses before the people" (13:31). Paul explains before the authorities that his experience on the road to Damascus designated him Christ's "witness before all" to what he had seen and heard (22:15; 26:16). While imprisoned in Jerusalem, the Lord assured Paul that "just as you have borne witness to my cause in Jerusalem, so you must also bear witness in Rome" (23:11). Paul speaks of Stephen as a witness whose blood was shed (22:20). In Acts 6:3 seven "reputable men" (literally, *andres martyroumenous*) are chosen for table ministry.

It is not clear that there are any women among those commissioned by Jesus to be witnesses. In Acts those who claim to be witnesses are Peter and Paul. The others to whom they refer as witnesses appear to be men. In 10:39 the subject of "we" is unspecified and the identity of those to whom Jesus appeared and with whom he ate and drank after the resurrection is obscure. The first resurrection appearance and eating together is with Cleopas and his companion (Luke 24:13-35), but the identity of the latter is never disclosed. The second such instance (24:36-49) is to the "eleven and those with them" in Jerusalem (24:33). Again, Luke obfuscates any reference to women in the group. That the group included women can only be inferred from his later note in Acts 1:14 that women, including Mary the mother of Jesus, were staying in the upper room with the Eleven. Luke does not disclose whether women were among the "eleven and all the others" when Mary Magdalene, Joanna, Mary the mother of James, and the other women announce the news of the empty tomb (24:9-10). In Acts 1:2-3 those to whom Jesus presented himself alive were the "apostles whom he had chosen." Luke tends to equate the "apostles" with the twelve men listed in Luke 6:13. It seems Luke envisions only male disciples as witnesses.

Praying *(proseuchomai)*

Prayer is a particular emphasis of the third evangelist.[17] The first episode of the Gospel relates that "the whole assembly of the people was praying outside" while Zechariah was burning incense in the sanctuary (Luke 1:9-10). In 2:37 appears the prophet Anna who "never left the temple, but worshiped night and day with fasting and prayer." Luke shows Jesus at prayer as a regular occurrence (5:16) and at critical turning points: at his baptism (3:21), before his choice of the Twelve (6:12), before Peter's confession of him as the Messiah (9:18), at the transfiguration (9:28-29), before his arrest on the Mount of Olives (22:39-46), and on the cross (23:46). A spontaneous prayer of Jesus giving

[17] See Fitzmyer, *The Gospel According to Luke*, 244-247, 268-269.

thanks is found in 10:21-23. Jesus assures Peter that he has prayed for him that his faith may not fail (22:32).[18] Luke emphasizes Jesus' intimate union with God through prayer and the unfolding of the course of Jesus' life and ministry in accord with God's saving plan.

Prayer is likewise an important practice for disciples in Luke and Acts.[19] Jesus instructs his disciples on prayer.[20] In Acts, the early Christians are portrayed as constantly at prayer. The Eleven "devoted themselves with one accord to prayer, together with some women, and Mary the mother of Jesus, and his brothers" (1:14). The group of about one hundred twenty brothers pray during the selection of Judas' successor (1:24). Acts 1:15 begins this episode by saying that Peter stood up in the midst of the brothers *(adelphōn)*, who numbered about one hundred twenty. Having just listed in 1:14 the group of gathered disciples as a mixed group of men and women, *adelphōn* might be thought to include both men and women. But in the next verse Peter addresses them as *andres aldelphoi*, "men, brothers," which indicates that at 1:15 there is a change of audience from 1:14 and that he is now speaking only to the men.

The community in Jerusalem "devoted themselves to the teaching of the apostles and to the communal life, to the breaking of the bread and to the prayers" (2:42; similarly 4:31). The community is found at prayer in the house of Mary (12:12). Peter and John went to the Temple at the hour of prayer (3:1). The Twelve are said to devote themselves to prayer and the ministry of the word (6:4). When choosing seven men to serve at table the apostles prayed and laid hands on them (6:6). Stephen prayed while being

[18]Luke inserts references to prayer in his redaction of Markan material in 3:21; 5:16, 33. Eight of the instances in which prayer is mentioned occur in material peculiar to Luke: 1:10, 13; 2:37; 18:1, 10, 11; 21:36; 22:32. There are four instances in which the Lukan version of Q material contains a reference to prayer: 6:28; 10:2; 11:1, 2. The Matthean parallels to Luke 10:2 and 11:2 have the references to prayer as well. Five times Luke's mention of prayer comes from the Markan source: 9:18; 20:47; 22:40, 41, 46.

[19]That prayer and fasting were expected of disciples of a religious leader is evident from Luke 5:33 where the Pharisees and their scribes charge that Jesus' disciples eat and drink in contrast to the disciples of John and those of the Pharisees who "frequently fast and pray."

[20]Luke 6:28; 10:2; 11:1-13; 18:1-14; 20:45-47; 21:36; 22:40, 46.

stoned to death (7:59). Peter and John prayed for the Samaritans who had accepted the word to receive the holy Spirit (8:15). Peter instructs Simon the magician to pray for forgiveness (8:22). In turn, Simon begs Peter to pray for him (8:24). When Ananias is directed to go to Saul he finds him praying (9:11). Peter prays over Tabitha and resuscitates her (9:40). Cornelius is a devout man who prayed constantly to God (10:2; see also 10:4, 30, 31). Peter is praying on the rooftop when he receives a vision (10:9; 11:5). When Peter was in prison the Church prayed fervently for him (12:5). The community[21] prays before sending off Saul and Barnabas as missionaries (13:3). Paul and Barnabas likewise pray and fast as they appoint elders in the churches of Lystra, Iconium, and Antioch (14:23). Paul goes in search of a place of prayer in Philippi (16:13,16). While in prison, Paul and Silas prayed and sang hymns to God (16:25). Before leaving the elders at Miletus and the disciples at Tyre, Paul knelt and prayed with them (20:36; 21:5). Paul recounts directions he received from the Lord while praying in the Temple (22:17). Paul exclaims to King Agrippa that he prays to God that he might become a Christian (26:29). The sailors in 27:29 prayed in the midst of the storm for day to come. Paul cures the father of Publius by praying and putting his hands on him (28:8).

To recap: at the outset of the Third Gospel, the whole assembly of the people are praying (1:10). Zechariah (1:13) and Anna (2:37) are singled out as specific individuals who pray. Beyond the infancy narratives, however, only Jesus is shown to be at prayer.[22] One parable told by Jesus features a widow as an example of

---

[21]It is not entirely clear in the text who does the praying. Acts 13:1-3 says "there were in the church at Antioch prophets and teachers: Barnabas, Symeon who was called Niger, Lucius of Cyrene, Manaen, who was a close friend of Herod the tetrarch, and Saul. While they were worshiping the Lord and fasting, the holy Spirit said, 'Set apart for me Barnabas and Saul for the work to which I have called them.' Then, completing their fasting and prayer, they laid hands on them and sent them off." Ernst Haenchen observes, "the presence of the congregation is not mentioned, but probably presupposed" (*The Acts of the Apostles* [Philadelphia: Westminster, 1971] 395).

[22]In a few instances disciples accompany him while he prays (Luke 9:18, 28, 29; 11:1; 22:40-46), but they are not said to be praying.

persistence in prayer (18:1-8).[23] In Acts, there is only one explicit mention of women praying: 1:14 lists "some women, and Mary the mother of Jesus" among the believers gathered in the upper room praying. We can presume women were present in the communities that are said to pray in 2:42; 4:31; 12:5, 12; 13:3, but they are not explicitly mentioned. One may also infer that Lydia and the women whom Paul found gathered at the river when he searched for a place of prayer (16:13) were, indeed, praying there. In contrast, the prayer of the men, i.e., the Twelve (6:4), the apostles (6:6), Peter (3:1; 8:15, 24; 9:40; 10:9; 11:5; 12:5), John (3:1; 8:15), Stephen (7:59), Cornelius (10:2, 4, 30, 31), Paul (9:11; 14:23; 16:13, 16, 25; 20:36; 21:5; 22:17; 26:29; 28:8), Barnabas (14:23), and Silas (16:25), stands out as exemplary. Women disciples who pray are scarcely mentioned in Acts; no impressive stories of women effecting healings, exorcisms, resuscitations, or reception of the Spirit by their prayer are recounted in Acts.

Sharing Life in Community

Throughout his public ministry Jesus is portrayed not as a lone itinerant prophet, but rather as one who is surrounded by a community of disciples.[24] Accordingly, the life of his disciples is life together in community, characterized by corporate mission, shared decision-making, accountability to one another, networking and hospitality among the communities, and sharing of material possessions.[25]

One aspect of Christian community is that mission is not undertaken alone. In the Gospel, Jesus sent out the Twelve, seemingly as a group (9:1-6).[26] He directs the further seventy(-two) to go out two by two (10:1). In Acts pairs of missionaries appear fre-

---

[23]The parable itself illustrates persistence in the pursuit of justice. Luke's introduction in verse 1 interprets it as "a parable about the need to pray always without becoming weary."

[24]E.g., Luke 6:1, 13-16, 17, 20; 7:11; 8:1-3, 9, 22, 45; 9:1, 10-17, 18, 28, 43, 46, 52, 54, 57; 10:1, 17, 23; 11:1; 12:1, 22; 16:1; 17:1, 5, 22; 18:15, 28, 31; 19:29, 37, 39; 20:45; 22:11, 14, 39; 23:49.

[25]Talbert, "Discipleship in Luke-Acts," 71–73.

[26]Compare Mark 6:7 where Jesus sends them out two-by-two. This detail is not found in Luke 9:1-6.

quently: Peter and John,[27] Paul and Barnabas,[28] Judas and Silas,[29] Paul and Silas,[30] Silas and Timothy,[31] Priscilla and Aquila.[32]

In Acts shared decision-making and accountability to one another show another aspect of community. The story of Ananias and Sapphira (5:1-11) relates the dire consequences of selfish holding back and lying to the community. In Acts 6:1-7 the whole community of disciples is called together to select the seven who are to serve at table. Acts 11:27-30 relates the decision of the disciples that each member, according to ability, would participate in the collection for the community of Judea. Accountability of disciples to one another is reflected in Acts 11:1-18, where Peter is called upon to explain his eating with Gentiles. Another instance of a communal decision occurs in Acts 15:1-35, where the issue of circumcision of Gentiles and their observance of dietary regulations is resolved by a meeting of Paul and Barnabas, with the apostles and presbyters of the Jerusalem community. Their decision is made "in agreement with the whole church" (15:22).

The corporate nature of the Christian movement is also evident in the way Luke portrays in Acts the linking of the various faith communities with that in Jerusalem. The apostles in Jerusalem send Peter and John to the Samaritans who had accepted the word (8:14) after Philip's preaching (8:1-13). The Gentile believers in Joppa are connected to the Jerusalem Church through Peter (11:1-18). After news of new believers in Antioch reaches the Church in Jerusalem, they send Barnabas, who in turn brings Saul to teach the disciples in Antioch (11:22-26). The decisions in Acts 15 about the practices of the Gentile converts bring the latter into accord with the Jerusalem community. Each of Paul's missionary journeys begins and ends in Jerusalem, creating the impression of a network of communities bound together in union with that of Jerusalem.

Hosts of house churches play an important role in fostering the life of the communities. Hosts named in Acts include Judas

[27]Acts 3:1, 3, 11; 4:1, 13, 19; 8:14, 17, 25.
[28]Acts 11:30; 12:25; 13:2-3, 7, 42, 43, 46, 50; 14:1, 12, 14, 20; 15:2, 12, 22, 25, 35, 36.
[29]Acts 15:22, 27, 32.
[30]Acts 15:40; 16:19–17:10.
[31]Acts 17:14, 15; 18:5.
[32]Acts 18:2, 18, 26.

(9:11), Simon the tanner (10:6), Mary (12:12), Lydia (16:40), Jason (17:5), Titius Justus (18:7), Philip (21:8), and Mnason of Cyprus (21:16). Their forerunners are those who offer hospitality to Jesus in the Gospel: Simon (4:38), Levi (5:29), Simon the Pharisee (7:36), Martha and Mary (10:38-42), a leader of the Pharisees (14:1), and Zacchaeus (19:5).

Community also entails sharing material possessions. More than any other evangelist, Luke stresses the relation between a person's use of material goods and their response to God's word.[33] In the Magnificat Mary announces God's exaltation of the lowly, filling the hungry, and sending the rich away empty (Luke 1:51-53). Jesus declares his mission "to bring glad tidings to the poor" (4:18). He pronounces the poor blessed (6:20) and remarks on how difficult it is for a rich person to enter the realm of God (18:25). He insists that a person cannot serve both God and mammon (16:13). Jesus invites a rich official to leave everything to follow him (18:22). Peter, James, John (5:11), and Levi (5:28) do precisely that. Mary Magdalene, Joanna, Susanna, and other Galilean women accompany Jesus and the Twelve, providing for them out of their resources (8:1-3). A poor widow who puts into the treasury all she had to live on is favorably contrasted with the rich who gave from their abundance (21:1-4). The parables of the rich fool (12:16-21) and of the rich man and Lazarus (16:19-23) illustrate the dire consequences of accumulating riches for oneself. Salvation comes to the house of the rich tax collector Zacchaeus, who gives half his possessions to the poor (19:1-10).

Acts 2:42-47 and 4:32-34 describes the total sharing, both spiritual and material, of the fledgling Jerusalem community. Acts 5:1-11 relates the horror of selfish holding back and lying to the community. Tabitha (Acts 9:36) and Cornelius (Acts 10:2, 4, 31) are upheld for their almsgiving. Paul reminds the Ephesian elders of a saying of Jesus, "It is more blessed to give than to receive" (Acts 20:35).

---

[33]See John Gillman, *Possessions and the Life of Faith: A Reading of Luke-Acts,* Zacchaeus Studies, New Testament (Collegeville, Minn.: The Liturgical Press, 1991); Luke T. Johnson, *The Literary Function of Possessions in Luke-Acts,* SBLDS 39 (Missoula: Scholars Press, 1977); Sweetland, *Journey,* 186–190.

Luke infrequently names women as contributing to the communal life. Although six missionary pairs are named in Acts, only one includes a woman: Priscilla and Aquila. No women are explicitly said to be among those sent out by Jesus. The Galilean women who travel with Jesus and the Twelve appear to be supporting them out of gratitude (8:1-3). With regard to decisions shared by the community, only by envisioning women among the "community of the disciples" in Acts 6:2 and "the whole church" in 15:22 do we glimpse their presence. The networking of Christian communities is accomplished predominantly by male apostles: Peter, John, Barnabas, Paul, the apostles and presbyters in Jerusalem. Along with her husband Aquila, Priscilla is the only woman who is said to participate in inter-community work (Acts 18). Among those who offer hospitality, the majority are male. Martha and Mary, Mary of Jerusalem, and Lydia are the exceptions. The Galilean women (8:1-3), the poor widow (21:1-4), and Tabitha (Acts 9:36) are the few women who appear among the numerous examples of right use of possessions. Sapphira, with her husband Ananias (Acts 5:1-11), provides a negative example.

Commissioned / Sent Forth
(apostellō, apoluō, ekpempō)

In his inaugural proclamation of his mission, Jesus relates that he has been sent *(apostellein)* "to proclaim liberty to captives and recovery of sight to the blind, to let the oppressed go free, to proclaim a year acceptable to the Lord" (4:18-19). In 4:43 Jesus explains to the crowds, "To the other towns also I must proclaim the good news of the kingdom of God, because for this purpose I have been sent *[apestalēn]*." Twice in his speech at Solomon's portico, Peter refers to Jesus' having been sent *(apostellō)* by God (Acts 3:20, 26).

Jesus, in turn, commissions the Twelve, sending them out *(apostellō)* with power and authority over demons, to cure diseases, to preach the reign of God, and to heal (9:1-2).[34] In 10:1-

---

[34]Cf. Mark 6:7 where Jesus gives them authority over unclean spirits and then proceeds to give instructions about what to take. Lukan redaction has expanded their mission to preaching and healing as well as exorcising.

12 a further seventy(-two) are appointed and sent out *(apostellō)* to heal the sick and to proclaim the reign of God (10:9). Although the word *apostellō* is not used, the disciples are commissioned by the risen Christ to proclaim repentance and forgiveness in his name to all nations (24:47) and to be his witnesses to the ends of the earth (Acts 1:8). In Luke 8:38 Jesus sends away *(apoluō)* the man from whom he had cast out a legion of demons, commissioning him to "return home and recount what God has done for you" (8:39).[35]

In Acts 8:14 Peter and John are sent *(apostellō)* by the apostles in Jerusalem to those who had accepted the word in Samaria. Ananias is sent *(apostellō)* by Jesus to Saul that he might regain his sight (9:17). When the collection is taken up for the community in Jerusalem, it is sent *(apostellō)* to the presbyters in care of Barnabas and Saul (11:30). Saul and Barnabas are sent off *(apoluō)* on their first missionary journey by the Church at Antioch (13:1-3). In 13:4 they are said to be sent forth *(ekpemphthentes)* by the holy Spirit. In 15:27 Judas and Silas are sent by the Church *(apostellō)* in Jerusalem to deliver the decision about Gentile observance of dietary regulations. The Church in Antioch in turn sent off *(apoluō)* Judas and Silas with greetings of peace to those who had commissioned them (15:33). After a disturbance in Thessalonica, the community there sent *(ekpempō)* Paul and Silas to Beroea (17:10). From Ephesus Paul sends forth *(apostellō)* two of his assistants, Timothy and Erastus, to Macedonia (19:22). Paul reports in 22:21 and 26:17 that God has sent *(apostellō)* him to the Gentiles.

There are no instances in the Gospel or Acts in which a woman is clearly commissioned or sent forth. It is possible that Luke envisions women among the pairs of disciples sent forth in Luke 10:1-12, but the identity of the pairs is not revealed. In Luke 24:47-49 those whom Jesus names as witnesses and who are given the promise of the Spirit are presumably "the eleven and those with them" (24:33). However, in Acts 1:4 when Luke is recapping the instructions to those who will receive the promise, the audience is "the apostles whom he had chosen" (1:2). Luke equates the "apostles" with the twelve men chosen in Luke 6:13. And in Acts 1:11 the two men dressed in white address the "witnesses" as

---

[35]In Luke 14:4 *apoluō* is not a commissioning, but rather a simple dismissal.

"men *[andres]* of Galilee." Acts 1:13-14 indicates that the men return to the upper room, where they join the women and Mary and Jesus' siblings. In other words, the women are not present at the commissioning at the ascension. In the remainder of Acts, only male disciples are named as apostolic emissaries sent forth by the Christian communities.

Teaching *(didaskō)*

One of Jesus' prime activities in his ministry is teaching.[36] In the Gospel, once Jesus begins his ministry, no one else is called teacher[37] and no follower of Jesus teaches. In Acts the Jerusalem community "devoted themselves to the teaching of the apostles" (2:42). Further references to the apostles' teaching are made in 5:21, 25, 28, 42. In 4:2 the Jewish leaders are disturbed because Peter and John "were teaching the people" and forbid them to teach further in 4:18. Gamaliel, "a teacher of the law," is cited in 5:34. Five teachers in the Church at Antioch are named in 13:1: "Barnabas, Symeon who was called Niger, Lucius of Cyrene, Manaen who was a close friend of Herod the tetrarch, and Saul." The teaching activity of Barnabas and Saul/Paul in Antioch is noted in 11:26 and 15:35. References to Paul's teaching appear frequently.[38] Apollos "taught accurately about Jesus, although he knew only the baptism of John" (18:25).

All those named as teachers or said to be teaching are men. The one woman in Acts who is usually thought to be teaching

[36]Jesus is said to be teaching in Luke 4:15, 31, 32; 5:3, 17; 6:6; 10:39; 11:1; 13:10, 22, 26; 19:47; 20:1; 21:37; 23:5. The numerous Lukan parables are also didactic. In Acts 1:1 Luke claims to have dealt with "all that Jesus did and taught" in his first volume.

[37]In Luke 2:46 the twelve-year-old Jesus is found "sitting in the midst of the teachers, listening to them and asking them questions." Tax collectors coming to be baptized address John as "teacher" in 3:12. Jesus is called "Teacher" in 7:40; 8:49; 9:38; 10:25; 11:45; 12:13; 18:18; 19:39; 20:21, 28, 39; 21:7; 22:11. Five times Luke takes this title from his Markan source (Luke 9:38 = Mark 9:17; Luke 18:18 = Mark 10:17; Luke 20:21 = Mark 12:14; Luke 20:28 = Mark 12:19; Luke 22:11 = Mark 14:14). The remaining instances occur in peculiarly Lukan material and Lukan redaction of his sources.

[38]Acts 13:12; 17:19; 18:11; 20:20; 21:21, 28; 28:31.

is Priscilla, along with her husband, Aquila. In 18:26 Luke relates that they heard Apollos preach in Ephesus, and "they took him aside and explained *[exethento]* to him the Way [of God] more accurately." However, here Luke does not use the verb "to teach," *didaskō,* but rather *ektithēmi,* meaning "to explain, set forth." One wonders if this is deliberate, so as to restrict the teaching ministry to male disciples.

Healing *(therapeuein; iasthai)*

Jesus commissions his disciples to heal the sick and cure diseases (9:1, 2, 6; 10:9), as he himself does.[39] In the Gospel Luke does not relate whether, indeed, they do heal anyone. It is only in Acts that Jesus' disciples are shown to take up this part of the mission. In Acts 3:1-10 Peter and John heal a man crippled from birth, as does Paul in 14:8-10. The community in Jerusalem prays that the Lord continue to "stretch forth [your] hand to heal" (4:30). Acts 5:16 relates that all those who were sick from the towns around Jerusalem were all cured by Peter and the apostles. "They even carried the sick out into the streets and laid them on cots and mats so that when Peter came by, at least his shadow might fall on one or another of them" (5:15). In Samaria many who were paralyzed or lame were cured by Philip (8:7). In Joppa Peter heals Aeneas, a man paralyzed for eight years (9:32-35). In Ephesus when the handkerchiefs or aprons that had touched Paul's skin were brought to the sick, their diseases left them (19:12). In Malta Paul cured the father of Publius who lay sick in bed with fever and dysentery (28:8). After this happened, the rest of the people on the island who had diseases also came and were cured (28:9).

In no instance does a woman disciple share in the mission of healing.

[39]Luke 4:38-40; 5:12-14, 17; 6:6-11, 18-19; 7:1-10, 21; 8:2, 40-56; 9:11, 42; 13:10-17; 14:1-6; 17:11-17; 18:35-43; 22:51; Acts 10:38.

Exorcising

In Luke 9:1-2 the Twelve are given power and authority over demons. In this they imitate Jesus who exorcises demons.[40] One incident is related in which Jesus' disciples are unable to perform an exorcism (Luke 9:40). When the seventy(-two) return from their first missionary expedition they rejoice that the demons are subject to them (10:17). In Acts 5:12-16 all those tormented by unclean spirits were cured by the apostles and Peter. Philip effects the same in Samaria (8:7). In Philippi Paul exorcises a slave girl with an oracular spirit (16:18). He also heals those with evil spirits in Ephesus (19:12).

No women are explicitly said to participate in the ministry of exorcism.

Forgiving *(aphesis hamartiōn)*

A particular emphasis of Luke is forgiveness of sins. John the Baptist, as Jesus' predecessor, "went throughout [the] whole region of the Jordan, proclaiming a baptism of repentance for the forgiveness of sins" (3:3), as prophesied by Zechariah (1:77). In his inaugural proclamation of his mission, Jesus says he has been sent "to proclaim liberty *[aphesis]* to captives" (4:18).

Narratives in the Gospel that highlight forgiveness by Jesus include the story of the paralytic (5:20), the episode with the woman who loved greatly (7:47-48),[41] and the forgiveness of his crucifiers (23:34) and the criminal hanged with him (23:43).[42]

In his Sermon on the Plain Jesus teaches his disciples, "forgive and you will be forgiven" (6:37). Jesus teaches them further to pray for forgiveness as they themselves forgive those who are indebted to them (11:4). He also instructs them that if another disciple sins, they must rebuke the offender, and if there is repentance, they must forgive (17:3). There is no limit to how often a disciple shall forgive (17:4). In his final commissioning of the

[40]Luke 4:31-37, 41; 6:18; 8:26-39; 9:37-43; 11:14.

[41]The perfect passive *apheōntai* in verse 47 and the parable in verses 41-43 point to the forgiveness having occurred prior to the incident at Simon's house.

[42]Luke 5:17-26 is based on Mark 2:1-12; the other examples are unique to Luke.

disciples Jesus tells them that repentance for forgiveness of sins is to be proclaimed in his name to all nations, beginning from Jerusalem (24:47).

In Acts, Peter invites people to repentance and forgiveness in his Pentecost speech (2:38). He does the same in Samaria with Simon the magician (8:22). In his speeches to the Sanhedrin (5:31) and to Cornelius (10:43) Peter speaks of the forgiveness of sins through Jesus. Similarly, Paul preaches forgiveness of sins in his address in the synagogue at Antioch in Pisidia (13:38) and in his speech to King Agrippa (26:18).

There is only one story in Luke of a woman who is the beneficiary of Jesus' forgiveness (7:36-50). In Acts only Peter and Paul preach forgiveness.

Serving *(diakonein)*

In the farewell instructions Jesus gives his disciples (22:26-27) he tells them that the one who would be the leader among them must be the one who serves *(ho diakonōn)*. He points to the example he himself has given them, "I am among you as the one who serves *[ho diakonōn]*." The verb *diakonein* occurs in three episodes in the Gospel. After Jesus rebuked her fever, Simon's mother-in-law "got up immediately and waited on them" (4:39). Mary Magdalene, Joanna, Susanna, and many other women accompanied Jesus and the Twelve as they journeyed through Galilee, and "provided for them *[diēkonoun autois]* out of their resources" (8:3). Finally, in Luke 10:40 Martha, burdened with much serving *(diakonian)*, asks Jesus, "Lord, do you not care that my sister has left me by myself to do the serving *[diakonein]*?"[43]

In Acts 1:17, 25, where Judas' successor is chosen, the noun *diakonia* refers to the apostolic ministry of the Twelve. In 6:1 the Hellenists complain against the Hebrews that their widows are being neglected in the daily distribution *(diakonia)*. The solution devised by the Twelve, who want to devote themselves solely to the ministry of the word *(diakonia tou logou,* 6:4) is to have the community select seven men to serve at table *(diakonein trapezais,*

---

[43]The other instances of *diakonein* are in sayings of Jesus referring to servants: 12:37; 17:8.

6:2). The noun *diakonia* is used of the relief mission to the community in Judea (11:29) carried out by Barnabas and Saul (12:25), and of Paul's ministry in general (20:24; 21:19). The participle form of *diakonein* describes Timothy and Erastus, two of Paul's assistants (19:22).

In the Gospel only women characters are the subjects of *diakonein*. In contrast, *diakonein* and *diakonia* are used only of men in Acts.[44]

Enduring Conflicts and Persecution

From the beginning of his mission, Jesus experiences rejection (Luke 4:24-30) and opposition (5:21-24, 33; 6:1-11; 7:34, 39). Jesus instructs his disciples repeatedly about his own coming persecution, trials, suffering, and death (9:22, 44-45; 18:31-34). At the transfiguration he and Moses and Elijah discuss his "exodus," his liberating death, that will be accomplished in Jerusalem (9:31). As Jesus moves closer to the city that kills the prophets (13:34) Herod is plotting against him (13:31-33). Following the Temple cleansing incident, the chief priests, scribes, and leaders of the people repeatedly seek a way to put him to death (19:47; 20:19; 22:2). Jesus endures agony (22:39-46), betrayal and arrest (22:47-54), denial and mockery (22:54-65), interrogations and trials (22:66–23:16), flogging (23:16), crucifixion (23:33-43), and death (23:44-49).

Jesus warns his disciples that such will be their fate as well (21:12-19), that his disciples must take up their cross daily and be willing to lose their lives (9:23-27). But he also encourages them not to fear "those who kill the body but after that can do no more" (12:4). He further assures them that the holy Spirit will teach them what to say when they are taken "before synagogues and before rulers and authorities" (12:11-12).

In Acts Peter and John are the first to be arrested and interrogated for their preaching of the gospel (4:5-22). This is repeated

---

[44]The issue of what is connoted by *diakonein* and *diakonia* in each of these references in Luke and Acts will be taken up below. See John N. Collins, *DIAKONIA: Reinterpreting the Ancient Sources* (New York: Oxford University Press, 1990).

in 5:17-42, when Peter and the apostles are put in the public jail and then tried before the Sanhedrin. The Jewish leaders wanted to put them to death (5:33) but Gamaliel persuades them to release them after a flogging (5:40). The first to be martyred for his faith in Christ is Stephen (7:54-60). James is the next to die at the hands of Herod, who also arrests Peter (12:1-5). After the death of Stephen "a severe persecution of the church in Jerusalem" (8:1) causes all but the apostles to scatter throughout the countryside. Saul, trying to destroy the Church, was "entering house after house and dragging out men and women," handing them over for imprisonment (8:3). It was while "breathing murderous threats against the disciples" and seeking to bring back in chains "any men or women who belonged to the Way" (9:1-2) that Saul experienced his conversion.

Paul himself then becomes the object of persecution, beginning with a conspiracy to kill him in Damascus (9:23-25). Jews oppose him at Antioch in Pisidia (13:45-47). There is an attempt to attack and stone him and Barnabas at Iconium (14:1-7). At Lystra Paul is stoned and left for dead (14:19-20) and at Philippi he is beaten with rods and imprisoned (16:40). In Thessalonica, Jason, Paul's host, is dragged before the magistrates in Paul's stead (17:5-9). In Beroea Jews of Thessalonica stir up the crowds against Paul, causing him to flee to Athens (17:10-16). In Corinth he is brought before the tribunal (18:12-16) and when his accusers are not satisfied with the outcome, they beat Sosthenes, the synagogue official (18:17). Paul's preaching causes a riot in Ephesus (19:23-40), from which he escapes to Macedonia, where another plot is made against him (20:3). In Caesarea Agabus predicts that Paul will be bound and handed over to the Gentiles (21:11). In Jerusalem he is beaten and arrested (21:27-36) while the mob shouts "Away with him!" (21:36). Paul stages defenses before Jewish and Gentile rulers (22:1–26:32), endures shipwreck (27:6-44), and ends in chains in Rome (28:11-31).

In sum, the only explicit mention of women who endure suffering for their faith are those whom Saul persecutes before his conversion. In the first chapters of Acts the sufferings of Peter, the apostles (whom Luke equates with the Twelve), Stephen, and James are narrated. From chapter 9 on Paul's tribulations predominate, with occasional mention of a male associate suffering in Paul's stead.

Filled With the Holy Spirit

What empowers disciples of Jesus is the gift of the holy Spirit. The action of the Spirit in Jesus and his disciples is a theme that is particularly emphasized by Luke. Luke's first mention of the Spirit is in 1:15 where Gabriel informs Zechariah that John "will be filled with the holy Spirit even from his mother's womb." The angel likewise assures Mary when announcing to her the birth of Jesus that the holy Spirit will come upon her (1:35). Elizabeth is filled with the holy Spirit (1:41), as is Zechariah (1:67). The child Jesus is said to grow and become strong in spirit (1:80). The holy Spirit rested upon Simeon and revealed to him that he would not see death before he had seen the Messiah (2:25-26). The Spirit guided him to come to the Temple when the parents of Jesus brought the child there (2:27). John the Baptist proclaims that Jesus will baptize with the holy Spirit and fire (3:16).

The holy Spirit led Jesus to the wilderness (4:1) where he was tempted; when he returned to Galilee he was "in the power of the Spirit" (4:14). Jesus opens his proclamation of his mission declaring, "The Spirit of the Lord is upon me" (4:18). Jesus rejoices in the holy Spirit (10:21). He assures his followers that the holy Spirit will be given to those who ask (11:13) and that the Spirit will teach them what to say in defense before authorities (12:12). He also warns of blasphemy against the holy Spirit (12:10). After his resurrection Jesus directs his followers to stay in the city to await the promise of his Father (24:49), that is, the Spirit.

In the post-resurrection time with them, Jesus gave "instructions through the holy Spirit to the apostles whom he had chosen" (Acts 1:2). He told them they would soon be "baptized with the holy Spirit" (1:5) and that they would receive power when the holy Spirit comes upon them (1:8). This is fulfilled at Pentecost when "they were all filled with the holy Spirit and began to speak in different tongues, as the Spirit enabled them to proclaim" (2:4). It is not said explicitly who is included in "all." The preceding references are to the Eleven (1:13), the women, Mary, the mother of Jesus, and his siblings (1:14), and the group of about one hundred twenty persons gathered in the one place (1:15). In Peter's Pentecost speech he quotes the prophet Joel (3:1-5) to interpret these new manifestations of the Spirit: "I will pour out a portion of my spirit upon all flesh. Your sons and your daughters shall prophesy, your young men shall see visions, your old men shall dream dreams. Indeed, upon my servants and my handmaids I will pour out a portion of my spirit in those days, and they shall prophesy" (Acts 2:17-18). Here it is clear that both men and women have received the Spirit. Peter also speaks of Jesus as "having received the promise of the holy Spirit from the Father," which he has poured out (Acts 2:33; see also 10:38). He ends his speech by inviting his hearers to repent and be baptized "and you will receive the gift of the holy Spirit" (2:38). About three thousand persons *(psychai)* accepted his message (2:41).

When Peter addresses the Sanhedrin he is filled with the Spirit (4:8). David is said to have spoken by the holy Spirit (4:25). The community in Jerusalem who pray with Peter and John after their release from prison are "all filled with the holy Spirit" (4:31). Ananias and Sapphira lie to the holy Spirit (5:3, 9). Peter and the apostles pronounce the Christian kerygma before the Sanhedrin, asserting, "we are witnesses of these things, as is the holy Spirit that God has given to those who obey him" (5:32).

The seven men selected for table ministry are full of the Spirit (6:3). Among them, Stephen is singled out as "a man filled with faith and the holy Spirit" (6:5). Those who debated with him "could not withstand the wisdom and the spirit with which he spoke" (6:10). Stephen accuses his fellow Jews of always opposing the holy Spirit (7:51). At the end of his speech, just before he was stoned to death, Stephen was filled with the holy Spirit as he "looked up intently to heaven and saw the glory of God and Jesus standing at the right hand of God" (7:55).

The Samaritans received the Spirit when Peter and John went down and prayed for them (8:15-17). The Spirit gives directions to Philip (8:29, 39), Peter (10:19; 11:12), and the prophets and teachers at Antioch: Barnabas, Symeon, Lucius, Manaen, and Saul (13:1-2). Saul received the Spirit when Ananias laid hands on him (9:17). He is filled with the holy Spirit when he confronts Elymas the magician (13:9). The Church throughout Judea, Galilee, and Samaria lived in peace, the fear of the Lord, and with "the consolation of the holy Spirit" (9:31).

The Spirit fell on "all who heard the word" (10:44; 11:15) when Peter preached to Cornelius and his relatives and friends (10:24). That the holy Spirit had been poured out even on the Gentiles astounded the circumcised believers who had come with Peter to Joppa (10:45). Peter speaks at the council of Jerusalem of how God gave the holy Spirit to the Gentiles "just as he did us" (15:8). The apostles and presbyters at the council of Jerusalem make their decisions in accord with the holy Spirit (15:28).

Barnabas is said to be "a good man, filled with the Holy Spirit and faith" (11:24). He and Saul are sent forth on mission by the holy Spirit (13:4). The disciples "were filled with joy and with the holy Spirit" at the conclusion of the episode at Antioch in Pisidia (13:52). The Spirit prevents Paul, Silas, and Timothy from preaching in Asia (16:6) and Bythinia (16:7). But Paul "resolved in the spirit" to go through Macedonia and Achaia, and then to go on to Jerusalem (19:21). The twelve men in Ephesus upon whom Paul laid hands received the Spirit (19:6). In his farewell to the Ephesian elders, Paul mentions that the holy Spirit has made them overseers of the flock (20:28).

Paul speaks of himself as "compelled by the Spirit" (20:22) and asserts that the holy Spirit testifies to him in every city that imprisonment and persecutions await him (20:23). In Tyre the disciples told Paul through the Spirit not to go on to Jerusalem (21:4). Agabus, who had predicted by the Spirit that there would be a severe famine over all the world (11:28), also prophesied by the Spirit that Paul would be bound by the Jews in Jerusalem (21:11). The last reference to the Spirit in Acts is in 28:25 where Paul affirms the correctness of what the Spirit said through the prophet Isaiah.

To summarize, in the Gospel the only characters besides Jesus who are said to be filled with the Spirit are found in the infancy narratives: Elizabeth, Zechariah, John, Mary, and Simeon. These figures are not disciples. Once Jesus' ministry begins, only he is said to be filled with the Spirit. He speaks of the promised Spirit to his disciples and they experience the power of the Spirit throughout Acts.

In Acts there are no individual women disciples who are said to be filled with the Spirit or who are directed by the Spirit or who speak or act through the Spirit, as do Peter, Stephen, Philip, Barnabas, Symeon, Lucius, Manaen, Paul, Silas, Timothy, and Agabus. David and Isaiah are affirmed in what they spoke through the Spirit. Groups of men who act by the Spirit appear in Acts: the apostles, presbyters, the male deacons, the twelve men in Ephesus, the Ephesian elders. The only mention of women in connection with the Spirit is that they were in the gathered community at the first outpouring of the Spirit at Pentecost (2:4 with 1:14, 15 and 2:17-18). It may be that Luke presumes the presence of women among the three thousand persons who accepted Peter's message (2:41), the community in Jerusalem (4:31), the Samaritans (8:15-17), the Church throughout Judea, Galilee, and Samaria who lived in the comfort of the holy Spirit (9:31), Cornelius' relatives and friends (10:24), the disciples at Antioch in Pisidia (13:52), and the disciples in Tyre (21:4). But no stories of women ministering by the power of the Spirit are related in Acts.

Conclusion

While it is undeniable that there are women disciples[45] in Luke and Acts who receive the word, believe, are baptized, follow Jesus, and host house churches, their role is presented by the third evangelist as clearly different from that of the men. There are no narratives showing individual women disciples as called, commissioned, enduring persecution, or ministering by the power of the Spirit. Women in Luke and Acts do not imitate Jesus' mission of preaching, teaching, healing, exorcising, forgiving, or praying.

The powerfully prophetic women Elizabeth, Mary, and Anna in the infancy narratives are not disciples; they belong to the era of Judaism. Women who speak in the rest of the gospel are reprimanded by Jesus or are disbelieved. Women in the Third Gospel are healed by Jesus and are objects of his compassion. One (7:36-50) is exemplary for her great love, but nothing is related about how the love she demonstrated toward Jesus achieves a missionary dimension. The Galilean women who had been healed provided for Jesus and the Twelve (8:1-3). Luke portrays their ministry as an ancillary service to the mission of Jesus and his twelve chosen male apostles in gratitude for their healing. In Luke 10:38-42 Mary is praised for listening to Jesus, but nothing is related of how she acts on what she hears. Martha, who is serving, is reprimanded. In Acts 9:36 Tabitha is said to have been "completely occupied with good deeds and almsgiving." Her

---

[45]In Acts 9:36 Tabitha is explicitly called *mathētria*.

ministry is one that is silent and behind-the-scenes, making tunics and clothing (9:39). Philip's four daughters gifted with prophecy never speak (Acts 21:9).

Since Luke claims to have investigated "everything accurately anew, to write it down in an orderly sequence" (1:3), it is unlikely that he does not know of women who participate actively and visibly in the apostolic ministries, including that of leadership. Abundant references to such are found in Paul's letters.[46] We must conclude that Luke, like the author of the Pastoral letters, knowing of such women, is intent on restricting them to silent, passive, supporting roles. He is conveying the message that women and men have different ways of being disciples.

In today's Church, as we come to recognize that because women are equally created in God's image, equally redeemed by Christ, equally called to be disciples, equally entrusted with his mission, equally endowed with the Spirit, and equally gifted for ministry, what are we to do with Luke's stories that reinforce gender divisions? Some have decided to jettison the Bible entirely, and begin afresh, a choice that removes one from traditional Christian communities. Others look for ways to reinterpret the tradition so that good news may yet be found in it. To simply take the Lukan narrative at face value, women would have to read as though they were men if they would hear themselves called by Jesus, commissioned to proclaim and heal, empowered by the Spirit for mission.[47] Or women would have to be content with finding themselves in the story only as part of the amorphous crowds who follow and believe. Some have tried to construct tales that fill in the missing pieces of the stories of women disciples, of which we catch only a glimpse in the canonical text.

It is preferable to engage in a process of recontextualization and reinterpretation, in which Luke's patriarchal biases are recog-

[46]E.g., Phoebe, the deacon and patron of the Church at Cenchreae (Rom 16:1-2); Junia, a notable apostle (Rom 16:7); Mary, Tryphaena, Tryphosa, and Persis, coworkers of Paul (Rom 16:6, 12); Prisca, a coworker who "risked her neck" for Paul and was host of a house church at Corinth and then Ephesus (Rom 16:3-4); Euodia and Syntyche, coworkers of Paul who he says "have struggled at my side in promoting the gospel" (Phil 4:2-4).

[47]Jane Schaberg, "Luke," *The Women's Bible Commentary,* ed. Carol A. Newsom and Sharon H. Ringe (Louisville: Westminster/John Knox, 1992) 281.

nized and challenged. In order to promote a vision of church in which both women and men are called equally to discipleship and to share in the same mission, the Lukan stories cannot be taught, preached, or passed on uncritically. Luke is a master story-teller and each of his episodes has a powerful identity-forming potential. But unless their patriarchal framework is unmasked and addressed head-on, preachers and teachers will reinforce, rather than challenge, their inscribed gender role divisions. And the possibility of a church of equal disciples will recede away yet further from us. Choosing the better part would be to read with new eyes against Luke's intent.[48]

[48]Ibid., 291; See also Judith Fetterley, *The Resisting Reader: A Feminist Approach to American Fiction* (Bloomington & London: Indiana University Press, 1978).

Chapter 4

Elizabeth and Mary:
Women of Spirit Birthing Hope

The Gospel of Luke opens with stories not found elsewhere of three women who play key roles in the drama of salvation history: Elizabeth, Mary, and Anna. It is striking that the first two chapters of Luke invite the reader into the world of women and begin the story of Jesus from their perspective. By contrast, the opening chapters of the Gospel of Matthew are told through the lens of Joseph's experience. The revelations of God's plan are made to him, not to Mary, in a series of dreams (Matt 1:20-21; 2:13-15; 2:19-21). The Gospels of Mark and John have no infancy narratives; Mark begins his Gospel with John the Baptist's desert heralding; the hymn to the Word opens the Fourth Gospel.

The many differences between the infancy narratives of Luke and Matthew make it clear that they did not have a common source. Each evangelist shaped the traditions he received according to his own theological purposes. It is most likely that Luke composed these first two chapters after the rest of the Gospel was complete. The infancy narratives serve as an overture to the entire Gospel; they sound themes that will play out through the whole of Luke's story.[1]

---

[1]See further Raymond E. Brown, *The Birth of the Messiah* (Garden City, N.Y.: Doubleday, 1977).

LUKE 1:5-7

> [5]In the days of King Herod of Judea there was a priest named Zechariah of the priestly division of Abijah; his wife was from the daughters of Aaron, and her name was Elizabeth. [6]Both were righteous in the eyes of God, observing all the commandments and ordinances of the Lord blamelessly. [7]But they had no child, because Elizabeth was barren, and both were advanced in years.

Luke, more than any other evangelist, punctuates his Gospel with historical references (e.g., Luke 2:1-2; 3:1-2; Acts 18:12). The result is that the reader perceives Jesus' story from the start as immersed in a real place and time known to the first audience. For any Jewish members of Luke's community, and those who are not hearing the story for the first time, mention of "King Herod" sounds an ominous tone. The reference is to Herod the Great, who ruthlessly defended his throne as king of the Jews from 37–4 B.C.E.

The other Lukan references to Herod[2] are to his son, Herod Antipas, who was tetrarch of Galilee and Perea from his father's death until 39 C.E. It was he who had been censured by John the Baptist "because of Herodias, his brother's wife, and because of all the evil deeds Herod had committed," including putting John into prison (Luke 3:19-20). He was curious to see Jesus (Luke 9:7-9), but when he finally meets Jesus after his arrest, Herod mocks him and sends him back to Pilate (23:6-16). In his second volume, Luke includes Herod among those guilty for Jesus' death (Acts 4:27) and depicts him as a persecutor of the early Christians (Acts 12:1-24). The joy-filled setting for the births of the children of Elizabeth and Mary is tinged with seriousness at the mention of Herod, whose son will be instrumental in the deaths of John and Jesus.

The setting of these opening verses also immerses the reader into the world of pious Jews. Zechariah is offering priestly sacrifice in the sanctuary of the Lord (1:8-9); Elizabeth and Zechariah "observe all the commandments and ordinances of the Lord blamelessly" (1:6); Joseph and Mary take Jesus to Jerusalem for

---

[2]Luke 3:1, 19; 9:7, 9; 13:31; 23:6-16; Acts 4:27; 12:1-24; 13:1.

the Presentation and to offer sacrifice (2:22-24); Simeon and Anna are keeping vigil in the Temple (2:25-38). It will not surprise the reader, then, when Luke's Jesus is found praying at every key moment of the Gospel. The story of Jesus continues the story of the faithful God of Israel.

The stage is set and the scene opens on Zechariah and Elizabeth. For the most part Elizabeth's story has been overlooked while that of her husband and son receive the attention. Zechariah, because of the intriguing story of his silencing, has been the subject of study, as has John, because of the role he plays as the precursor of Christ.[3] But few have observed that from the start, Luke introduces Elizabeth as a character of equal importance in the gospel story. Every statement made of Zechariah is matched by what Luke says of Elizabeth. The priestly lineage and the names of both are given (v. 5). Both are righteous before God, both are childless, and both were getting on in years.

It is significant that Luke tells us Elizabeth's name. Countless biblical women are left unnamed, identified only as the daughter, wife, or mother of a male character. Luke adheres to this convention with Simon's mother-in-law (4:38-39) and the daughter of Jairus (8:40-42, 49-56), subsuming their identity into that of a male.[4] Although Luke first describes Elizabeth as Zechariah's

---

[3]E.g., R. E. Brown, "The Annunciation to Zechariah, the Birth of the Baptist, and the Benedictus (Luke 1:5-25, 57-80)," *Worship* 62 (1988) 482–496. The surveys by R. E. Brown, "Gospel Infancy Narrative Research From 1976 to 1986: Part I (Matthew)," *CBQ* 48 (1986) 468–483; "Gospel Infancy Narrative Research From 1976 to 1986: Part II (Luke)," *CBQ* 48 (1986) 660–680 show no studies on Elizabeth. In *But She Said: Feminist Practices of Biblical Interpretation* ([Boston: Beacon, 1992] 193–194), Elisabeth Schüssler Fiorenza includes a short reflection on Elizabeth from a feminist perspective by one of her students, Diana Scholl.

[4]Other unnamed Lukan women characters are the widow of Nain (7:11-17); the woman who showed great love (7:36-50); the woman healed of hemorrhages, whom Jesus calls "daughter" (8:48); the bent woman, whom Jesus calls "daughter of Abraham" (13:16); and the "daughters of Jerusalem" who weep for Jesus (23:28). The widow of Zarephath (Luke 4:26) and the wife of Lot (Luke 17:32) also remain nameless, as in 1 Kings 17:7-16 and Genesis 19:26. Interestingly, all of these women, with the exception of the woman healed of hemorrhages, are characters who appear only in Luke's Gospel.

wife (repeated in 1:13, 18, 24), and a daughter of Aaron, he does give her own name, thus individuating her as a character with a particular role to play.[5] With her name also comes further emphasis on her Aaronic lineage, as the only Elizabeth in the First Testament was the wife of the high priest Aaron (Exod 6:23).

Furthermore, a biblical name reveals something of the person's character. In Hebrew *'Elîšeba'* means either "My God is the one by whom to swear," or "my God is satiety, fortune." In either case, Elizabeth's name declares that she is a woman who depends utterly on God and who is filled to satisfaction by God. This paves the way for Luke's next statement about Elizabeth.

Luke emphasizes that both Elizabeth and Zechariah were righteous *(dikaios)* in the eyes of God, observing all the commandments and ordinances of the Lord blamelessly.[6] What is astonishing about this is that rarely in the Bible is the adjective "righteous" used to describe a woman. In the Greek translation of the Hebrew Bible *dikaios* is frequently attributed to God.[7] The few individuals that are said to be upright include Noah (Gen 6:9); Job (Job 1:1); Daniel (4 Macc 16:21); Ishbaal, the son of Saul (2 Sam 4:11); and the Servant of God (Isa 53:11). The only woman said to be "righteous" is Tamar (Gen 38:26), whose deception of Judah earns her the title!

In the New Testament God is said to be upright[8] and is addressed as *pater dikaie,* "Righteous Father," by Jesus (John 17:25). The term is often used of Jesus.[9] Other individuals said to be righteous in the New Testament are Joseph (Matt 1:19), John the Baptist (Mark 6:20), Simeon (Luke 2:25), Joseph of Arimathea

---

[5]Other women who are named by Luke include Mary (1:27, 30, 34, 38, 39, 41, 46, 56; 2:5, 16, 19, 34); Anna (2:36-38); Mary Magdalene (8:2; 24:10); Joanna (8:3; 24:10); Susanna (8:3); Martha and Mary (10:38-42); and Mary, the mother of James (24:10).

[6]This last phrase has strong echoes, both in structure and vocabulary of 1 Kings 8:61 (LXX), where Solomon's blessing over the community of Israel concludes, "You must be wholly devoted to the LORD, our God, observing his statutes and keeping his commandments, as on this day."

[7]E.g., Pss 7:12; 114:5; Isa 45:21; Jer 12:1; Dan 9:14; 2 Chr 12:6.

[8]Rom 3:26; 2 Tim 4:8; 1 John 1:9.

[9]Matt 27:19; 27:24 (some mss, e.g., ℵ, K, L, W); Luke 23:47; Acts 3:14; 7:52; 22:14; 1 Pet 3:18; 1 John 2:1, 29; 3:7.

(Luke 23:50), Cornelius (Acts 10:22), Abel (Heb 11:4; 1 John 3:12), and Lot (2 Pet 2:7). Elizabeth is the only woman to whom the term is applied.

It is particularly significant that Luke uses *dikaios* of Elizabeth in light of the importance he gives this term in reference to Jesus. Luke has changed Mark's climactic declaration of the centurion at the death of Jesus from, "Truly this man was the Son of God!" (Mark 15:39) to "Certainly this man was innocent *[dikaios]*" (Luke 23:47). And in his second volume, "the Righteous One" *(ho dikaios)* becomes a title of Jesus in three key speeches: Peter's speech in the Temple (3:14); Stephen's speech (7:52); and Paul's speech before the Jerusalem Jews (22:14). In this overture to the Gospel and Acts, Elizabeth, as well as Zechariah, prefigure Jesus in his righteousness.[10]

In saying that Elizabeth was "observing all the commandments and ordinances of the Lord blamelessly," Luke sets the stage for the story of a woman who has been faithfully walking in the way of God for many long years. It is clear from this statement that her childlessness is not a punishment for sin. Luke would have us see her rather as a woman who has been freer to devote her attentions to God since she has been unfettered by the duties of motherhood.

The equal pairing of statements about Elizabeth and Zechariah ends with verse 7, where Luke asserts that it is Elizabeth's barrenness that is the cause of their childlessness. The possibility that Zechariah was responsible for their inability to conceive a child did not arise in Luke's worldview.

A person familiar with the First Testament cannot help but recognize that Luke situates Elizabeth among a long line of childless biblical women: Sarah (Gen 16:1), Rebecca (Gen 25:21), Rachel (Gen 30:1), the mother of Samson (Judg 13:2), and Hannah (1 Samuel 1–2). Continuity is a theme throughout the Third Gospel: the same faithful God of Israel is present and active in the New Age. Like her predecessors, Elizabeth will play an im-

---

[10]J. M. Ford ("Zealotism and the Lukan Infancy Narratives," *NovT* 18 [1976] 280-292) uses the description of John the Baptist's parents as "righteous" as part of her evidence that they were zealots. I am not convinced that this was either historically probable or theologically suited to Luke's purpose.

portant role in salvation history by conceiving and bearing a child who will be a key figure in God's interaction with humankind.

The fact that both Elizabeth and Zechariah are advanced in years underlines the great improbability of their ever having a child and highlights the divine element in John's conception.[11] At the same time, the detail about Elizabeth's age accents her many long years of faithful relationship with God. Like her barren ancestors, Elizabeth's faith, although seemingly long unrewarded, is unshakable. In this she once again prefigures Jesus, who resolutely trusts in God even as he is confronted with his passion and death.

In the next scene (Luke 1:8-23) the focus narrows to Zechariah in the familiar story of the announcement of John's birth. There are strong resemblances to the story of the birth of Samuel to Hannah and Elkanah.[12] Luke depicts Zechariah as fearful and disbelieving. He is a priest, a mediator of the divine, but he is unable to believe this new act of God and is silenced. In accord with Luke's theme of the surprising ways of God and the reversal of expectations, Elizabeth becomes the one who understands and proclaims.

LUKE 1:23-24

> [23]Then, when his days of ministry were completed, he went home. [24]After this time his wife Elizabeth conceived, and she went into seclusion for five months, saying, "So has the Lord done for me at a time when he has seen fit to take away my disgrace before others."

The setting now shifts to the private sphere of Elizabeth's home and to her interior thoughts. It is striking how easily Elizabeth, in contrast to Zechariah, recognizes God's grace. From the way Luke tells the story, we have the impression that Elizabeth is a woman whose lifelong relationship with God has taught her to

[11]The parallels between the situation of Elizabeth and Zechariah and that of Sarah and Abraham (Gen 18:11) are most evident.

[12]The introductions of both stories (Luke 1:5; 1 Sam 1:1) are very similar. In both the annunciation of the birth of the child is made to the father and comes during the offering of priestly sacrifice (1 Sam 1:3, 17; Luke 1:13). These parallels are outlined in Brown, *Birth,* 268-269.

know the ways of God, even when God does the unexpected. There is no questioning or objecting from Elizabeth; only the declaration: "So has the Lord done for me."

Luke often gives us access to the thoughts or interior dialogue of his characters. Most often the inner reflections reveal mistaken notions, as in 2:44 where Mary and Joseph thought *(nomisantes)* Jesus was in the caravan returning from the Passover feast in Jerusalem. John the Baptist admonishes the crowd, "do not begin to say to yourselves *[legein en heautois]*, 'We have Abraham as our father' " (3:18). It is mistaken to think that membership among God's chosen is automatic by birth. In 3:15 people "were asking in their hearts *[dialogizomenōn]* whether John might be the Messiah." Simon the Pharisee tells himself *(eipen en heautǫ̣)* that Jesus is not really a prophet (7:39). In 11:17 Jesus knew the thoughts *(dianoēmata)* of those who asked for a sign because they wanted to test him. The rich fool first asks himself *(dialogizeto en heautǫ̣)* what he should do with his bountiful harvest (12:17), and then says, "I shall say to myself *[erō tę̣ psychę̣ mou]*, 'Now as for you, you have so many good things stored up for many years, rest, eat, drink, be merry!' " (12:19). In the parable of the judge and the widow, after her persistent demands for justice, he said to himself *(eipen en heautǫ̣)*, "While it is true that I neither fear God nor respect any human being . . ." (18:4). In 19:11 people "thought *[dokein]* that the kingdom of God would appear there [near Jerusalem] immediately." In 24:37 when the resurrected Jesus appeared to the startled disciples they "thought *[edokoun]* that they were seeing a ghost." In every instance of interior dialogue in the Gospel of Luke, the speakers articulate mistaken notions or misguided judgments. Elizabeth is unique in making a significant theological statement in what she says to herself.

Despite the many years that she has been the one carrying the onus for the couple's childlessness, Elizabeth's statement asserts that suffering and humiliation is not God's intent for her. In her day, bearing children, especially sons, was considered a woman's main function. With childbearing came status, approval, and security.[13] With barrenness came disdain (as that of Hagar for Sarah

---

[13]See P. Bird, "Images of Women in the Old Testament," *Religion and Sexism,* ed. R. Ruether (New York: Simon and Schuster, 1974) 62–63.

in Gen 16:4-5), envy (as that of Rachel for Leah in Gen 30:1), deep sorrow, and misery (as that of Hannah in 1 Sam 1:16). A barren woman could also suffer the shame of divorce and be returned to her father's house (Lev 22:13).[14] Worse yet, barrenness was also considered a punishment for sin (Lev 20:21) or being forgotten by God (1 Sam 1:11). In the case of Elizabeth, Luke's statement of her uprightness dispels any thought that her barrenness is a punishment from God. Nonetheless, Elizabeth has suffered public humiliation being known as the one who is barren (1:36).[15]

This vignette is the first in Luke's Gospel to raise the question of suffering and how to understand it. Although Elizabeth has suffered humiliation in her childlessness, she does not identify the suffering with God's will. Rather, she sees God's hand in the new life she bears and in the lifting of her public disgrace. She expresses a deeply incarnational theology, recognizing God in bodiliness. Her perspective questions a spirituality that seeks out suffering and exalts as closest to God one who suffers most. In her suffering she prefigures the suffering Messiah (Luke 24:26), but like him, does not seek suffering for its own sake. Jesus will show that suffering is a direct consequence of the mission of proclaiming the good news, but is not to be sought after for itself.

What Elizabeth articulates is that God's delight is not in how she endures tribulation. Rather, Elizabeth is intimately familiar with the God who delivers oppressed people from their plight and who rejoices in their liberation. This is the Mighty One who brought the Israelites out of bondage from Egypt to the Promised Land, a land flowing with milk and honey. This is the Holy One who also brought back the captives from Babylon, restoring divine favor and blessings. It is the same God that Jesus will proclaim in his opening address in Nazareth, the God who had anointed him to preach good news to the poor, release to captives, recovery of sight to the blind, and liberty to those who are oppressed (Luke 4:18-19).

---

[14]These examples are given by Jane Schaberg, *The Illegitimacy of Jesus* (San Francisco: Harper & Row, 1987) 103.

[15]Elizabeth's declaration that God has removed her humiliation in verse 24 has strong echoes of Rachel's exclamation at the birth of Joseph, "God has removed my disgrace" (Gen 30:23).

Anyone familiar with the Scriptures knows well that God, time after time, showed compassion to the people of the covenant through the wombs of women. The very words "compassion" and "womb" have a semantic connection. In Hebrew the verb "to show compassion," so often used of Yahweh (e.g., Isa 49:13; Hos 2:25), and the noun "womb" come from the same root *(rhm)*. Once again, it is through the womb of a woman, Elizabeth, that Yahweh's compassion is manifest.

Elizabeth is portrayed as a woman who is aware of herself as valuable and loved in God's eyes. "So has the Lord done for *me*," she asserts. One might expect that in her culture the conception of John would be seen as what God is doing for Zechariah, or for God's people. What Elizabeth articulates is that God is equally concerned to show graciousness to her.

For five months Elizabeth remains in seclusion. From the point of view of narrative logic, Elizabeth's seclusion is for the sake of the story. Mary is not to know yet of her relative's pregnancy because news of it will be the sign given to her by the angel Gabriel when he announces the birth of Jesus to her (1:36).[16] From a sociocultural perspective, Elizabeth would be seen to behave correctly by secluding herself in her condition. She would be acting according to the attitudes deemed proper for females: inwardness, submission, shyness, passivity, timidity, and restraint.[17] This portrait of Elizabeth contrasts greatly with that of 1:57-66, where she will speak out at John's naming with authority, daring, and boldness, taking up a stance that is more properly male, by the mores of her day.

These months of seclusion for Elizabeth can also be seen as a time of contemplation. Having experienced a profound moment of God's compassion, Elizabeth now nurtures the Word within. Alone with God and her silent husband, she reflects on the grace of God in her life before naming that grace to others. The next episode, told in parallel fashion to the announcement of the birth of John, is the annunciation to Mary (Luke 1:26-38).

---

[16]Brown, *Birth,* 282.

[17]Bruce J. Malina, *The New Testament World: Insights from Cultural Anthropology* (Rev. ed. Louisville: Westminster/John Knox, 1993) 51. See also David Daube, "Shame Culture in Luke," *Paul and Paulinism: Essays in Honour of C. K. Barrett,* ed. M. D. Hooker and S. G. Wilson (London:

LUKE 1:26-38

²⁶In the sixth month, the angel Gabriel was sent from God to a town of Galilee called Nazareth, ²⁷to a virgin betrothed to a man named Joseph, of the house of David, and the virgin's name was Mary. ²⁸And coming to her, he said, "Hail, favored one! The Lord is with you." ²⁹But she was greatly troubled at what was said and pondered what sort of greeting this might be. ³⁰Then the angel said to her, "Do not be afraid, Mary, for you have found favor with God. ³¹Behold, you will conceive in your womb and bear a son, and you shall name him Jesus. ³²He will be great and will be called Son of the Most High, and the Lord God will give him the throne of David his father, ³³and he will rule over the house of Jacob forever, and of his kingdom there will be no end." ³⁴But Mary said to the angel, "How can this be, since I have no relations with a man?" ³⁵And the angel said to her in reply, "The holy Spirit will come upon you, and the power of the Most High will overshadow you. Therefore the child to be born will be called holy, the Son of God. ³⁶And behold, Elizabeth, your relative, has also conceived a son in her old age, and this is the sixth month for her who was called barren; ³⁷for nothing will be impossible for God." ³⁸Mary said, "Behold, I am the handmaid of the Lord. May it be done to me according to your word." Then the angel departed from her.

As is his custom, Luke opens a new scene with a time marker. "In the sixth month" situates the annunciation to Mary in relation to that of Elizabeth and prepares for the sign in verse 36. The same messenger that announced the birth of John (1:19) now comes to Mary. Of the many angelic appearances in the Hebrew Scriptures, only twice does God's messenger appear to women: to Hagar (Gen 16:7-16) and to Samson's mother (Judg 13:1-25).[18]

SPCK, 1982) 355–372; and Karen J. Torjesen, "In Praise of Noble Women: Gender and Honor in Ascetic Texts," *Semeia* 57 (1992) 41–64, especially p. 53 on a woman's seclusion as a public sign of her chastity.

[18]Randall D. Chestnutt ("Revelatory Experiences Attributed to Biblical Women in Early Jewish Literature," *"Women Like This": New Perspectives on Jewish Women in the Greco-Roman World,* ed. Amy-Jill Levine, SBL Early Judaism and Its Literature 1 [Atlanta: Scholars Press, 1991] 107–

In both stories the angel announces the birth of a son. The annunciation to Mary will follow the same pattern.[19] The function of angelic appearances in which God's messenger speaks of a future happening is to enable the reader to understand the coming event as part of God's plan for salvation.

It is striking that although Mary is introduced in terms of her relation to Joseph, she becomes the focus and active agent in the annunciation scene, and not him. Her name, Mary (*Mariam* in Greek; *Miryām* in Hebrew), is a Semitic name, probably derived from the Hebrew noun *mrym,* meaning "height, summit." As a feminine name, it likely connoted, "Excellence."[20] No one familiar with the Bible can fail to recognize that the mother of Jesus bears the same name as Moses' sister. Both women play important roles in the unfolding of the drama of salvation, and their stories bear some resemblance to each other.[21]

Luke gives us less information about Mary than about any of the other characters he presents in the infancy narrative. He tells

---

125) discusses how the roles of other women, such as Rebekah in *Jubilees,* Aseneth in *Joseph and Aseneth,* and Job's wife in *Testament of Job,* are embellished with revelatory experiences in diverse early Jewish texts.

[19] See Brown, *Birth,* 292–296. For a form analysis of Mandatory, Interpretative, and Predictive Angelophanies see Barbara E. Reid, *The Transfiguration: A Source- and Redaction-Critical Study of Luke 9:28-36,* Cahiers de la Revue Biblique 32 (Paris: Gabalda, 1993) 80–86. The annunciation to Mary is a predictive angelophany like the annunciation of the births of Ishmael (Gen 16:1-16), Isaac (Gen 18:1-16), Samson (Judg 13:2-23), and John the Baptist (Luke 1:5-23). The prediction of Enoch's ascension (*2 Enoch* 1:1-10) and the Lukan account of the transfiguration (9:28-36) also conform to this type. There are eight standard elements in these stories: (1) Introduction; (2) Appearance of the angel; (3) Prostration or Fear by the one to whom the angel appears; (4) Prediction and Interpretation of a future saving event; (5) Protestation or Questioning; (6) Reassurance, sometimes involving a sign; (7) further witnesses are mentioned; (8) Departure of the angel or the one(s) to whom the angel appears.

[20] Joseph Fitzmyer, *The Gospel According to Luke,* AB 28 (Garden City, N.Y.: Doubleday, 1981) 344.

[21] See Rita J. Burns, *Has the Lord Indeed Spoken Only Through Moses? A Study of the Biblical Portrait of Miriam,* SBLDS 84 (Atlanta: Scholars Press, 1987); Phyllis Trible, "Bringing Miriam Out of the Shadows," *BibRev* 5 (1989) 14–25, 34; J. Gerald Janzen, "Song of Moses, Song of Miriam: Who Is Seconding Whom?" *CBQ* 54 (1992) 211–220.

us nothing of her genealogy, unlike his introductions of Elizabeth, Zechariah (1:5), Joseph (1:27), and Anna (2:36). Nor does he remark on her piety as he does with Elizabeth, Zechariah (1:6, 8), Simeon (2:25, 27), and Anna (2:37). It is Gabriel's greeting, "Hail, favored one! The Lord is with you" (1:28), that informs us of Mary's high status with God. The common Greek greeting "hail!" *(chaire)* also carries a connotation of "rejoice" and may recall prophecies of restoration that open thus.[22] From Gabriel's greeting and Luke's twice repeated mention of Mary's virginity, the reader knows God's estimation of her, and knows that Mary is upright despite contrary appearances. In Luke's story, unlike that of Matthew (1:19), there is no suspicion voiced of any impropriety on the part of Mary.

In verse 29 the point of view shifts to Mary. Luke says "she was greatly troubled at what was said and pondered what sort of greeting this might be." Some think that Mary's fearful reaction comes from the realization that she, a woman, was being greeted by a man, which was not proper according to Jewish prescriptions.[23] But a better explanation is that in biblical stories of angelic apparitions fear or prostration is the standard reaction of those to whom a heavenly messenger comes.[24] Moreover, Luke stresses that it is *what the angel said* that disturbed Mary.

Since *chaire* is a very normal greeting, we must query what it is about being called "favored one" or the assertion, "the Lord is with you" that is troubling. The expression "favored one" *(kecharitōmenē)* is unique in the New Testament.[25] Gabriel will repeat in verse 30, "you have found favor *[charis]* with God." To find favor with God or with another person is a frequent ex-

[22]In the Septuagint: Zeph 3:14; Joel 2:21; Zech 9:9.

[23]Fitzmyer, *The Gospel According to Luke,* 346. He bases this on the later rabbinical tradition that males extend no greeting to women (*b. Qiddušin* 70a).

[24]E.g., Gen 18:2; 19:1; Num 22:31; Josh 5:14; Judg 13:20, 22; 1 Chr 21:16; 2 Macc 3:27; Matt 28:4-5; Mark 16:5; Luke 1:12; 2:9; 24:5; Acts 10:4. Some manuscripts of Luke 1:29 stress the visual aspect of the appearance by adding *idousa,* "seeing (him)." Curiously, the usual fearful reaction is absent in the stories of the angelic appearances to Hagar (Gen 16:7-16) and Samson's mother (Judg 13:1-25).

[25]The perfect participle passive *kecharitōmenos* occurs in Sir 18:17 (LXX) with the connotation "gracious."

pression in the First Testament. Particular individuals who found favor with God include Noah (Gen 6:8), Moses (Exod 33:12-17); Gideon (Judg 6:17), and Samuel (1 Sam 2:26). Perhaps the troubling thing from the perspective of a patriarchal world view is that in Luke it is a *woman* whom God favors. A woman is graced by God and will be the vehicle for salvation for God's people. And God's messenger speaks directly to her; the message is not mediated through her father or her intended husband.

Mary's troubledness may also be associated with the great demands that are made on those who find favor with God. Moses, for example, favored by God (Exod 33:12-27), finds that the burden of carrying the people by himself is too great and prays, "please do me the favor of killing me at once, so that I need no longer face this distress" (Num 11:15). In the Third Gospel Jesus is also characterized as God's favored one. After Mary and Joseph have fulfilled their obligations at the Temple, they return to Nazareth, where "the child grew and became strong, filled with wisdom; and the favor *[charis]* of God was upon him" (2:40). Similarly, at the conclusion of the story of the twelve-year-old Jesus in the Temple, Luke comments that the boy Jesus "advanced in wisdom and age and favor *[charis]* before God" (2:52). And in Jesus' inaugural proclamation of his mission, the crowd is amazed at Jesus' gracious words (*logois tēs charitos,* 4:22). Being favored by God carries a heavy price. A favored one carries out God's will, laying down their own life. Mary has good reason to be troubled that she is so regarded by God.

The declaration "The LORD is with you" is the same as that made to Gideon (Judg 6:12).[26] This statement prefaces a command from God for Gideon to save Israel from the power of Midian. In the same way, Gabriel's declaration to Mary prepares for her participation in God's action to save.

In verse 30 the angel reassures Mary. This is a standard feature in stories of angelic apparitions that predict and interpret God's future actions.[27] The heart of Gabriel's message comes in verses 31-33: Mary is told she will bear a son, what his name is to be,

---

[26]A similar phrase on the lips of Boaz in Ruth 2:4, "The Lord be with you!" is more a wish than a declaration.

[27]E.g., Gen 18:14; Judg 13:20, 23; Luke 1:35-37.

and what will be his role in God's design. From the way Luke tells the story, what the angel declares seems all predetermined.

Mary's response (v. 34) does not question *that* all will happen according to what Gabriel has said, but rather, queries *how* such can be. There is a difference between Mary's question and that of Zechariah.[28] Both state why the announced birth is humanly impossible. Zechariah says, "For I am an old man, and my wife is advanced in years" (1:18). Mary asserts, "since I have no relations with a man" (v. 34). But Zechariah's question, "How shall I know this?" reflects disbelief, whereas Mary's is a practical one: "How can this be, since I have no relations with a man?" Mary's response presumes acceptance and requests an explanation of the logistics. The reader wonders with Mary, how will God accomplish this—that she can conceive without having relations with a man? Her question serves to advance the story; it allows the angel to explain more fully.

Gabriel's reply is that it will be accomplished by God's Spirit and power. The words "come upon" *(eperchesthai)* and "overshadow" *(episkiazein)* have no sexual connotation, i.e., in the sense of divine-human intercourse. They are figurative language that speak of God's intervention. There may be an allusion to the cloud of God's presence that settled upon *(episkiazein)* the tent of meeting (Exod 40:35, LXX). The angel further assures Mary that all will take place in the realm of the holy. Her child will be called "holy, the Son of God" (v. 35), not illegitimate. The reader may infer that the holiness of her son will redound to her and that she, too, will continue to be perceived as favored by God, although she has conceived before the proper time.

This is the second reference to the holy Spirit, who figures prominently throughout Luke and Acts. Gabriel had told Zechariah that John "will be filled with the holy Spirit even from his mother's womb" (1:15). So too, the holy Spirit will come upon Mary (1:35). Elizabeth is also filled with the holy Spirit (1:41), as is Zechariah (1:67); John the Baptist grows and becomes strong in spirit (1:80); the holy Spirit rested upon Simeon and revealed to him that he would not see death before he had seen the Messiah (2:25-26). Once the holy Spirit descends on Jesus at his bap-

---

[28]Protestation or questioning is another standard element in predictive angelophanies: Gen 16:13; 18:12; Judg 13:12, 17.

tism (3:22) only Jesus is said to have the Spirit for the remainder of the Gospel.[29] It is not until he gives the Spirit to his disciples after his resurrection that they, too, will act in the power of the Spirit.

In verses 36-37 Gabriel further reassures Mary by giving her a concrete sign: her relative Elizabeth has also conceived a son.[30] The notation that this is Elizabeth's sixth month informs the reader how much narrative time has elapsed and points forward to the visit in 1:39-45. The statement that "nothing will be impossible for God" (v. 37) echoes the words of God to Abraham, reassuring him about the future birth of Isaac, "Is anything too marvelous for the LORD to do?" (Gen 18:14).[31] The assurance in verse 37 also points ahead to Luke 18:27, where Jesus, remarking on God's ability to save those with wealth, says, "What is impossible for human beings is possible for God."

The scene concludes with Mary's acceptance, "Behold I am the handmaid of the Lord" (v. 38). Her assertion, "May it be done to me according to your word" casts her as a model for future disciples: one who hears the word of God and responds positively to it. She prefigures, as well, her son's acceptance of God's will, despite the high price that it demands. Immediately before his arrest, Jesus prays, "Father if you are willing, take this cup away from me; still, not my will but yours be done" (22:42). Just as Gabriel offers a sign of assurance that results in Mary's acquies-

---

[29]In Luke 4:1 the holy Spirit leads Jesus to the wilderness; in 4:14 Jesus returns to Galilee filled with the power of the Spirit; in 4:18 Jesus opens his inaugural proclamation of his mission declaring, "The Spirit of the Lord is upon me"; in 10:21 Jesus rejoices in the holy Spirit; in 11:13 he assures his followers that the holy Spirit will be given to those who ask; and in 12:12 that the Spirit will teach them what to say in defense before authorities. See further, Odette Mainville, *L'esprit dans l'oeuvre de luc,* Héritage et Projet 45 (Quebec: Fides, 1991); M. B. Turner, "Jesus and the Spirit in Lucan Perspective," *TynB* 32 (1981) 3–42.

[30]Reassurance by the angel is another standard element in predictive angelophanies: Gen 18:14; Judg 13:20, 23; Luke 1:19-20.

[31]Similar words are also pronounced by Job at the conclusion of his ordeals, "I know that you can do all things, and that no purpose of yours can be hindered" (42:2). The prophet Zechariah likewise assures rescue for the remnant of Israel and their restoration to Jerusalem, though this seems impossible (8:6).

cence, so an angel from heaven strengthens Jesus (22:43), as he makes a final decision of acceptance that results in passion and death. The next scene brings the two expectant kinswomen together.

LUKE 1:39-45

[39]Mary set out and traveled to the hill country in haste to a town of Judah, [40]where she entered the house of Zechariah and greeted Elizabeth. [41]When Elizabeth heard Mary's greeting, the infant leaped in her womb, and Elizabeth, filled with the holy Spirit, [42]cried out in a loud voice and said, "Most blessed are you among women, and blessed is the fruit of your womb. [43]And how does this happen to me, that the mother of my Lord should come to me? [44]For at the moment the sound of your greeting reached my ears, the infant in my womb leaped for joy. [45]Blessed are you who believed that what was spoken to you by the Lord would be fulfilled."

This scene brings Elizabeth and Mary together and preserves a rare biblical vignette of a conversation between two women. Mary's journey, according to Luke's arrangement, is from Nazareth to the hill country near Jerusalem, a distance slightly more than one hundred miles. Such a trip would take the better part of a week or more.[32] By not mentioning any traveling companions, Luke leaves a disturbing impression: a maiden making such a journey alone would be highly unusual and improper. This

---

[32]Roman legions traveled at a pace of twenty-five miles per day. Most Jews making a trip from Galilee to Jerusalem would cross over into Perea, on the east side of the Jordan, to avoid going through Samaria (Mark 10:1). This would add even more time. Matthew's infancy narrative presumes that Mary and Joseph live in Bethlehem and that Jesus was born at home. Luke, knowing the tradition about Jesus' birth in Bethlehem, as well as the tradition that he was raised in Nazareth, and a tradition about a census, puts the pieces together in a way that is probably not historically accurate. Luke's connecting the birth of Jesus to a census under Quirinius is notoriously difficult. The known universal registrations of Roman citizens were in 28 B.C.E., 8 B.C.E., and 14 C.E.; Quirinius' term as legate of Syria began in 6–7 C.E.

tension in the narrative is resolved various ways by commentators. The popular fourteenth-century writer Ludolph of Saxony,[33] for example, fills in the details, saying that a train of virgins and angels accompanied Mary to protect her. More recently, Malina and Rohrbaugh assert, "It seems Mary considers the son she conceives as apotropaic, clearly capable of warding off evil."[34]

Mary enters "the house of Zechariah" and greets Elizabeth (v. 40). Zechariah will play no part in this scene; it is the private sphere of the women that the reader glimpses. Moreover, he is yet unable to speak. It is Mary and Elizabeth who will theologize and speak authoritatively about God's newest deeds. Luke has painted these two as trustworthy characters; the reader is meant to adopt their theological interpretation of the impending births.

At Mary's greeting, Elizabeth is "filled with the holy Spirit," thus aligned with others in Luke's Gospel of whom this is said: John (1:15), Mary (1:35), Zechariah (1:67), and Jesus (4:1). Elizabeth, in turn, proclaims to Mary, "Most blessed are you among women." Her acclamation calls to mind that of Deborah, "Blessed among women be Jael" (Judg 5:24), and Uzziah's exclamation to Judith, "Blessed are you, daughter . . . above all of the women on earth" (Jdt 13:18).[35] Another OT echo is heard in Elizabeth's declaration, "blessed is the fruit of your womb." This was the same blessing promised by Moses to the Israelites if they were obedient to the voice of God (Deut 28:1, 4).[36]

Elizabeth's blessing (1:42, 45) is the first of many in Luke. Mary's Magnificat affirms her blessedness (1:48). Simeon blesses Mary and Joseph (2:34). Jesus pronounces blessed those who are poor, hungry, and hated (6:20-22). He admonishes his followers to bless those who curse them (6:28). He calls blessed whoever does not take offense at him (7:23) and those who hear and obey the word of God (11:28). Alert and hardworking servants are blessed (12:37, 38, 43), as are those who hold banquets without repayment (14:14). Jesus declares blessed the eyes of his disciples

---

[33]His *Vita Domini nostri Jesu Christi ex quatuor evangeliis* was one of the most widely read books of the Middle Ages.

[34]Bruce J. Malina and Richard L. Rohrbaugh, *Social Science Commentary on the Synoptic Gospels* (Minneapolis: Fortress Press, 1992) 291.

[35]Brown, *Birth*, 342.

[36]Ibid.

for what they see (10:23). Most significant is Jesus' blessing of the bread at the Last Supper (24:30), prefigured in the feeding of the five thousand in 9:16. Jesus himself is blessed by the throng at his entrance into Jerusalem (19:38). And at the ascension, his final departure, Jesus blesses his disciples (24:50-51). The Gospel ends on a note of blessing as Luke concludes, "they [the disciples] were continually in the temple praising God."

In the narrative setting of Zechariah and Elizabeth's house, it is startling that Elizabeth "cried out in a loud voice" (v. 42) when she greeted Mary. Although this is the only instance in which Luke uses the phrase *kraugē megalē,* there are six other instances in which a "loud voice" is expressed with *phōnē megalē.* In 4:33 and 8:28 the loud cry comes from a possessed man; in 17:15 the healed leper glorifies God in a loud voice; similarly, in 19:37 the disciples who acclaimed Jesus at his entry to Jerusalem praised God with a loud voice; in 23:23 the loud shouts of the chief priests, rulers, and the people demand Jesus' crucifixion; and in 23:46 Jesus cries out in a loud voice, commending his spirit to God as he breathes his last. Another verb Luke uses four times for "crying out" is *boaō.* John the Baptist quotes Isaiah's words about a voice crying out in the desert in reference to his own mission (3:4); a man with an ill son cries out for Jesus to come and look at him (9:38); the blind beggar near Jericho shouts for pity from Jesus (18:38); and the parable of the widow and the judge ends with a reassurance that God secures the rights of the chosen ones who call out to God day and night (18:7). In the context of these Lukan voices, Elizabeth's is the first great cry of blessing (1:42); Jesus' is the final shout of trust in God (23:46).

It is notable that Elizabeth's blessing begins by first affirming Mary, "blessed are *you,*" and only secondarily blessing the fruit of her womb (v. 42). She blesses Mary as a woman in her own right first, and then for her childbearing. Elizabeth's blessing, however, goes far beyond a purely personal one; she acclaims the salvific significance for the whole people of God in the obedience of her sister, Mary.

In calling Mary "the mother of my Lord" (v. 43) Elizabeth makes a significant theological statement. She is the first in this Gospel to call Jesus "Lord," *kyrios.* This is the most frequently used title for Jesus by Luke: ninety-seven times. Before Elizabeth's declaration, it is God, not Jesus, who is called "Lord."[37] In verse 43 Elizabeth verbally surrounds Mary: "me . . . mother of my Lord . . . me," symbolizing her taking in and nurturing of her relative.

In verse 45 it is not the blessedness of motherhood that Elizabeth exalts, but Mary's obedient response to God's word. "Blessed are you who believed that what was spoken to you by the Lord would be fulfilled" describes how the ideal disciple will later respond in Luke's Gospel. Such a one hears the word of God and believes. In Luke 11:27-28, a pericope peculiar to Luke, we find a parallel statement on the lips of Jesus. A woman in a crowd exclaims, "Blessed is the womb that carried you and the breasts at which you nursed." Jesus' reply is, "Rather, blessed are those who hear the word of God and observe it." Jesus does not negate the blessedness of his mother, but asserts that close relationship to him is not only by blood relation. Even more important than mother-son ties are the bonds of discipleship based on hearing and acting on the word of God. Like Elizabeth he affirms the blessedness of his mother not only because God is manifest through her womb. First and foremost she hears and acts on God's word.

Together Mary and Elizabeth affirm the grace of God in their own lives and help one another to name that grace. The cooperation of Elizabeth and Mary stands in great contrast to the rivalry and competition in the stories of other pairs of mothers in the Hebrew Scriptures. Athalya Brenner describes two variations on a paradigm of "Birth of the Hero" stories in the Hebrew Scriptures.[38]

One type is exemplified in the stories of Sarah and Hagar (Genesis 16, 21), Leah and Rachel (Genesis 29–31), and Peninnah and Hannah (1 Samuel 1). In each instance, two women share one overriding ambition: to bear a son and heir to the same husband.

[37] Luke 1:6, 9, 11, 15, 16, 17, 25, 28, 32, 38. The titular use of *kyrios* for Jesus is a post-resurrection understanding retrojected into the time of the earthly ministry of Jesus. See Fitzmyer, *The Gospel According to Luke*, 200–204, for background on the origin of the use of the title. See also James M. Dawsey, "What's in a Name? Characterization in Luke," *BTB* 16 (1986) 143–147.

[38] "Female Social Behavior: Two Descriptive Patterns Within the 'Birth of the Hero' Paradigm," *VT* 36 (1986) 257–273.

Rather than cooperating, they are locked in deadly rivalry. Even after the birth of their respective sons, each mother continues the power struggle to ensure the economic status of her own son over that of the other. Her motivation is depicted as coming not from motherly love, but rather, from calculating power politics. Such an effort to place her own ambitions above the concern for the community's survival puts each of these women in a very poor light.

A second type of "birth of the hero" narrative is found in the stories of Naomi and Ruth (Ruth 1–4) and the birth of Moses (Exod 2:1-10). In the first instance, it is Ruth's generous and unselfish behavior that makes cooperation between the two women possible, and ultimately saves the family line from extinction. In the latter instance, the laudable act of Moses' mother in giving up her child leads not only to his salvation, but to the liberation of the whole people of Israel. This occurs with the cooperation of three women: Moses' biological mother, his adoptive mother, and his sister.

Brenner sees the Lukan infancy narratives as having motifs and themes of both types of "birth of the hero" stories. Mary and Elizabeth could easily be presented as rivals. Instead, they exemplify faith triumphing over personal ambition. They are mutually supportive and understanding, each accepting her own role in salvation history, and not threatened by that of the other. They serve as models of the power of cooperation over the destructiveness of competition.[39] The collaboration of Mary and Elizabeth are a prelude to that of the Galilean women who cooperate in their service for Jesus' mission (8:1-3), who labor together to prepare the spices and perfumed oils for his embalming (23:56), and who together announce the resurrection to the other disciples (24:9). Such a stance contrasts markedly with the disciples who argue at the Last Supper about which of them should be regarded as the greatest (22:24). The scene culminates in the canticle of Mary (1:46-56) which also holds up a radically different model of power.

---

[39]However, see Fitzmyer, *The Gospel According to Luke,* 313–315, on the step-parallelism in the infancy narratives, particularly in the annunciation stories. There is a kind of "one-upmanship" that attempts to put John in the proper perspective in relation to Jesus.

LUKE 1:46-56

⁴⁶And Mary said: ⁴⁷"My soul proclaims the greatness of the Lord; my spirit rejoices in God my savior. ⁴⁸For he has looked upon his handmaid's lowliness; behold, from now on will all ages call me blessed. ⁴⁹The Mighty One has done great things for me, and holy is his name. ⁵⁰His mercy is from age to age to those who fear him. ⁵¹He has shown might with his arm, dispersed the arrogant of mind and heart. ⁵²He has thrown down the rulers from their thrones but lifted up the lowly. ⁵³The hungry he has filled with good things; the rich he has sent away empty. ⁵⁴He has helped Israel his servant, remembering his mercy, ⁵⁵according to his promise to our fathers, to Abraham and to his descendants forever." ⁵⁶Mary remained with her about three months and then returned to her home.

The Magnificat (1:46-55) is the first of four canticles in Luke's infancy narrative. The Benedictus of Zechariah (1:67-79), the Gloria in Excelsis of the angels (2:13-14), and Simeon's Nunc Dimittis (2:28-32) punctuate the narrative with praise for God's gracious deeds. Most probably these were Jewish Christian hymns that Luke wove into his story.[40] They echo themes from the First Testament and introduce strains that will play throughout the Gospel of Luke.

There are strong parallels between Mary's[41] Magnificat and the

---

[40]Their parallelism in style and religious outlook to Jewish hymns of the intertestamental period, their lack of Lukan stylistic traits, their echoing of themes from the First Testament, and their lack of direct correlation to their narrative context favor this hypothesis. Some scholars argue for their composition by Gentile Christians. Others believe they were composed by Luke either as he was formulating the infancy narratives or at a later point than the infancy narratives, to which he subsequently added them. The theory that they were composed by those who speak them in the narrative, i.e., Mary, Zechariah, and Simeon, has no support by serious scholars. See Brown, *Birth*, 346-355, for a fuller discussion of the various hypotheses and for the theories about their origin in a Christian community centered on Jewish Anawim piety.

[41]Some mss attribute it to Elizabeth, but all the Greek mss, and most of the ancient versions, have the speaker as Mary. See Fitzmyer, *The Gospel According to Luke*, 365-366.

victory hymn of her namesake, Miriam, in Exodus 15:1-18.[42] Both women speak prophetically, celebrating God's triumphs over the godless. Both Miriam and Mary begin by celebrating what God has done for her personally. Miriam sings, "My strength and my courage is the LORD, and he has been my savior. He is my God, I praise him." (Exod 15:2). Mary proclaims that God "has looked upon his handmaid's lowliness . . . the Mighty One has done great things for me" (Luke 1:48-49). Both list the powerful deeds God has done by the might of God's arm (Exod 15:16; Luke 1:51). Both exult in God's mercy and steadfast love (Exod 15:13; Luke 1:50).[43] Both speak of God as mighty (Exod 15:16; Luke 1:49) and holy (Exod 15:11; Luke 1:49). Both celebrate God bringing down the powerful who oppose God's plans (Exod 15:4, 7, 14, 15; Luke 1:52) and how God has helped Israel (Exod 15:16-17; Luke 1:54). Both songs expect God's reign and the divine promises to last forever (Exod 15:18; Luke 1:55).

Mary proclaims God's greatness with her whole being (v. 47). The Greek terms *psychē*, "soul," and *pneuma*, "spirit," are not different parts of the human, nor should they be understood as opposed to *sōma*, "body," or *sarx*, "flesh." Rather, each term describes the whole human person as viewed from a particular perspective.[44] Soul, *psychē*, refers to the whole living being, equivalent to the Hebrew *nepeš*. "It expresses the vitality, con-

---

[42] A number of scholars believe that originally the whole Exodus hymn was led by Miriam, and not simply verse 21, which mirrors verse 1. Like 1 Samuel 18:7 the women would be leading the victory songs and dancing. See further George J. Brooke, "A Long-Lost Song of Miriam," *BAR* 20 (1994) 62–65. Brooke suggests that a separate Song of Miriam, partially suppressed in the book of Exodus, has survived in part in a Qumran text, 4Q365. He also shows that Mary's Magnificat, the Song of Hannah (1 Sam 2:1-10), the victory hymn of Judith (Jdt 16:6, 7, 13), and two sections of the Qumran War Scroll (1QM 11, 14) all sing of how the powerful are brought low by God's action through those who are lowly. He proposes that the survival of this theme in songs associated with women may reflect an effort on the part of the then-current power structure to marginalize the threat of these poems.

[43] The Greek word *eleos* used in Luke 1:50 is the word that often translates *hesed*, the Hebrew word used in Exodus 15:13.

[44] See Joseph A. Fitzmyer, "Pauline Theology," *NJBC*, ed. Raymond E. Brown, Joseph A. Fitzmyer, and Roland E. Murphy (Englewood Cliffs, N.J.: Prentice Hall, 1990) 1406–1407.

sciousness, intelligence, and volition of a human being."[45] The meaning of *pneuma* is barely distinguishable from that of *psychē*.[46] It suggests the aspect of the self that is particularly able to receive the Spirit. Both terms can be used simply as a substitute for the personal pronoun, "I." Mary, like Elizabeth, recognizes God in bodiliness, conception, and incarnation, not as removed to a purely spiritual plane. She proclaims this with her whole being.

Mary's song celebrates reversals: the proud and confident are scattered; the powerful are dethroned; the lowly are lifted up; the hungry are filled while the rich are sent away empty (vv. 52-53). A theme of reversal continues throughout Luke's Gospel as those invited to share in Jesus' life and mission and those who exemplify right relation in the reign of God are often the least expected (e.g., Levi in 5:27-32; Mary Magdalene, Joanna, and Susanna in 8:1-3; the people from the streets, alleys, highways, and hedgerows in 14:15-24; the sinners and tax collectors in 15:1-2; Lazarus in 16:19-31; the toll collector in 18:9-14; Zacchaeus in 19:1-10).

Mary's song ends on the confident note that God has promised mercy not only to our ancestors, but to all their descendants, women and men of faith. At the conclusion of the canticle Luke notes that Mary remained about three months and then returned home. He leaves the impression that Mary left just before the birth of John—the time when Elizabeth would most need her! The best explanation is that Luke is simply finishing off Mary's part in the story. He tends to have the characters from one scene exit before beginning the next. With verse 57 the story shifts back again to Elizabeth, bringing her role to an important climax.

LUKE 1:57-66

[57]When the time arrived for Elizabeth to have her child she gave birth to a son. [58]Her neighbors and relatives heard that the Lord had shown his great mercy toward her, and they rejoiced with her. [59]When they came on the eighth day to circumcise the child, they were going to call him Zechariah after his father, [60]but his mother said in reply, "No. He will be called John." [61]But they answered her, "There is no one among your relatives who has

[45]Fitzmyer, "Pauline Theology," 1406.
[46]See, e.g., Philippians 1:27 where the two are used in parallelism.

this name." ⁶²So they made signs, asking his father what he wished him to be called. ⁶³He asked for a tablet and wrote, "John is his name," and all were amazed. ⁶⁴Immediately his mouth was opened, his tongue freed, and he spoke blessing God. ⁶⁵Then fear came upon all their neighbors, and all these matters were discussed throughout the hill country of Judea. ⁶⁶All who heard these things took them to heart, saying, "What, then, will this child be?" For surely the hand of the Lord was with him.

Now comes the time for a more public proclamation of God's grace. When Elizabeth gives birth to her son, all her neighbors and relations share her joy[47] and, like her, interpret the event as God's doing: God has shown great mercy toward her (Luke 1:57, 58). Throughout the Third Gospel each critical moment in the drama of salvation is marked by joy. The birth of John, herald of the Messiah, brings joy (1:14, 58). While still in his mother's womb, John leaped for joy at the sound of Mary's greeting (1:44). The annunciation of Jesus' birth causes Mary to rejoice (1:47) and will bring great joy to all the people (2:10). Hearing the word produces joy (8:13), as does success in mission (10:17). Persecution suffered because of Jesus is cause for rejoicing (6:23). Heaven rejoices over repentant sinners (15:7, 10), just as one does when finding what was lost (15:5, 6, 9, 32). Seeing the risen Christ brings his followers joy (24:41). The last note of the whole Gospel is one of great joy (24:52).

That Elizabeth is the one to name her child is significant. In the patriarchal narratives a child was often named by its mother,[48] though there are also examples where the father did so.[49] It is generally thought, however, that in New Testament times naming was the prerogative of the father (e.g., Matt 1:21). In the case of John (as also Jesus in Luke 1:31), it is God who names the child, and Gabriel conveys the name in the annunciation of his birth to Zechariah (Luke 1:13). How Elizabeth knew the name

[47]Brown (*Birth*, 375) notes the parallel to Sarah's joy at the birth of Isaac and the rejoicing of all who hear of it in Genesis 21:6.

[48]E.g., Gen 4:1, 25; 16:11; 19:37-38; 29:32-35; 30:6, 8; 35:18; 38:4-5; Judg 13:24; 1 Sam 1:20.

[49]E.g., Gen 4:26; 5:3, 28-29; 16:15; 17:19; Exod 2:22; Judg 8:31.

intended by God for her son, Luke does not explicitly say.[50] He had related that all her life she has been faithful to God (1:6). It is not surprising, then, that she is able to rightly convey God's intended name for her son. The drama of the episode is heightened when Luke tells that by the time of the circumcision,[51] everyone was already calling the child "Zechariah" after his father.[52] Elizabeth intervenes, asserting, "No, he is to be called John."

The choice of name is very significant. Biblical names often reflect the personality or character of the person.[53] Sometimes they signify the circumstances surrounding the birth.[54] Other names indicate the parents' wish for their child.[55] The child of a prophet might be given a name that symbolizes the main theme of the prophet's oracles.[56] John's name not only expresses his own character, but also describes well Elizabeth's experience of God. *Yôḥānān* literally declares "Yahweh has given grace" *(ḥnn)*. Com-

[50]Raymond E. Brown ("The Annunciation to Mary, the Visitation, and the Magnificat," *Worship* 62 [1988] 249–259) sees it as a marvelous coincidence that Elizabeth also chooses the name John, and that this is a miracle that provokes awe and wonder, as do the miracles of Jesus in his ministry.

[51]In the Hebrew Scriptures the name was given at birth or shortly after, but in Luke (1:59; 2:21) we find the giving of the name associated with circumcision. Brown (*Birth*, 369) notes that it is not certain how common it was in first-century Palestine to name a child at his circumcision. He points out that in rabbinic tradition it is at his circumcision that Moses is named (*Pirqe Rabbi Eliezar* 48 [27c]).

[52]According to G. Mussies ("Vernoemen in de antieke wereld. De historische achtergrond van Luk. 1,59-63," *NedTheolTijd* 42 [1988] 114–125) the first evidence of Jews naming children after parents or grandparents is found at Elephantine and dated to approximately 500 c.e. He believes the custom came to Palestine after Alexander, in imitation of the practice of the Ptolemies and Seleucids. Brown (*Birth,* 369) notes that the custom of naming a child after his father is attested in Wadi Murabba'at legal documents from the second century c.e., but that in priestly circles it seems to have been more common to name a child after his grandfather.

[53]E.g., "Eve" as "mother of all the living" in Genesis 3:20; "Esau," meaning "hairy," in Genesis 25:25.

[54]E.g., "Samuel," meaning "asked of God," in 1 Samuel 1:20.

[55]E.g., "Obadiah," meaning "worshiper/servant of Yahweh."

[56]E.g., Hosea's daughter "Lo-ruhamah," that is, "Not pitied" (1:4). See further, R. Abba, "Name," *IDB* 3, ed. George A. Buttrick, et al. (New York: Abingdon, 1962) 500–508.

passion *(rḥm)* and grace *(ḥnn)* characterize Yahweh time and again in the Hebrew Scriptures.[57]

Elizabeth, who has experienced God's grace in solitude and in the company of another woman, now shares the experience of that grace with all her family and neighbors. Like a pebble dropped in a lake that creates ever wider ripples, Elizabeth is the instrument by which God's grace becomes known to an ever expanding group of people. First, she leads her own husband to that recognition. After nine months of muteness from disbelief and incomprehension of God's ways, Zechariah is enabled by her to declare as Elizabeth did to all those assembled for the circumcision, "John is his name" (1:63). At this, amazement (v. 63) and fear (v. 65) come upon all their neighbors, and finally, "all these matters were discussed throughout the hill country of Judea. All who heard these things took them to heart" (1:65-66).

Luke's description of the reaction of the people to Elizabeth's proclamation makes it eminently clear that she is a special agent of God, who leads others to the source of grace. Numerous times in Luke's Gospel the evangelist uses the same verb, *thaumazō* (1:63), and the noun *phobos* (1:65) to describe the awestruck reaction of people to God's manifestation in the person of Jesus, his words, and his works.[58] As is the case with Elizabeth, news of God's actions through Jesus spreads throughout the whole countryside.[59] And Elizabeth leads people to treasure these things in their heart (1:66), just as Mary is said to do in 2:19 and 2:51. The action comes full circle: having begun with Elizabeth's contemplation of the grace of God, she has led the whole countryside to enter into a contemplative stance, pondering the divine favor and wondering, "What, then, will this child be?" (1:66).

CONTEMPORARY QUESTIONS

The Lukan portraits of Elizabeth and Mary offer mixed messages and raise a number of questions for contemporary believers. In the opening description of Elizabeth and Zechariah (1:5-6), the

---

[57]E.g., Exod 33:19; Pss 102:14; 116:5.

[58]It is used in relation to the person of Jesus in 2:18, 33; 9:34; to his words in 4:22; 20:26; 24:41; and to his works in 5:26; 7:16; 8:25, 37; 9:43; 11:14.

[59]This phrase occurs again in 4:14, 37; 5:15; 7:17; 8:34, 39; 23:5.

equal pairing of the two offers hope toward a vision of the equality of women and men in the Church. Elizabeth is named and known. Her credentials are priestly, as are Zechariah's. In her long years of faithfulness to God despite suffering and humiliation, she prefigures Jesus, who will trust in God even through his passion and death. She easily recognizes God's new saving act and articulates a profoundly incarnational theology. She knows God in bodiliness, in the tangibility of the new life that grows inside her. She is aware that she is loved, that God is doing this for her. She understands God as one who delights in new life, not in suffering. She retreats into contemplative seclusion, and awaits the completion of God's action in her with patience, even while not understanding God's timing (1:24-25).

One shadow that crosses Luke's initial positive portrayal of Elizabeth is that it is she who is said to be responsible for the couple's childlessness (1:7). The possibility that Zechariah was responsible for his and Elizabeth's inability to conceive a child did not arise in Luke's world view. For modern believers, this point raises the question of how often women assume the blame for whatever is not well within a relationship. Many women have interiorized so well the responsibility for peacemaking and bridge-building that their first reaction to a problem that arises in relationships is, "What have *I* done wrong?" Women today are learning not to accept too readily the responsibility for difficulties they have not caused.

In the Visitation scene (1:39-45), Elizabeth provides a marvelous example of the wisdom and care that older women believers can offer younger women. The word Elizabeth has contemplated in solitude must be shared. And how better than with her younger kinswoman, who receives from her the assurance that she does not face an uncertain future alone. Elizabeth precedes her in childbirth and in theologizing. A Spirit-filled woman, she exudes blessing: she blesses Mary, blesses her child, blesses her belief, and reassures her that God's word will be fulfilled. This scene invites those contemporary believers who mistrust women's ability to interpret God's word to accept that women as well as men know God's ways and reliably communicate them. It particularly encourages women to accept the companionship of other women as spiritual guides, theologians, confessors, retreat directors, teachers, and preachers in their faith journeys.

At the circumcision and naming of John (1:57-66) Elizabeth exemplifies the missionary dimension that follows upon contemplation of God's word. The revelation of God's grace is not to be kept to oneself. That word must go forth, and so, Elizabeth shares it first with Mary, and then proclaims it to a wider group of relatives and neighbors. Although the celebration of circumcision and naming would have been a private setting, Elizabeth's action can be seen as a model for contemporary women to exercise a ministry of public proclamation of the Word. Elizabeth steps out of the bounds of silence and passivity proper to women of her day, because she must name God's grace. By so doing she opens herself to criticism and has to contend with the objections of others. In the end her ability to truthfully convey God's word is confirmed. If, in our day, the patriarchal voices that have defined our images of God, self, and the world were to be silenced for a time, as was Zechariah's, would not feminist namings of God's grace bring the same blessing and truth as that word spoken by Elizabeth?

One drawback to Elizabeth's story is her participation in a male-designed ritual of circumcision. This presents a stumbling-block for those who would rather fashion new religious rituals that are inclusive and participative for all believers, not only for those of the male sex. Elizabeth, even as she asserts herself in an active way in this male-oriented service, could be seen to reinforce patriarchal practices, rather than undermine them. In addition, Elizabeth, who has been portrayed throughout Luke 1 as steadfast, unquestioning, contemplative, supportive of Mary, and faithful in speaking God's word, is overshadowed in the end by her husband. The people turn to him for confirmation of John's name, and only when Zechariah writes it on a tablet do they acquiesce. Though it is Elizabeth who first speaks out and ensures that God's plan is carried out, Zechariah has the last word. Elizabeth's word is finally eclipsed by the canticle placed on her husband's lips that concludes chapter one (1:67-79). In a church of equal disciples, contemporary believers would not replicate the pattern Luke presents of women in the background, allowing men to speak what they have formulated, or where women are heard only when men confirm what they say.

In the portrait of Mary we also find both pitfalls and promise. In the annunciation scene (1:26-38) a woman is positively presented as favored by God and one indispensable to God's plan for salvation. Mary's interaction with Gabriel can exemplify woman's ability to perceive God's word and act on it without the mediation of a man. Her positive response has always been upheld as the model of openness and receptivity to God.

But there are also distressing aspects to this scene. Mary's acquiescence can also be used to reinforce silent passivity for women. Gabriel's message can be heard as describing something that is already predetermined, over which she has little or no control. Her final words to Gabriel are, literally, "Behold I am the *slave* of the Lord." She responds as one who has no choice but to do the bidding of the master. Such an image is not helpful for contemporary women who struggle to assert themselves and to make choices for their own good in a male-dominated world that programs them to serve the desires and needs of men.[60] A positive use of this image is to see Mary as prefiguring Jesus in his stance as servant toward others (22:27). It is notable, though, that the term *doulos,* "slave," used of Mary in 1:38 is never used of Jesus, but rather, *ho diakonōn,* "one who serves." A further positive use of the image of Mary as totally open and receptive, even passive, is to present this as a stance to be emulated by both men and women believers, not for women alone.

A further pitfall to the portrait of Mary is that her own identity becomes submerged as the angel speaks about the child to be born. He assures her that despite the unusual circumstances of his birth he will be called "Son of the Most High" (1:32), and "holy, Son of God" (1:35), not "illegitimate son." The implication is that the honor that will accrue to her son will redound to her. The stories of both Elizabeth and Mary are problematic for contemporary believers in that the identity and public esteem of the women derive from the sons they bear. Today the value of women in themselves and in their giftedness, apart from childbearing, needs to be affirmed.

There is the further problem that glorifying Mary's virginal conception and birth can denigrate women who conceive and bear children in the ordinary way. We are better served by an incarnational theology that knows God to be revealed in bodiliness.

[60]Rosemary Radford Ruether, *New Woman New Earth: Sexist Ideologies & Human Liberation* (New York: Crossroad, 1975) 57.

Mary's story can also provide hope for women who are victims of sexual violence. The tendency to wrap Mary in an aura of romantic joy at the annunciation obscures the reality that in her culture, to be found with child before she comes to live with her betrothed is a horrendously shameful situation. Luke 1:27 makes it clear that Mary is already engaged to Joseph, the first of two formal steps in first-century Jewish marriages. This entails an official exchange of promises before witnesses, and payment of the dowry. From this stage forward the groom has legal rights over his woman. Any infringement on her chastity is a challenge to his honor. Only at the second stage does the husband take his wife into his home. Matthew 1:18 is more explicit that the annunciation of Jesus' birth comes between the two stages: after Mary and Joseph are betrothed, but before they have come to live together.

Although the reader of the Gospel is given to know that it is by God that this conception is accomplished, such would not be the conclusion of Mary's neighbors and relatives. She would be in a most irregular and shameful situation, facing suspicion and accusations. It may be out of alarm and fright that Mary went in haste to Elizabeth (1:39), not out of eagerness to share the joy of her news.[61] Women who have been victims of sexual abuse might find comfort in the words of Gabriel to Mary in her irregular situation. He repeatedly assures her that she is regarded by God as favored (1:28, 30), that God is with her (1:28), that she need not fear. Despite appearances to the contrary, her child will be called "holy, Son of God" (1:35), not "shameful, illegitimate child." God's holy Spirit and power will keep her from harm (1:35).[62]

Gabriel's message is that although this will not be how others regard it, all that will happen to her will take place in the realm of the holy. God is able to bring holiness and good from even the most apparently shameful situations, for nothing is impos-

---

[61]Schaberg, *Illegitimacy,* reconstructs the story of Jesus' conception as a story of terror, which has been reinterpreted by the evangelists as a miraculous virginal conception. For my review of her work see *CBQ* 52 (1990) 364–365.

[62]See Elisabeth Schüssler Fiorenza, *Jesus: Miriam's Child, Sophia's Prophet: Critical Issues in Feminist Christology* (New York: Continuum, 1994) 182–186.

sible for God. This incarnational God is to be found right in the midst of the messiness of painful human plights. Elizabeth, too, helps Mary to know her blessedness and God's trustworthiness. She can speak with authority, as one who also experiences the incomprehensibility of God's timing. As Luke will emphasize throughout his Gospel, it is those who are most disadvantaged who most clearly perceive and accept the good news. Elizabeth and Mary are the first such examples.

From this standpoint, the Magnificat can be read as Mary's song of vindication, and can serve as such today for all those unjustly oppressed. There is a drawback, however, to the way in which her canticle orders structures in dualistic terms: lowliness/might; rulers/ruled; full/empty. In a world cast in hierarchical divisions, bliss for the oppressed would be in the inversion of the current arrangement. But in the remainder of the Gospel the vision of Luke's Jesus is not simply the reversal of the status quo, so that those on the bottom are now on top. Rather, his Gospel proclaims inclusivity, where no one is automatically in or out, up or down. All are invited as equal participants, across boundaries of status, gender, and race.

In contemporary terms, Mary's canticle would serve us best not as a call to replace patriarchy with matriarchy. Rather, when seen against the practice of Jesus, it challenges women and men to work together to "dethrone" the current patriarchal order and to design circular structures that fully embody God's mercy for all. In the canticle, God's mercy (vv. 50, 54) frames the list of the divine saving deeds on behalf of the whole of God's people and their descendants. Just so, a new order would best be constructed with the ethos of God's mercy and inclusivity.

In Luke's first chapter Mary has occupied center stage. But in the second, she recedes to the background as her son takes primacy. She gives birth to her firstborn son, wraps him in swaddling clothes, and lays him in a manger (2:1-7). When the shepherds relay to Mary and Joseph what they had been told about the child, "Mary kept all these things, reflecting on them in her heart" (2:19). This phrase is repeated in 2:51, conveying Mary's piety and her humanness in needing to continually ponder God's ways and God's words in order to understand their meaning. As with all believers, it is her constant reflection on experience and on God's word that reveals God's purposes over time to her. We move now to the scene of the Presentation.

Chapter 5

Anna: Prophetic Widow

The story of Anna is part of the larger episode of the Presentation of the child Jesus in the Temple. Because Mary also plays an important role in 2:22-35 we will first consider these verses.

LUKE 2:22-24

> [22]When the days were completed for their purification according to the law of Moses, they took him up to Jerusalem to present him to the Lord, [23]just as it is written in the law of the Lord, "Every male that opens the womb shall be consecrated to the Lord," [24]and to offer the sacrifice of "a pair of turtledoves or two young pigeons," in accordance with the dictate in the law of the Lord.

These verses are confusing in the use of "their" and "they" without antecedents. Presumably, "their purification" refers to Mary and Joseph, but in Jewish law purification was specified only for the woman (Lev 12:2-8). Some commentators have understood "their" as referring to Mary and Jesus, but there was no requirement of purification for a newborn. Since the main verb *anēgagon*, "they took him up," refers to Mary and Joseph, it is best to take "their purification" as referring to Mary and Joseph as well. The inaccuracy about who was required to undergo purification is usually explained as Luke's mistake, due to his being a non-Palestinian Gentile Christian, unfamiliar with the intricacies of Jewish law. When today we are concerned for gender equality, we might smile at Luke's unwitting inclusivity of Joseph in a ritual intended for women.

The scene has echoes of 1 Samuel 1:24, where Hannah and Elkanah presented Samuel to the Lord at the Temple in Shiloh and sacrificed a young bull. Mary and Joseph, however, offer the sacrifice of the poor (Lev 12:8). Like Elizabeth and Zechariah (1:6), Mary and Joseph are portrayed as obediently fulfilling the demands of the law of Moses. Contemporary believers may still recall the practice of women being "churched" after childbirth. Although Christians do not observe levitical laws of ritual purity it is curious that remnants of the notion that giving birth makes a woman unclean remained. Today any residual effects of this notion would need to be rejected. The same must be said for the higher valuation of male children as seen in their consecration to God (Luke 2:23; Exod 13:2)[1] and in the doubled time of purification after the birth of a female child (Lev 12:5).

LUKE 2:25-36

[25]Now there was a man in Jerusalem whose name was Simeon. This man was righteous and devout, awaiting the consolation of Israel, and the holy Spirit was upon him. [26]It had been revealed to him by the holy Spirit that he should not see death before he had seen the Messiah of the Lord. [27]He came in the Spirit into the temple; and when the parents brought in the child Jesus to perform the custom of the law in regard to him, [28]he took him into his arms and blessed God, saying: [29]"Now, Master, you may let your servant go in peace, according to your word, [30]for my eyes have seen your salvation, [31]which you prepared in sight of all the peoples, [32]a light for revelation to the Gentiles, and glory for your people Israel." [33]The child's father and mother were amazed at what was said about him; [34]and Simeon blessed them and said to Mary his mother, "Behold, this child is destined for the fall and rise of many in Israel, and

---

[1]Luke's quotation of Exodus 13:2 in reference to "every male that opens the womb" in 2:23 reflects that he does not have in view the later notions of Mary retaining her virginity *in partu*.

to be a sign that will be contradicted [35](and you yourself a sword will pierce) so that the thoughts of many hearts may be revealed.

In the scene with Simeon, Mary and Joseph are amazed at what this devout man says about Jesus (v. 33). According to narrative logic, Mary should not be startled by what Simeon says; she has already been told by Gabriel about her son's role (1:32-33). Rather than surprise, Mary and Joseph's amazement might instead be understood as the kind of reverential awe that will be the reaction of many to Jesus' words and deeds.[2]

Simeon blesses Mary and Joseph and then directs his message to Mary. He first speaks about the destiny of her child and then of the sword that will pierce her own soul (v. 35). "Soul," *psychē,* should be understood here as connoting the whole self, as in 1:46. The first image that Simeon's words bring to mind for most believers is that of Mary at the foot of the cross. But it must be remembered that vignette belongs to the Fourth Gospel (John 19:25-27). In Luke, Jesus' mother is not mentioned among his acquaintances and the women who had followed him from Galilee, who stood at a distance and saw everything (23:49; see also 23:55; 24:10). Simeon's message to Mary is linked, rather, to what he says about Jesus causing the rise and fall of many in Israel. The image is drawn from Ezekiel 14:17, where a sword of discrimination goes through the midst of the people, separating out those destined for destruction from those who will have mercy. What Simeon intimates is that Mary, like all disciples, will experience difficulty in understanding God's word. She was not given automatic knowledge and insight about her son and his mission at the annunciation. Rather, she continually pondered these things "reflecting on them in her heart" (2:19, 51).

Mary will not play any significant role in the remainder of Luke's narrative. The scene of the presentation ends with Mary, Joseph, and Jesus returning to their home in Nazareth, where "the child grew and became strong, filled with wisdom; and the favor of God was upon him" (2:40). The final episode of the infancy narratives relates how the twelve-year-old Jesus astounded the teachers in the Temple when his parents took him to Jerusalem for the feast of Passover, as they did each year (2:41). Mary and

[2]Luke 4:22; 8:25; 9:43; 11:14, 38; 20:26; 24:12, 41.

Joseph are shown as observant of Jewish custom (2:42), but unknowing of Jesus' plans (2:43, 49). They have great anxiety in their search for him (2:48) and do not understand his reply (2:50). As in 2:19, "his mother kept all these things in her heart" (2:51).

In the rest of the Gospel, Mary is mentioned only twice. In 8:19-21 Luke relates that Jesus' mother and siblings came to him, but they could not reach him because of the crowd. When he was told that they wished to see him, he replied, "My mother and my brothers [and sisters] are those who hear the word of God and act on it." Although the source for this episode is Markan, Luke's redaction has changed it considerably. Luke does not include in his Gospel the vignette found in Mark 3:21, where Jesus' relatives set out to seize him, thinking he is "out of his mind." In Mark 3:31-35, Jesus' mother and siblings are "outside" the circle of Jesus' followers. His reply to their desire to see him is, " 'Who are my mother and my brothers?' And looking around at those seated in the circle he said, 'Here are my mother and my brothers. (For) whoever does the will of God is my brother and sister and mother.' " Luke's version is much less harsh toward Jesus' relatives: Jesus' response does not contrast his mother and siblings with his disciples, but allows for the possibility of their inclusion within the circle of his followers. Luke has already portrayed Mary as one who hears the word of God and does it. She will not be mentioned as a disciple anywhere in the ministry of Jesus, nor will she appear at the foot of the cross, as in John 19:25-27. But in Acts 1:14 she, along with Jesus' siblings, is named among the disciples in the upper room awaiting the coming of the Spirit.

One last allusion to Jesus' mother occurs in Luke 11:27-28. These verses are peculiar to Luke. In the context of Jesus' journey to Jerusalem, a woman in the crowd called out, "Blessed is the womb that carried you and the breasts at which you nursed." Jesus' reply, "Rather, blessed are those who hear the word of God and observe it," does not deny the blessedness of Jesus' mother since she herself has been shown as a hearer and doer of the word.[3] The emphasis is shifted from blessedness based on bio-

---

[3]Fitzmyer (*The Gospel According to Luke,* AB 28A [Garden City, N.Y.: Doubleday, 1985] 928-929) shows that the particle *menoun* can have three different connotations: (1) adversative, as in Romans 9:20; 10:18, i.e., negat-

logical relation to Jesus to that based on discipleship. Today it can be read by women as an affirmation of their blessedness as disciples apart from roles of wife and mother, although the sacredness of the latter is not denied. In essence, Jesus' reply echoes Elizabeth's acclamation of Mary's blessedness. She extolled not only Mary's motherhood (1:42), but also her belief that what God had spoken to her would be fulfilled (1:45).

LUKE 2:36-38

[36]There was also a prophetess, Anna, the daughter of Phanuel, of the tribe of Asher. She was advanced in years, having lived seven years with her husband after her marriage, [37]and then as a widow until she was eighty-four. She never left the temple, but worshiped night and day with fasting and prayer. [38]And coming forward at that very time, she gave thanks to God and spoke about the child to all who were awaiting the redemption of Jerusalem.

Like many biblical women, Anna is identified in relation to a man: she is the daughter of Phanuel, of the tribe of Asher.[4] Anna's name is a feminine variation of John, from the root *ḥnn,* meaning "grace" or "favor." It is the Greek form of the Hebrew *Hannāh,* the name of Samuel's mother (1 Samuel 1–2). Like Hannah, she is found praying fervently in the Temple. Although Anna is not given a canticle, as is Hannah, or her counterpart, Simeon, that she prophesied and uttered praise of God are remembered.

Very few prophets besides Jesus appear in the Third Gospel. Zechariah prophesies as he speaks his canticle (1:67). Gabriel an-

---

ing the blessing of Jesus' mother and replacing it with the blessing on hearing and doing; (2) affirmative, as in Philippians 3:8, i.e., an intensifier, expressing agreement with the statement; (3) corrective, i.e., while not denying the first statement, it supplies a further truism. This third option is the more likely meaning in Luke 11:28. M. E. Thrall (*Greek Particles in the New Testament,* NTTS 3 [Leiden: Brill, 1962] 34–35) observes that Luke uses *ouchi, legō hymin* in adversative expressions (12:51; 13:3, 5), and *nai* in affirmations (e.g., 7:26; 10:21; 11:51; 12:5).

[4]See Joshua 19:24-31 for the delimitation of the boundaries of this northernmost tribe.

nounces that John the Baptist "will be called prophet of the Most High" (1:76; see also 3:2; 7:26; 20:6). Anna is the last prophet mentioned before Jesus assumes this role. Jesus is cast as the promised "prophet like Moses" of Deuteronomy 18:15 (Luke 9:28-36; Acts 3:22-23; 7:37). He also emulates the prophets Elijah and Elisha in his miracle working.[5] There is a double Elijah theme in Luke as John the Baptist also is cast as a new Elijah (1:17, 76; 7:27). A particular Lukan theme is that of Jesus as the rejected prophet.[6]

In Acts there are several prophets mentioned. In Peter's Pentecost speech he explains the speaking in different tongues in terms of prophesy, quoting the prophet Joel, "Indeed, upon my servants and my handmaids I will pour out a portion of my spirit in those days, and they shall prophesy" (Acts 2:18). In Acts 11:27-30 Luke tells of some prophets that came down from Jerusalem to Antioch, one of whom was named Agabus. He predicted a severe famine, which prompted a relief collection for the Christians in Judea. This same prophet later announced that Paul would be bound by the Jews and handed over to the Gentiles (Acts 21:10-11). In Acts 13:1 the names of prophets and teachers at Antioch are listed: "Barnabas, Symeon who was called Niger, Lucius of Cyrene, Manaen who was a close friend of Herod the tetrarch, and Saul." In 15:32 Judas and Silas also exhort the community in Antioch as prophets. A Jewish false prophet, Bar-Jesus, is mentioned in 13:6. In Ephesus, Paul laid hands on twelve men, upon whom the holy Spirit came, and they spoke in tongues and prophesied (19:6-7). The only women prophets mentioned are the four unmarried daughters of Philip (21:9).

Anna continues the line of notable women prophets from the First Testament: Miriam (Exod 15:20), Deborah (Judges 4-5), and Huldah (2 Kgs 22:14; 2 Chr 34:22). Her credentials are impeccable. As with Elizabeth (1:7), her advanced years (2:36) make her a reliable figure of maturity and wisdom. That she had lived with her husband seven years evokes the image of an ideal wife

---

[5] Luke 4:25-27; 7:11-17; 9:8, 10-17, 19, 30-33, 51. See Fitzmyer, *The Gospel According to Luke,* 213-215; R. O'Toole, "The Parallels Between Jesus and Moses," *BTB* 20 (1990) 22-29; Raymond E. Brown, "Jesus and Elisha," *Perspective* 12 (1971) 84-104.

[6] Luke 4:24, 39; 13:33; 24:19-20; Acts 7:52.

(seven being the number for perfection or completeness in biblical symbolism). Her worshiping in the Temple night and day with fasting and prayer prefigures Jesus' nights of communion with God (6:12), his fasting (4:2), and frequent prayer,[7] practices that would be continued by Jesus' disciples.[8] Anna typifies those who, like the widow of Luke 18:1-8, call out day and night and are heard by God.

Although many see Anna as paired with Simeon, the similarities between her and Judith are more notable. Judith was also a widow (Jdt 8:4) who "fasted all the days of her widowhood" (Jdt 8:6), and who prayed for the rescue of Israel "while the incense was being offered in the temple of God in Jerusalem" (Jdt 9:1). Overtones of Judith's urging the rulers of Bethulia to pray while waiting for salvation from God (Jdt 8:17) can be heard in Anna's speaking to all who were awaiting the redemption of Jerusalem (2:38). Finally, Anna's age can be calculated to be the same as Judith's. If Anna was married at fourteen, lived seven years with her husband, and eighty-four more as a widow,[9] she too had reached one hundred and five years (Jdt 16:23).[10] Anna is portrayed as an exemplary widow, comparable to the revered widow Judith.

Anna is the first widow to appear in the Lukan narrative. Luke has more episodes about widows than any other evangelist. Peculiar to his Gospel are Jesus' mention of the many widows in Israel while Elijah was sent to the widow in Zarephath (4:25-26), the incident of the resuscitation of the son of the widow at Nain (7:11-17), and the parable of the widow who persisted in demanding justice (18:1-8). In Acts 6:1-6 Luke relates a complaint of the Hellenists that their widows were being neglected in the daily distribution. At the death of Dorcas the widows are weeping over her and show Paul the clothing she had made (Acts 9:36-43). Luke

---

[7]Luke 3:21; 9:18, 28, 29; 11:1; 22:32, 41-45.

[8]Luke 24:53; Acts 1:14; 2:42, 46; 3:1; 4:31; 6:4, 6; 7:59; 8:15; 9:11, 40; 10:2, 9; 11:15; 12:5, 12; 13:2-3; 14:23; 16:25; 20:36; 21:5; 22:17; 26:29; 27:29; 28:8.

[9]The Greek *heōs etōn ogdoēkonta tessarōn*, "until" or "up to eighty-four years" in 2:37 can mean either her present age is eighty-four or she has been a widow for eighty-four years.

[10]See J. K. Elliott, "Anna's Age (Luke 2:36-37)," *NovT* 30 (1988) 100–102.

retains from Mark a warning about scribes who "devour the houses of widows" (Luke 20:47; Mark 12:40) and the story of the poor widow who contributes her whole livelihood to the temple treasury (Luke 21:1-4; Mark 12:41-44).[11]

It is often remarked that Luke's frequent featuring of widows is part of his concern to emphasize God's care for the poor and oppressed, as expressed in Jesus' ministry. Although this may be true for an episode such as the raising of the widow's son at Nain (7:11-17), many other Lukan scenes with widows do not portray them as destitute recipients of charity. They are shown, rather, as is Anna, to be ministering in the community. Regarded as "forsaken" or "left empty," as the Greek term for widow, *chēra,* signifies, Anna instead forsakes her home in Asher and fills her days with fasting and prayer and prophecy. As one "not spoken for" (the root of the Hebrew word for widow, *almanah,* means "unable to speak"), Anna, now freed from the responsibilities of caring for a husband and children, speaks of the child who will bring the redemption of Jerusalem.

Anna is a prototype of what would later develop into a clerical order of consecrated widows whose duties included praying, fasting, visiting and laying hands on the sick, making clothes, and doing good works.[12] The number of Lukan incidents with widows may reflect the growing numbers and importance of widows in the ministry of the Church of Luke's day.

Anna is a prophet, but in Luke the voices of woman prophets are never heard. Unlike Simeon, Anna's words of prophecy are not preserved, nor are those of Philip's four daughters who had the gift of prophecy (Acts 21:9). Unlike Simeon, Elizabeth, or Mary, she is not said to be filled with the holy Spirit. Anna kept speaking "about the child to all who were awaiting the redemption of Jerusalem" (2:38) but no reaction to her prophecy is related. Simeon's prophecy evokes amazement (2:33), as does the

---

[11]It may also be that some of the Galilean women mentioned in 8:1-3 are widows, as well as Tabitha (Acts 9:36-43), Mary (Acts 12:12), and Lydia (Acts 16:11-15).

[12]These are listed in the *Didascalia Apostolorum*. See R. Hugh Connolly, ed. *Didascalia Apostolorum* (Oxford: Clarendon, 1929) 132-145. See further Bonnie Bowman Thurston, *The Widows: A Women's Ministry in the Early Church* (Minneapolis: Fortress Press, 1989).

message of the shepherds (2:18) and the naming of John by Elizabeth and Zechariah (1:63). Amazement is likewise the constant reaction to Jesus' words (4:22; 20:26) and deeds (8:25; 9:43; 11:14, 38; 24:12, 41). By giving Anna no audience for her prophecy, Luke discourages the reader from giving her much notice.[13]

Luke's opening chapters tell stories of women that are liberative and life-giving. Elizabeth embodies contemplative faithfulness, and assertive naming of God's grace. Mary proclaims in inchoate form the very same good news that Jesus will bring. Anna prophetically heralds him for all Israel. Each prefigures Jesus in his unwavering faithfulness to God, his endurance of tribulation, and his mission of liberation for others. Luke has preserved stories of powerful, Spirit-filled women of vision who bring new life to birth. But a notable shift occurs from chapter three on. No longer will women speak out prophetically. They will cry out in pain and in need and be attended to by Jesus. When they do speak what they say will be corrected (10:38-42; 11:27-28) or disbelieved (24:11).

Such a shift could be explained by Luke having used separate sources for different parts of his narrative. For the stories of Elizabeth, Mary, and Anna, it may be that he had access to traditions preserved in circles of women believers and that the rest of the Gospel reflects more andro-centric traditions. If Luke's intent is to reinforce a portrait of women as silent, passive, and supportive as the proper stance for Christian women, it may seem strange at first that he should begin his Gospel with such powerful portraits of prophetic women.

This may be explained by Luke's understanding of salvation history as divided into two ages: the age of Israel, of promise and prophecy; and the new age of saving history begun by Jesus (Luke 16:16).[14] In this schema, Luke has cast Elizabeth, Mary, and

---

[13]There is a similar effort to silence widows in the *Didascalia Apostolorum*, where widows are forbidden to teach and baptize and "gad about," which refers, perhaps, to their answering and asking theological questions. See Connolly, *Didascalia*, 133, 134, 142.

[14]Hans Conzelmann (*The Theology of St. Luke* [Philadelphia: Fortress Press, 1961] 16) saw Luke's story of salvation delineated in three stages: (1) The period of Israel (Luke 16:16); (2) the period of Jesus' ministry; (3) the period since the Ascension, on earth the period of the *ecclesia pressa*. How-

Anna in the mold of the prophetic women of Israel. They belong to the age of promise. There is a distinct break with the new age. For Luke, Christian women do not emulate the Jewish women prophets of old. Rather, he would have them assume a quiet, private stance that he deems proper for women in his Greco-Roman world. In his view the public prophetic ministries belong to the men. As we proceed with these stories, we will approach Luke's restrictive portrayal of women with a hermeneutics of suspicion. We will be "choosing the better part" by looking for ways to read against Luke's intent so as to release their liberating potential.

---

ever, many Lukan scholars today speak of only two periods: (1) a time of preparation, prophecy, and promise; and (2) a time of fulfillment inaugurated by the Christ event and awaiting final fulfillment. See Mark Allan Powell, *What are They Saying About Luke?* (New York: Paulist Press, 1989) 76–81.

Chapter 6

Simon's Mother-in-Law:
Healed for Service

LUKE 4:38-39

[38]"After he left the synagogue, he entered the house of Simon. Simon's mother-in-law was afflicted with a severe fever, and they interceded with him about her. [39]"He stood over her, rebuked the fever, and it left her. She got up immediately and waited on them.

The first Lukan incident involving a female character beyond the infancy narratives is the story of the healing of Simon's mother-in-law (4:38-39). The narrative follows the basic contours of the Markan version (Mark 1:29-31), and is the first of several Lukan incidents in which women are healed by Jesus. Luke has arranged the opening episodes of Jesus' ministry differently from Mark. In both Gospels the cure of Simon's mother-in-law follows the cure of a man with an unclean spirit.[1] But Mark precedes the two healings with the call of the first disciples (1:16-20). Luke delays this episode until after the initial healings and preaching (5:1-11). In Luke's Gospel there is narrated no previous rela-

[1]Although the healing of Simon's mother-in-law apparently takes place on the same Sabbath as the healing in the synagogue of a man possessed by a demon (Luke 4:31-37), the issue of Jesus healing on the Sabbath is not addressed until Luke 6:1-11.

tion between Jesus and Simon. The healing of Simon's mother-in-law lays the foundation for Simon's call to be a disciple; in Mark the reverse is true.

Luke's account differs from Mark's in a number of details. In the Third Gospel Andrew, James, and John have not yet been called to be disciples, and so Luke does not mention them entering Simon's house with him and Jesus (cf. Mark 1:29). In describing the illness of Simon's mother-in-law, Luke heightens her plight, calling it a "severe" fever. In Mark's version they (presumably Simon, Andrew, James, and John) simply tell *(legousin)* Jesus about her. In Luke's account they (it is unclear to whom "they" refers) interceded *(erōtēsan)* with him for her.[2] Mark says that Jesus took her by the hand and lifted her up; Luke relates that Jesus stood over her and rebuked the fever. Luke eliminates the reference to Jesus touching her, and uses a verb he frequently employs: *epistas,* "stood over."[3] He has Jesus treat the fever in the same way as he does demons: he "rebuked" it *(epetimēsen;* see 4:35, 41; 9:42). Mark had opened his account with his typical *kai euthys,* "and immediately." Luke eliminates this, as well as *euthys* before the disciples' telling of the illness. Instead, Luke inserts *parachrēma,* "immediately," before her rising and serving.

As in all the gospel healing stories, the primary intent of the evangelist is to highlight the power of Jesus. Luke's intensification of the seriousness of the fever and the immediacy of the cure serve this end. Little attention is given to Simon's mother-in-law as a character in her own right. She remains nameless and voiceless throughout. She does not have her own home, but resides in that of her son-in-law. Whether she is merely visiting or whether she was living there with her daughter and her family Luke does

[2]The *NRSV* translation, "they asked him about her" is more vague about whether the household members are merely informing Jesus or are imploring him to do something for her. The latter is the meaning when *erōtaō* is used with the accusative pronoun + *peri* + the genitive, as also in John 16:26; 17:9, 10. Other instances in Luke where *erōtaō* is used for asking someone to do something are: 5:3; 7:3, 4, 36; 8:37; 11:37; 14:32; 16:27.

[3]The use of the verb *ephistēmi* in the New Testament is almost exclusively Lukan. Of its twenty-one occurrences, seven are in Luke: 2:9, 38; 4:39; 10:40; 20:1; 21:34; 24:4; and eleven in Acts: 4:1; 6:12; 10:17; 11:11; 12:7; 17:5; 22:13, 20; 23:11, 27; 28:2.

not say.[4] She is seriously ill but in the narrative she does not give voice to her own suffering, nor does she speak directly to Jesus. She is identified by her relationship to her son-in-law, who takes charge of speaking for her and about her.

In his version of the story, Luke alters the tender detail of Jesus touching her and lifting her up. His rendition is less personal: Jesus stands over her, and his interaction is with the fever, which he rebukes. Once the fever left her, she immediately got up and served *(diēkonei)* them. The imperfect verb *diēkonei* can be translated either "she began to serve" or "she kept on serving." The verb *diakonein* occurs eight times in the Gospel of Luke and twice in Acts. The noun form, *diakonia*, occurs once in the Gospel and eight times in Acts. In the story of Simon's mother-in-law (4:39) Luke retains *diakonein* from his Markan source (1:31).[5] In 8:1-3, a passage unique to Luke,[6] Mary Magdalene, Joanna, Susanna, and many other women who accompanied Jesus and the Twelve on their missionary journey "provided for *[diēkonoun]* them out of their resources." In 10:40, also unique to Luke, Martha is "burdened with much serving *[diakonia]*" and asks Jesus, "do you not care that my sister has left me by myself to do the serving

[4]Bruce Malina and Richard L. Rohrbaugh speculate, "Since marriages in first-century Palestine were patrilocal, the fact that Peter's mother-in-law was in his house may mean that she was a widow with no living family members to care for her" (*Social Science Commentary on the Synoptic Gospels* [Minneapolis: Fortress Press, 1992] 181). It seems odd, however, that if Luke intended us to understand her as a widow he would not mention this, being that he emphasizes stories of widows more than any other evangelist.

[5]Mark 1:13 recounts that angels ministered to *(diēkonoun)* Jesus during the time of his temptation in the desert. The Lukan account (4:1-13) does not have this detail, but rather has an angel appear to strengthen Jesus during his agony (22:43).

[6]Although unique to Luke, there are echoes in the passage of Mark's crucifixion scene, "There were also women looking on from a distance. Among them were Mary Magdalene, Mary the mother of the younger James and of Joses, and Salome. These women had followed him when he was in Galilee and ministered to *[diēkonoun]* him. There were also many other women who had come up with him to Jerusalem" (Mark 15:40-41). Luke's version of this scene adds "all his acquaintances" to the Galilean women witnesses (23:49).

[diakonein]?'' The meaning of *diakonein* in these two passages will be discussed in following chapters.

In two instances *diakonein* occurs in sayings about vigilant servants. In 12:37 Jesus proclaims blessed ''those servants whom the master finds vigilant on his arrival . . . he will gird himself, have them recline at table, and proceed to wait on *[diakonēsei]* them.'' In 17:8 Jesus illustrates a disciple's attitude of service with how a master says to a servant, ''Put on your apron and wait on *[diakonei]* me while I eat and drink,'' expecting that servant to comply. These two examples are also peculiar to Luke, and in both instances *diakonein* refers to table service.

In his farewell discourse to his disciples at the Last Supper, Jesus instructs them, ''The kings of the Gentiles lord it over them and those in authority over them are addressed as 'Benefactors'; but among you it shall not be so. Rather, let the greatest among you be as the youngest, and the leader as the servant *[ho diakonōn]*. For who is greater: the one who is at the table or the one who serves *[ho diakonōn]*? Is it not the one seated at the table? I am among you as one who serves *[ho diakonōn]*'' (22:25-27). This passage has no parallel in the Gospels of Mark or Matthew, but it echoes Mark 10:43-45, ''whoever wishes to be great among you will be your servant *[diakonos]*; whoever wishes to be first among you will be the slave *[doulos]* of all. For the Son of Man did not come to be served *[diakonēthēnai]* but to serve *[diakonēsai]* and to give his life as a ransom for many.'' In Mark this saying occurs after the third passion prediction, before Jesus' entrance into Jerusalem.

In Acts there are two instances of *diakonein*. In 6:2 the Twelve assert, ''it is not right for us to neglect the word of God to serve *[diakonein]* at table.'' They propose that the community select seven others for this task while they devote themselves to the ministry of the word (*diakonia tou logou,* 6:4). In 19:22 Paul sends two envoys *(duo tōn diakonountōn autọ̄)* to Macedonia while he remained in Asia.

The noun form, *diakonia,* occurs once in the Gospel of Luke: in 10:40, where Martha is ''burdened with much serving *[diakonia].*'' In Acts it is found eight times. In 1:17, Peter speaks of Judas' allotted share ''in this ministry *[diakonia].*'' The apostles pray for God to show who is to replace Judas ''in this apostolic ministry'' (*diakonia,* 1:25). In 6:1 the Hellenists complain against the Hebrews because their widows were being neglected in the daily distribution *(tç diakonią).*[7] In 6:4 *diakonia* refers to the ministry of the word *(diakonia tou logou).* In 11:29 and 12:25 *diakonia* denotes the relief mission conducted by Barnabas and Saul for the community in Judea suffering from famine. In 20:24 and 21:19 it refers to the whole of Paul's ministry.

The basic meaning of the verb *diakonein* is to act as a "go-between."[8] It applies to persons who perform errands, deliver messages, execute tasks for another, or attend another person. In all New Testament examples *diakonein* has the general connotation of "to carry out a charge."[9] The task is established either by God or by an authority within the community. In some instances attendance on another is concretely waiting on them at table. In both Mark 10:43-45 and Luke 22:25-27 *diakonein* expresses the epitome of Jesus' mission; Mark equates it with the very giving of Jesus' life. In both accounts Jesus advises his disciples that leadership is equivalent to serving. In the context of the Last Supper meal, *diakonein* in Luke 22:25-27 elicits the image of table service rendered by a waiter. In the narrative, Jesus is not actually serving the meal. But he instructs his disciples to adopt the stance that his actions symbolize: to be "as the one who serves" (22:27).

Interestingly, the only characters in the Third Gospel with whom the verb *diakonein* is used are women; in Acts it is used exclusively of men. Given its wide range of meanings, how is it to be

---

[7]Elisabeth Schüssler Fiorenza (*In Memory of Her: A Feminist Theological Reconstruction of Christian Origins* [New York: Crossroad, 1983] 165–166) argues that the conflict involved the role and participation of women at the Eucharistic meal: that the Hellenist widows were not being assigned their turn in the table service or that they were not properly served.

[8]John Collins, *Diakonia: Re-Interpreting the Ancient Sources* (New York: Oxford University Press, 1990) 77–95.

[9]It is important to remember that the ministries of the early Church were still very fluid at the time of Luke's writing. There were no set job descriptions. In the Pastoral letters, written not long after Luke and Acts, the qualifications for *diakonoi,* "deacons" (1 Tim 3:8-13), are essentially the same as those for *episkopoi,* "overseers" or "bishops" (1 Tim 3:2-7), and *presbyteroi,* "elders" (Titus 1:5-6; 2:2-3). Titus 1:5-7 uses *presbyteros* and *episkopos* interchangeably.

understood in each instance? Kathleen Corley[10] observes that when women serve, Luke casts it as table service; when men do, it is distribution of goods, and it symbolizes leadership. Accordingly, Luke apparently intends that we see Simon's mother-in-law as carrying out the domestic duties proper to women of first-century Palestine.

By reading against Luke's intent, we may see a deeper, theological significance to her service. She serves as a prototype of the disciple whose ministry of faithful attendance on another is modeled after the service that Jesus exemplified. In fact, in the Matthean version there are clues that this is a call story in which she illustrates the ideal response by serving.

Matthew 8:14-15 takes the form not of a healing story, but of a call story with a healing motif.[11] It is briefer than the versions of Mark and Luke and is missing some of the standard elements of a healing miracle: "Jesus entered the house of Peter, and saw his mother-in-law lying in bed with a fever. He touched her hand, the fever left her, and she rose and waited on him." Matthew's account has the same form elements as the story of the call of Matthew (9:9). In both stories Jesus takes the initiative; he sees *(eiden)* the one to be called; there is a description of the person to be called; there is a word or action by Jesus; and the person responds to him. It is only in the Matthean version of the story of Simon's mother-in-law that Jesus takes the initiative. Likewise, the detail of Jesus seeing her is unique to Matthew. Only in Matthew is the pronoun *(autǫ,* "him") singular, i.e., her response is directed to Jesus alone, as in a call story. Just as the tax collector "got up and followed him" (9:9), she got up and served him (8:15).

The Matthean account preserves the only call story of a woman disciple in the New Testament. Most probably it was told within circles of women followers of Jesus, and its function was to legitimate not only the discipleship of women, but their participation in ministries of service. In Luke's Gospel, however, the story has been reformulated into a healing story. Simon's mother-in-law

[10]Kathleen Corley, *Private Women, Public Meals: Social Conflict and Women in the Synoptic Tradition* (Peabody, Mass.: Hendrickson, 1993) 121.

[11]Elaine M. Wainwright, *Towards a Feminist Critical Reading of the Gospel according to Matthew* (Berlin: de Gruyter, 1991) 177-191.

thus appears to be serving out of gratitude for having been healed, not from having heard the word. Luke accents not a woman's call to discipleship, nor the serving ministry of women, but rather, uses this story to prepare for the call of Simon in 5:1-11 and the participation of the male disciples in Jesus' mission. One way of "choosing the better part" is to retrieve from Matthew's account the story of a woman called by Jesus who responds with service.

There is one caution, however, in speaking of "service" as the exemplary Christian response. As Elisabeth Schüssler Fiorenza has shown, a theology of service has different implications for women than for men.[12] When women are socialized to "be for others," and when, because of their gender, they have assumed subservient tasks in the Church, to speak of ministry as service causes women to "internalize and legitimate the patriarchal-hierarchical status quo in theological-spiritual terms."[13] It is often argued that service is liberating when it is freely chosen. But this is true only for those who actually have the power and freedom of choice. In the present patriarchal structure women do not have such freedom. Thus, to speak of ministry as service does not empower women. Other New Testament concepts such as *dynamis*, "power," *exousia*, "authority," and *sōtēria*, "well-being," could be employed in a liberating theology of ministry by those who are marginalized. When coupled with a stance of ministerial servanthood by those who do have actual power and privilege, the Church could then be transformed into a community of equal disciples.

---

[12]Elisabeth Schüssler Fiorenza, " 'Waiting at Table': A Critical Feminist Theological Reflection on Diakonia," *Concilium 198. Diakonia: Church for the Others,* ed. N. Greinacher and N. Mette (Edinburgh: T. & T. Clark, 1988) 84–94.

[13]Ibid., 86.

Chapter 7

The Widow of Nain:
Voiceless Protester Against Death

LUKE 7:11-17

[11]Soon afterward he journeyed to a city called Nain, and his disciples and a large crowd accompanied him. [12]As he drew near to the gate of the city, a man who had died was being carried out, the only son of his mother, and she was a widow. A large crowd from the city was with her. [13]When the Lord saw her, he was moved with pity for her and said to her, "Do not weep." [14]He stepped forward and touched the coffin; at this the bearers halted and he said, "Young man, I tell you, arise!" [15]The dead man sat up and began to speak, and Jesus gave him to his mother. [16]Fear seized them all, and they glorified God, exclaiming, "A great prophet has arisen in our midst," and "God has visited his people." [17]This report about him spread through the whole of Judea and in all the surrounding region.

Following the cure of Simon's mother-in-law, Luke sketches numerous other healings, all pointing to God's reign breaking into the human realm in a powerful new way through the person and ministry of Jesus. In addition to healings, there are call stories, as Jesus gathers a community of followers and then sends them out on mission. Teachings of Jesus, particularly the "Sermon on the Plain" (6:17-49) show him powerful in word as well as deed.

The story of the raising of the widow's son (7:11-17) is unique to Luke. Unlike the stories of widows who actively exercise their gifts, such as Anna (2:36-38), the widow demanding justice (18:1-8), and the woman who gave her whole livelihood to the Temple (21:1-4), the woman of 7:11-17 is cast in the more traditional widow's role. She is a nameless, silent object of pity. Her only son, her only means of support and status, is dead. She bears not only the grief of losing her child, but also anxiety for her own future.

Jesus, accompanied by his disciples and a large crowd, encounters the sizable funeral procession and is moved with pity for the widow. He says to her, "Do not weep," touches the coffin, commands the young man to arise, and returns him to his mother. Not only the son, but his mother as well, is restored to life in the community.

Like the other accounts of resuscitations and healings, this story's main effect is to point to Jesus and the power of God at work in him. The crowd reacts by glorifying God[1] and acclaiming Jesus as a prophet (v. 16).[2] The widow fades into the background. We hear nothing of her reaction. There is no mention of faith in this story. We know nothing more about whether the widow became a disciple of Jesus or whether others were drawn to him through her testimony. Luke concludes the story by attesting that "this report about him spread through the whole of Judea and in all the surrounding region" (v. 17), but who it is that spreads the word is left unspecified.

The parallels between this incident and that of Elijah and the widow of Zarephath (1 Kgs 17:8-24) are striking.[3] In both stories the prophet initially meets the widow at the gate of the city (1 Kgs 17:10; Luke 17:12). In both the dead son is an only son

[1]The acclamation "God has visited his people" in 7:16 echoes 1:68, where Zechariah sings of God's blessedness for visiting and bringing redemption to Israel. Further, Jesus' compassion (7:13) demonstrates the "tender mercy of our God" (1:78).

[2]Fear *(phobos)* also seized them, as often in Luke and Acts, as a response to a God's saving deeds: 1:12, 65; 2:9; 5:26; 8:37; 21:26; Acts 2:43; 5:5, 11; 9:31; 19:17.

[3]See T. L. Brodie, "Towards Unravelling Luke's Use of the Old Testament: Luke 7:11-17 as an *Imitatio* of 1 Kings 17:17-24," *NTS* 32 (1986) 247-267.

(monogenēs),[4] heightening the distress of the widow. Whether God does care for the plight of widows (as affirmed in Exodus 22:23 and many other times in the Hebrew Scriptures) is the theological point at issue. In 1 Kings 17:20 Elijah complains to God about the affliction visited upon his host; in Luke 7:13 Jesus' compassion reflects that of God (v. 16). Both stories have identical wording when the prophet gives the raised son back to his mother (1 Kgs 17:23; Luke 7:15). In both incidents the healer is acclaimed as one who acts and speaks for God (1 Kgs 17:24; Luke 7:16).

This is one of many Lukan episodes in which Jesus is cast as the prophet Elijah.[5] In Jesus' initial proclamation of his mission (4:26), which stirred his audience to fury (4:28), he cited this very incident of Elijah and the widow of Zarephath, implying that his own mission would be similar. In Luke 9:8, 19 some thought that Jesus was Elijah reappeared. Jesus, like Elijah, fasted forty days in the wilderness (Luke 4:2; 1 Kgs 19:8). Jesus' feeding of the five thousand (Luke 9:10-17) is comparable to Elijah's miraculous provision of food in 1 Kings 17:7-16. As Elijah controlled the weather (1 Kgs 17:1; 18:41- 45), so too Jesus (Luke 8:22-25). Both Elijah and Jesus were men of prayer;[6] both were "taken up" to heaven (2 Kgs 2:11; Luke 9:51; Acts 1:9).[7]

There is ambiguity, however, as to whether the Lukan Jesus is the new Elijah. Three times (Luke 7:27; 9:54, 61-62) Jesus rejects this role. In the aspects of eschatological prophet and miracle worker, Jesus is like Elijah; but the functions of fiery social reformer and precursor are not played by Jesus, but rather by John the Baptist (Luke 1:17, 76; 7:27). By casting Jesus like Elijah, yet unlike him, Luke is showing Jesus as a prophet in line with those of old, yet inaugurating a new age of salvation.

At first reading, this story of a silent, pitied widow, an object of compassion, may seem devoid of liberating potential for con-

[4]In two other episodes, Luke 8:42 (cf. Mark 5:23) and Luke 9:38 (cf. Mark 9:17) Luke heightens the distress of the parents by making the ill child an only child.

[5]See above, pp. 90–91, for references to Jesus as prophet.

[6]1 Kgs 17:21-22; 18:36-37; 19:9; Luke 3:21; 5:16; 6:12; 9:18, 28, 29; 10:21-22; 11:1-13; 22:3, 32, 41-42; 23:46.

[7]Other allusions to Elijah are found in Luke 9:61-62 (see 1 Kgs 19:19-21); Luke 9:54 and 12:49 (see 1 Kgs 1:10, 12); Luke 19:1 (see 2 Kgs 2:4); Luke 22:33 (see 2 Kgs 2:4); Luke 24:49 (see 2 Kgs 2:13).

temporary women who would not want to be so regarded. One direction for "choosing the better part" is to see the way in which she prompts Jesus to take up the cause of one who is voiceless.[8] It is her very silence that brings Jesus to compassion. Her tears and voiceless protest against death are more eloquent than words and have the effect of moving Jesus to restore life. She and her fellow mourners can be seen as prototypical of contemporary groups of women who gather in so many places of our globe to protest against death. The Madres de la Plaza de Mayo are one such group, who march every Thursday, silently demanding to know the fate of their disappeared husbands and brothers and sons from Argentina's "dirty war" of the 1970s. Although they cannot bring back to life the 30,000 *desaparecidos,* their weekly march for human rights has been thought to be partially responsible for toppling the military dictatorship in 1982. Like the widow of Nain, powerlessness in the face of death can be converted into silent protest that brings forth life.

[8] I am indebted to one of my students, Gioacchino Campese, for this insight.

Chapter 8

The Woman Who Showed Great Love

LUKE 7:36-50

[36]A Pharisee invited him to dine with him, and he entered the Pharisee's house and reclined at table. [37]Now there was a sinful woman in the city who learned that he was at table in the house of the Pharisee. Bringing an alabaster flask of ointment, [38]she stood behind him at his feet weeping and began to bathe his feet with her tears. Then she wiped them with her hair, kissed them, and anointed them with the ointment. [39]When the Pharisee who had invited him saw this he said to himself, "If this man were a prophet, he would know who and what sort of woman this is who is touching him, that she is a sinner." [40]Jesus said to him in reply, "Simon, I have something to say to you." "Tell me, teacher," he said. [41]"Two people were in debt to a certain creditor; one owed five hundred days' wages and the other owed fifty. [42]Since they were unable to repay the debt, he forgave it for both. Which of them will love him more?" [43]Simon said in reply, "The one, I suppose, whose larger debt was forgiven." He said to him, "You have judged rightly." [44]Then he turned to the woman and said to Simon, "Do you see this woman? When I entered your house, you did not give me water for my feet, but she has bathed them with her tears and wiped them with her hair. [45]You did not give me a kiss, but she has not ceased kissing my feet since the time I entered. [46]You did not anoint my head with oil, but she anointed my

feet with ointment. ⁴⁷So I tell you, her many sins have been for-given; hence, she has shown great love. But the one to whom little is forgiven, loves little." ⁴⁸He said to her, "Your sins are forgiven." ⁴⁹The others at table said to themselves, "Who is this who even forgives sins?" ⁵⁰But he said to the woman, "Your faith has saved you; go in peace."

The story of this nameless woman is often confused with that of the woman who anointed Jesus for burial (Mark 14:3-9; Matt 26:6-13; John 12:1-8). There are strong parallels between Mark 14:3-9 and Luke 7:36-50. In both the woman is unnamed; she enters the house of Simon; Jesus is reclining at table; the woman carries an alabaster flask of ointment with which she anoints Jesus; observers react negatively, whereas Jesus affirms her ac-tion. Luke's account shares other details with the Johannine ver-sion: the woman's ministrations are to Jesus' feet, which she also wipes with her hair.

There are also important differences between the Lukan story and the other three. In Luke the setting is Galilee,[1] rather than Bethany. In Mark (14:3) and Matthew (26:6) the host is Simon the leper, while in Luke Simon is a Pharisee. In John (12:2) the supper is served by Martha, in the home she shares with Mary and Lazarus. In John (12:3) it is Mary who anoints Jesus, whereas in the synoptic stories the woman is unnamed.[2] In Matthew, Mark, and John, the anointing occurs shortly before Jesus' passion and is a prophetic action related to his burial; in Luke it happens dur-ing the Galilean ministry and the focus is on repentance, forgive-ness, and love. In Luke the objection comes from Simon; in John (12:4-6) it is Judas who objects; in Matthew (26:8) "the disciples;"

[1]The pericope itself has no place indicator, but Luke sets it in the midst of Jesus' Galilean ministry.

[2]In the Western Church, traditions about Mary of Bethany, Mary Mag-dalene, the woman who showed great love, and the woman caught in adul-tery (John 8:1-11) have been interwoven and confused. These Marys and unnamed women have, for the most part, maintained their own identities in the traditions of the Greek Church. In the Gospel of Luke, Mary of Bethany appears only in 10:38-42, the episode with her sister Martha. Mary Magda-lene is introduced in 8:2 and appears again in 24:10. In light of 24:10 she is probably to be understood as one of "the women who had followed him from Galilee" and witnessed Jesus' death and burial in Luke 23:49, 55.

and in Mark (14:4) "some." In Luke Simon's objection centers on the woman's sinful past; in the other three versions the indignance revolves around the extravagance of the anointing when the ointment could have been sold for money to use for the poor.

The best explanation for these similarities and differences is that there are two strands of tradition: one tells of a woman who entered a dinner gathering in Galilee, at which Jesus was a guest. She had experienced forgiveness from Jesus and wept over his feet and dried them with her hair. The other strand relates that a woman at a dinner in Bethany anointed Jesus' head with costly perfume shortly before his passion. Whether the two strands of tradition represent two separate incidents in the life of Jesus or only one that has been variously preserved is impossible to determine. Because the two had many points of similarity, they became intertwined, and details from one passed over to the other in the oral retelling.[3] Each evangelist has further shaped the episode to his own theological purposes.

As it stands in Luke's Gospel, the story is a moving illustration of the desired response to Jesus' preaching. It comes on the heels of the episode in which the disciples of John the Baptist inquire of Jesus, "Are you the one who is to come, or should we look for another?" (7:20). Jesus replies by reminding them of what they have seen and heard: "the blind regain their sight, the lame walk, lepers are cleansed, the deaf hear, the dead are raised, the poor have the good news proclaimed to them" (7:22). He concludes, "And blessed is the one who takes no offense at me" (7:23). The issue is how one evaluates what one sees and hears concerning Jesus: does it draw you to faith in him, or do you take offense?[4]

The divided response is further illustrated in 7:24-35. There Jesus quizzes the crowds about what they went out to the desert to see (vv. 24, 26) when they followed John. The issue of seeing a prophet is raised in verse 26, preparing for Simon's objection in verse 39, regarding Jesus' identification as a prophet. Verses

[3]See A. Legault, "An Application of the Form-Critique Method to the Anointings in Galilee (Lk. 7.37-50) and Bethany (Mt. 26.6-13; Mk. 4.3-9; John 12.1-8)," *CBQ* 16 (1954) 131-145.

[4]See above, pp. 22-24, on seeing as a metaphor for perceiving the word of God, and the various responses exhibited in the Gospel.

29-30 highlight the positive response of "all the people . . . including tax collectors" to John and to the righteousness of God, in contrast to "the Pharisees and scholars of the law, who were not baptized by him" and who "rejected the plan of God for themselves."[5]

A parable in verses 31-32 continues to contrast actual responses to those desired. Verse 32, "We sang a dirge, but you did not weep," leads into the story in 7:36-50, where the woman who exemplifies the desired response stands behind Jesus, "at his feet weeping" (v. 38). Following the parable, verses 33-34 return to the issue of seeing. For those determined not to "see" in a way that leads to faith, they will see what they want: in John, who "came neither eating food nor drinking wine," they will see a man "possessed by a demon" (v. 33); in Jesus who "came eating and drinking" they see "a glutton and a drunkard, a friend of tax collectors and sinners" (v. 34).[6]

The central point of the story in Luke 7:36-50 concerns the interaction between Jesus and Simon.[7] The whole story hinges on Jesus' question to Simon in verse 44, "Do you see this woman?" This challenge of Jesus to Simon arises from Simon's misperception of the woman in verse 39. Two perceptions are intimately related: what Simon sees in the woman as she interacts with Jesus determines how Simon sees Jesus. Simon is clear about what he sees: she is a sinner and Jesus is not a prophet. The question that the story poses is: can Simon see differently? Can he see what Jesus sees: a forgiven woman who shows great love (v. 47)? If he can see her this way, then he may perceive Jesus aright: not only as prophet, but also as the agent of God's forgiving love.

As most often in this Gospel, Jesus' way of getting people to see God's realm as he does is through parables. And so, Jesus

[5] See J. T. Carroll ("Luke's Portrayal of the Pharisees," *CBQ* 50 [1988] 604–621) for further detail on how Luke uses Jesus' encounters with the Pharisees to demonstrate competing understandings of the realm of God.

[6] See also David A. Neale, *None But the Sinners: Religious Categories in the Gospel of Luke*, JSNTSup 58 (Sheffield: JSOT, 1991) 135–147 for connections between Luke 7:28-35 and 7:36-50.

[7] Contrary to Evelyn Thibeaux, " 'Known to Be a Sinner': The Narrative Rhetoric of Luke 7:36-50," *BTB* 23/4 (1993) 151–160, esp. 152, who asserts that the main plot is the interaction between Jesus and the woman.

replies to Simon's perception of the woman as a sinner by telling a parable. What Simon "sees" (vv. 39, 44) frames the parable of the two debtors in 7:41-43. The parable in verses 41-43 is not an allegory that corresponds point by point with the narrative of 7:36-40, 44-50. Nothing is said in the story about Simon being a sinner or that he is in need of forgiveness. The parable is not meant to contrast Simon's puny love after being forgiven little with the woman's lavish love after being forgiven much. Rather, the parable has a single point: that one who has been forgiven much loves greatly the one who remitted the debt.

Jesus contrasts the behavior of Simon with that of the woman (vv. 44-46) to show Simon that his actions reveal his shortsightedness. Simon provided none of the amenities of hospitality, which would express his respect for Jesus and his concern for his guest's comfort.[8] Simon gave no water for Jesus to wash his feet to refresh himself after walking dry, dusty roads.[9] He did not greet Jesus with a kiss,[10] nor did he anoint Jesus' head with oil.[11] The

---

[8]G. Bouwman ("La pécheresse hospitalière [Lc. vii, 36–50]," *ETL* 45 [1969] 172–179) asserts that the insertion of elements from John 12:1-11 and the parable in verse 41-44 shift the accent of the story: the woman's gestures of contrition have become expressions of hospitality. He postulates that this episode reflects a tension in the early Church over women of questionable pasts who offered hospitality to apostles. However, J. Delobel ("Encore la pécheresse. Quelques réflexions critiques," *ETL* 45 [1969] 180–183) rightly points out that the woman's actions in 7:38 are not about hospitality; it is when they are contrasted with Simon's omissions (vv. 44-46) that that nuance emerges. Furthermore, Jesus is not the guest of the woman; rather, of Simon. If this theme were a concern to Luke it is odd that it does not emerge in Acts, where numerous episodes mention hospitality toward apostles.

[9]In Gen 18:4; 19:2; 24:32; 43:24 this is part of the hospitality extended to guests.

[10]It was customary to greet or bid farewell to relatives and friends (of the same or opposite sex) with a kiss (e.g., Gen 27:26; 29:11, 13; 31:28; 1 Sam 20:41; Luke 15:20). Christians habitually greeted one another with a kiss (Rom 16:16; 1 Cor 16:20; 1 Thess 5:26). It would be expected that Simon would greet Jesus with a kiss on the cheek. A kiss on the hand would signal even greater respect.

[11]The custom of providing dinner guests with a cone of oil that would drip down on their heads during the course of the meal is seen in Egyptian representations of banquet scenes (James B. Pritchard, ed., *ANEP* [Princeton: Princeton University Press, 1969] 209). This would cool and refresh the guests.

woman, by contrast, went to extravagant lengths: she bathed his feet with her tears and wiped them with her hair, kissed his feet ceaselessly,[12] and anointed them with ointment.[13]

Jesus points out these actions to Simon so that he can make the same conclusion Jesus has. When presented with the matter in parable form, Simon easily judges rightly (v. 43). In verse 44 the question moves to the real woman that faces Simon. If Simon still does not see the link between the parable and the woman after Jesus recites what he sees (vv. 44-46), he proceeds to interpret it: "So I tell you, her many sins have been forgiven; hence, she has shown great love" (v. 47).[14] The choice lies before Simon: can he let go of seeing her as a sinner and see, rather, her great love? If so, then this will also enable him to perceive Jesus correctly: that he is the prophet. Simon's fate rests on whether he can be persuaded to see as Jesus does. In the end, we don't know if he does. As with all good parables, the story is open-ended. It invites the reader to take up the challenge presented to Simon, and to be converted to Jesus' way of seeing.

Like Simon the Pharisee, modern readers come to this episode with their own presuppositions, which can blind them to its liberating potential. It is surprising how many commentators and translators reinforce Simon's initial perception of the woman, and

---

For the custom among Jews, see H. Strack and P. Billerbeck, *Kommentar zum Neuen Testament*, 6 vols. (Munich: Beck, 1922–1961) 427, 428. Psalm 23:5 and Ecclesiastes 9:7-8 associate anointing of the head with banqueting. Not only was the ointment on the head refreshing, but its fragrance would fill the room (John 12:3), masking other less pleasant odors. In Matthew 6:17 Jesus instructs his disciples to anoint their head and wash their face when fasting.

[12]Kissing the feet was a sign of deep reverence, often extended to leading rabbis (Xen. *Cyr.* vii.5.32; Polyb. xv.1.7; Aristoph. *Vesp.* 608).

[13]Legault, "Anointings," 131–145, asserts that anointing feet is an unheard of action and that this detail is best explained as having crossed into the story from the tradition about the anointing of Jesus' head. However, J. Coakley ("The Anointing at Bethany and the Priority of John," *JBL* 107 [1988] 247) offers eight literary references to anointing of feet.

[14]The end of verse 47, "But the one to whom little is forgiven, loves little," does not refer to Simon; it simply provides a contrast to highlight the woman's great love.

never move beyond that. The episode has no title in the Greek text,[15] but modern translators have entitled it: "The Pardon of a Sinful Woman" *(NAB)*; "The Woman Who Was a Sinner" *(NJB, NRSV)*; "A Sinful Woman Forgiven" *(Harper Collins Study Bible)*. *La Nueva Biblia Latinoamericana* confuses matters entirely by making her "La mujer pecadora de Magdala," "The sinful woman from Magdala." *The Christian Community Bible* is noncommittal: "Jesus, the Woman and the Pharisee." None has thought to point the reader to the way Jesus perceives her by entitling it: "A Woman Who Shows Great Love" (v. 47).

Verse 37 does clearly say the woman was a sinner, but the imperfect verb *ēn* has the connotation "used to be"; she is no longer the sinner she once was. That she had been forgiven before this dinner party is clear from verse 47.[16] How or when the woman's sins were forgiven is not narrated. In verse 47 the perfect tense of the verb *apheōntai*, "have been forgiven," expresses a past action whose effects endure into the present.[17] This story has often

[15]The original Greek text of the New Testament has no subtitles of individual pericopes. Modern translators add these to help the reader find discreet episodes more easily.

[16]See B.-M. Ferry, "La pécheresse pardonnée (Lc 7,36-50). Pourquoi verse-t-elle des pleurs?" *EspVie* 99 (1989) 174–176. Understanding that the woman's sins have already been forgiven before the banquet scene means that the point in 7:36-50 is not that Jesus "has violated, or perhaps transcended, the letter of the law of clean and unclean in the presence of a Pharisee" by allowing an unclean woman to touch him and by passing over her act in silence (see Ben Witherington III, *Women and the Genesis of Christianity* [New York: Cambridge University Press, 1990] 67). Nor does it illustrate the curative power that flows from Jesus when one touches him (see P. Delobel, "L'onction par la pécheresse. La composition littéraire de Lc.: VII, 36-50," *ETL* 42 [1966] 441). That point emerges in the story of the woman with a hemorrhage (8:43-48), not 7:36-50.

[17]Ferry, "La pécheresse pardonnée," 176, would likewise translate *ēgapēsen* as present, "she loves much." J. Kilgallen ("John the Baptist, the Sinful Woman, and the Pharisee," *JBL* 104 [1985] 675–679) postulates that the woman had been forgiven her sins in the baptism of John (reading 7:36-50 in light of 7:24-35). This hypothesis, however, does not adequately explain why the woman's demonstrations of gratitude are directed toward Jesus. Kilgallen is right in connecting 7:36-50 with the previous episode, but to assert that the central issue is whether a person accepts the efficacy of John's bap-

been understood as telling of a woman who is forgiven because of her lavish love; that is, her pardon is a consequence of her loving actions. The Greek phrase *hoti ēgapēsen poly* allows this meaning, taking the conjunction *hoti* in a consecutive sense. However, the conclusion in verse 47c, "But the one to whom little is forgiven, loves little," and the parable in verses 41-43 have the opposite point: that the love follows the forgiveness. In this context it is clear that *hoti* must be understood in the causal sense, pointing not to the reason why the fact *is* so, but whereby it is *known* to be so.

This interpretation makes an important theological point: divine forgiveness is not dependent on a person's demonstrations of love; the remittance of sin is prior. The *NAB* rendering of verse 37, "Now there was a sinful woman in the city," completely obscures that her being a sinner was in the past. Moreover, this translation juxtaposes "sinful" and "woman," making it all the more difficult to eradicate the yet pervasive linking of women with sinfulness. The *NRSV* is far preferable, and translates the Greek more literally, "And a woman in the city, who was a sinner. . . ." The whole point of the episode is that she had already been forgiven and is not seen by Jesus as a sinner.

The verb *apheōntai*, "have been forgiven," in verse 47 may be understood as a theological passive, that is, that the forgiving has been done by God. But the demonstrations of love directed toward Jesus and the question of the others at table in verse 49, "Who is this who even forgives sins?" clearly connect the forgiveness to Jesus. The central point of the episode, however, does not concern Jesus' ability to forgive sins, but rather Simon's misperception of a forgiven sinner. Verses 48-50 append sayings found in other Lukan stories that have a loose connection to 7:36-

---

tism to forgive sins is forcing a connection that does not exist. John has already been imprisoned (3:20) and has pointed the way to the "one more powerful" coming after him (3:16). The focus is the identity of *Jesus* and the proper response to him, not his predecessor. In 9:7-9 the question is clearly stated by Herod: John is dead, who is Jesus? That the reader must presume prior contact of the woman in 7:36-50 with Jesus is not the problem that Kilgallen supposes. Many gospel incidents presuppose that the characters have had prior contact with Jesus that is not related in the narrative, e.g., Luke 8:1-3; 10:38-42; Mark 15:40.

47. In the story of the man who had been paralyzed (Luke 5:17-26) Jesus also says, "Your sins are forgiven" (5:20). The scribes and Pharisees react by asking themselves, "Who is this who speaks blasphemies? Who but God alone can forgive sins?" (5:21). Simon's asking himself about Jesus' identity in 7:39 recalls 5:20-21 and prompts Luke to end the episode in chapter 7 with the same statement, "Your sins are forgiven" (7:48), and the same question, "Who is this?" (7:49). The concluding verse, "Your faith has saved you; go in peace" (7:50) is identical to the closing line of the healing of the woman with a hemorrhage (8:43-48).[18] In the latter story, faith is at the heart of the message; in 7:36-50 faith only appears in the final verse, and is not the point of the episode. The similarities of the two narratives, in which a woman thought to be unclean approaches Jesus without his bidding and touches him, followed by objections from a character named Simon,[19] causes Luke to append 7:50 to the story of the woman who loved greatly, giving the two episodes identical endings.

It is curious that although the text does not say what sort of sins the woman had committed, much attention is given to speculation on the nature of her sinful past. By contrast, commentators never discuss what might be the type of sins Simon Peter has committed when he says he is "a sinful man" in the story of his call (5:7). The usual presumption is that the woman in 7:36-50 was a prostitute.[20] In verse 47 Jesus acknowledges that her sins

[18]Luke's source is Mark 5:25-34.

[19]In 7:39 it is Simon the Pharisee; in 8:45 it is Peter, whom we know also as Simon (4:38; 5:1-11; 6:14).

[20]E.g., J.D.M. Derrett, *Law in the New Testament* (London: Darton, Longman & Todd, 1970) 167–168; E. Schweizer, *The Good News According to Luke* (Atlanta: John Knox, 1984) 139; Alfred Plummer, *The Gospel According to S. Luke,* 5th ed., ICC (Edinburgh: T. & T. Clark, 1981) 210; Witherington, *Genesis,* 66; Luise Schottroff, "Through German and Feminist Eyes: A Liberationist Reading of Luke 7:36-50," paper presented at the AAR/SBL Annual Meeting, November 21, 1994; Kathleen Corley, *Private Women: Public Meals* (Peabody, Mass.: Hendrickson, 1993) 124; E. Moltmann-Wendel, *The Women Around Jesus* (New York: Crossroad, 1987) 65. Fitzmyer, *The Gospel According to Luke,* 1.689 dissents: "No hint is given of the kind of sins that she has committed." M. Black (*An Aramaic Approach to the Gospels and Acts,* 3d ed. [Oxford: Clarendon, 1967] 181–183) thinks that the Lukan text is playing on the Aramaic word for "sinner," *hayyābtā',* "debtor," and

had been many, and Luke hints in verse 37 that the whole city also knows this. But does that warrant the conclusion that she is a prostitute? In a first-century Galilean city everyone knows everyone else's business. This woman need only have been ill or disabled or have contact with Gentiles to be considered a sinner by Jews in the city.[21] Simon's remark in verse 39 implies that the woman's sinfulness is not immediately apparent to a stranger. A possible scenario is that the woman is employed in work that brings her into frequent contact with Gentiles,[22] perhaps midwifery or dyeing. Everyone in the city would know her occupation and Jews would consider her sinful from her association with the unclean. Simon, unaware of any prior contact between her and Jesus, remarks to himself that if Jesus were indeed a prophet, he too would know that she is a sinner.

Her mere presence[23] at the banquet does open her up to the accusation of being a prostitute.[24] Women who attended banquets were prostitutes who were there to enhance the pleasure of the men. Although in the Roman period respectable women became more liberated and were beginning to attend banquets with men, the pervasive attitude was that such actions made a woman sexually suspect. But the woman who comes to Simon's house is not a participant in the banquet. Nor does she do any of the things

---

is thus providing a connection between the pronouncement-story and the parable.

[21]That sickness and disability were equated with sinfulness in Jesus' day is evident from the question of Jesus' disciples in John 9:2, "Rabbi, who sinned, this man or his parents, that he was born blind?" Jesus' reply is, "Neither this man nor his parents sinned; it is so that the works of God might be made visible through him" (John 9:3). The equation of Gentile with "sinner" can be seen in 1 Maccabees 2:44; Galatians 2:15, and is implied in Luke 6:32-33; 24:7.

[22]The phrase *hai hamartiai autēs hai pollai,* "her many sins," in verse 47 indicates that her sinfulness came from numerous acts.

[23]John Koenig (*New Testament Hospitality,* Overtures to Biblical Theology 17 [Philadelphia: Fortress Press, 1985] 16–17) notes that rabbinic texts ('*Abot.* 1:5; *t.Ber.* 4:8; *Ta'an.* 20.b) speak of virtuous Jews who were known to open their houses to the needy, particularly for Sabbath eve supper. This explains how the woman could have gained access to a Pharisee's meal.

[24]Corley, *Private Women,* 126.

that banquet courtesans were known to do: engage in witty conversation or discussion with the banqueters, drink with them, recline beside them, dance, act, play the flute or harp, or in any way entertain.[25] Nor is she named by any of the known terms for such women: *pornē*, "prostitute," or "whore"; *koinē*, "common," i.e., "shared by all"; *gynai pagkoine*, "public woman"; *pilasōtos*, "wanton"; or *hetaira*, "companion to men," the term for the highest class prostitutes.

That any of the women who associated with Jesus were prostitutes is pure conjecture. Such speculation is based on one lone saying unique to Matthew. It occurs on the lips of Jesus at the end of the parable of the two sons. He says to the chief priests and elders, "Amen, I say to you, tax collectors and prostitutes are entering the kingdom of God before you. When John came to you in the way of righteousness, you did not believe him; but tax collectors and prostitutes did. Yet even when you saw that, you did not later change your minds and believe him" (Matt 21:31-32). The saying serves as a warning to the religious leaders, who think themselves upright, but who, in fact, may not be. It contrasts their negative response to Jesus with that of those least expected to be upright: tax collectors and prostitutes. It is a warning to the leaders, set forth in polemical terms, not a historical attestation on the makeup of Jesus' itinerant band of followers.

It is also important to note that this Matthean saying is parallel to Luke 7:29-30. If the mention of prostitutes was present in the original Q form of the saying, it is curious that Luke should drop it from his version of the saying. The mention of the positive response of prostitutes to John would have served Luke's interest if, indeed, he had wanted the woman in 7:36-50 to be understood as a prostitute. The accusation that Jesus is "a glutton and a drunkard, a friend of tax collectors and sinners" (Luke 7:34) evokes the image of a man who eats and drinks with courtesans, but it is more likely that this saying recalls an accusation by Jesus' opponents that "has its roots in a common slur used rhetorically when one wanted to question the public morality of

---

[25]See descriptions of banquet courtesans in Corley, *Private Women*, 38-48; see also Sarah Pomeroy, *Goddesses, Whores, Wives, and Slaves: Women in Classical Antiquity* (New York: Dorset, 1975) 88-92.

an individual.''[26] The greater probability is that the women who followed Jesus or dined with him were not, in fact, prostitutes, but were so maligned for overstepping ideal societal roles.

Nonetheless, some find in 7:36-50 proof of the woman's prostitution in the details of her loosening her hair, possessing an expensive alabaster flask of perfume, and emptying it out on Jesus' feet.[27] It is true that in Leviticus and Numbers there are references to disheveled hair as a sign of mourning, uncleanness, and shame.[28] Numbers 5:18 prescribes as part of the ordeal for a woman suspected of adultery, that the priest have the woman come forward and stand before the Lord; he would dishevel her hair, and place in her hands the cereal offering of her appeal. The disheveled hair was a sign of uncleanness and shame. However, there is no indication in Luke 7:36-50 that this woman's loosened hair connotes adultery, shame, or uncleanness. The narrative does not say that she entered with her hair disheveled, or that it was already loosened. In fact, had she been a prostitute, her hair would have been beautifully groomed.

[26]Kathleen Corley, "Were the Women Around Jesus Really Prostitutes? Women in the Context of Greco-Roman Meals," *SBL 1989 Seminar Papers* (Atlanta: Scholars Press, 1989) 520.

[27]Coakley ("Anointing," 250) rightly observes that if letting down the hair in public was such a gross act of immodesty such as only a "sinner" would have done, then why did the woman, who was supposed to be penitent, perform such a shocking action? And why, in the narrative, did no one comment on its offensiveness? Moreover, if it were so obvious from her actions that she is a prostitute, why would Jesus have to be a prophet to realize what sort of woman this is? Luise Schottroff ("Through German and Feminist Eyes") resolves the tension in the opposite direction. She asserts that the woman is a whore but is not repentant. Because of economic necessity she remains a prostitute, but has experienced and given love. She believes the story is not about prostitution that can be overcome by Christian repentance. Rather, the issue is mercy and respect toward prostitutes exhibited by Jesus contrasted with prejudice against them shown by Simon. Schottroff states that it is the moralizing tendency of Christians that prevents us from accepting such an interpretation.

[28]In Leviticus 13:45 the instructions for a person with a leprous disease include wearing torn clothes and letting their hair be disheveled as a sign of their uncleanness. In Leviticus 10:6; 21:10 are directions that priests were not to perform the mourning observances, including disheveling their hair, since they were to maintain themselves in a state of ritual purity.

According to the Talmud (e.g., *t. Sota* 5.9; *y. Git.* 9.50d) a married Jewish woman was not to let down her hair in the presence of other men.[29] But a mishnaic text (*m. Ketub.* 2.1) seems to assume that an unmarried woman did not bind up her hair until her marriage. The woman in 7:36-50 might then be unmarried and acting decently in a neighbor's house among friends.[30] There are also references in the Song of Songs to the young woman having loose, flowing hair. Among the charms extolled by the bridegroom-to-be of his beloved is her beautiful hair that is "like a flock of goats, streaming down the mountains of Gilead" (4:1; 6:5). Her dark, flowing hair evokes in him awe and love; there is nothing of shame or uncleanness. As in the Song of Songs, the flowing hair of the woman in Luke 7:38 evokes an image of beauty. Like the bridegroom of the Song of Songs, Jesus sees this woman as lovely and loving and attempts to get his host to perceive the same.

Another possible New Testament reference to loosened hair is 1 Corinthians 11:2-16. It is notoriously difficult to determine precisely what is the issue Paul addresses here.[31] One possibility is

[29]Plummer (*Luke,* 211) asserts that although it was shameful for the woman to let down her hair in public, she chooses to sacrifice her own honor so as to minister to Jesus.

[30]Coakley, "Anointing," 250.

[31]J. Murphy-O'Connor ("Sex and Logic in 1 Corinthians 11:2-16," *CBQ* 42 [1980] 482-500 and "1 Cor 11:2-16 Once Again," *CBQ* 50 [1988] 265-274) understands the problem as one of hairstyles, and thinks that Paul's underlying concern is homosexuality and the proper differentiation of the sexes. J. P. Meier ("On the Veiling of Hermeneutics [1 Cor 11:2-16]," *CBQ* 40 [1978] 212-226) thinks the problem is that liberated Corinthian women were creating scandal by doffing their veils in public. A. C. Wire (*The Corinthian Women Prophets: A Reconstruction Through Paul's Rhetoric* [Minneapolis: Fortress Press, 1990]) also believes that in this passage Paul is trying to persuade the women prophets to cover their heads. C. Thompson ("Hairstyles, Head-coverings, and St. Paul," *BA* 51 [1988] 99-115) believes Paul is recognizing women's right to choose among two acceptable alternatives: to cover their heads or not, but he recommends the former. A. Padgett ("Paul on Women in the Church: The Contradictions of Coiffure in 1 Corinthians 11.2-16," *JSNT* 20 [1984] 69-86) also understands Paul to be championing the rights of women to do what they wish with their heads. H. W. House ("Should a Woman Prophesy or Preach before Men?" *BibSac*

that Corinthian women prophets were prophesying in the assembly with loosened hair. Paul wants them to braid or bind up their hair, as was the fashion for Hellenistic and Roman women, for the sake of propriety and so that they would not be mistakenly identified with ecstatic worshipers of oriental divinities for whom disheveled hair was a sign of true prophecy.[32] However, in Luke 7:36-50 it is not the woman who is a prophet, but rather, Jesus. This is a deliberate recasting on the part of Luke if he is working from the tradition that stands behind Mark 14:3-9. In the Markan version, the woman's action is prophetic: she anoints Jesus' head, a political gesture, properly identifying the king at the propitious moment, as did Samuel for Saul (1 Sam 10:1) and David (1 Sam 16:13). In the Lukan story, the anointing has lost all prophetic significance;[33] it is a gesture of love.

The identity of Jesus as prophet is, however, central to the whole of Luke's chapter 7. Jesus' healing of the centurion's slave (7:2-10) strongly resembles Elisha's healing of Naaman (2 Kgs 5:1-14). Jesus' restoring the widow's son to life (7:11-17) echoes Elijah's raising of the widow's son at Zarephath (1 Kgs 17:17-24) and Elisha's resuscitation of the Shunammite woman's son (2 Kgs 4:18-37). This causes the onlookers to exclaim, "A great prophet has arisen in our midst" (7:16). The deeds Jesus has performed (7:18-23) recall those of Elijah and Elisha. And 7:24-35 plants the question, "What did you go out to see? A prophet?" (v. 26). The themes of seeing rightly and thus being able to correctly identify the prophet culminate in 7:36-50. Jesus' parabolic response to Simon is meant to lead Simon and the hearer of Luke's story to recognize Jesus as the prophet by seeing as he sees.

---

145 [1988] 141–161) sees "headship" of man over woman as the central concept in 1 Corinthians 11:2-16. To him Paul's concern is that women who pray or prophesy be submissive to their husbands.

[32]Elisabeth Schüssler Fiorenza, *In Memory of Her: A Feminist Theological Reconstruction of Christian Origins* (New York: Crossroad, 1983) 226–233.

[33]D.A.S. Ravens ("The Setting of Luke's Account of the Anointing: Luke 7.2-8.3," *NTS* 34 [1988] 282–292) sees the woman's anointing as the beautifying preparation of Jesus' feet (his feet are referred to seven times in 7:36-50) for announcing the good news to Jerusalem. She also identifies vocabulary in Luke 7:36-8:1 that echoes Isa 52:7: *euangelizomai* (8:1); *eirēnē* (7:50); *sōtēria/sōzō* (7:50); *basileusei sou ho theos/basileia tou theou* (8:1).

Another possibility is that the woman's gesture of wiping Jesus' feet with her hair may simply signify that her tears were not premeditated and that, lacking a towel, her hair was the only means at hand for drying Jesus' feet.[34] Or, one may wonder if the woman's tears were so copious as to need wiping up at all. This detail could simply be a poetic expression, such as found in Psalm 6:7, "every night I flood my bed with weeping; I drench my couch with my tears."[35] The tearful psalmist's prayer is accepted and his enemies are put to shame (vv. 10-11). This weeping woman's ministrations are accepted by Jesus and the adversarial Simon is put to shame.

With regard to the expensive alabaster flask of ointment, that the woman possessed such attests to her wealth.[36] But prostitution was not the only source of wealth for women in antiquity. According to Numbers 27:8 an unmarried woman without brothers could inherit money and property from her father.[37] A woman could also acquire money by working, either on her own or by sharing in her husband's work. From Acts 16:14, for example, we know of Lydia of Thyatira, who was a dealer in purple goods, luxury items. Acts 18:3 tells of Prisca working together with her husband Aquila at tentmaking. There is evidence of Greco-Roman women employed as weavers, midwives, doctors, hairdressers, wet nurses, masseuses, attendants, and musicians.[38]

It is curious that although the anonymous women who anoint Jesus in Mark 14:3-9 and Matthew 26:6-13 use alabaster flasks of very expensive ointment, commentators never conclude that they are prostitutes. Nor is such a slur directed at Mary of Bethany,

[34]I. Howard Marshall, *Commentary on Luke,* New International Greek Testament Commentary (Grand Rapids: Eerdmans, 1978) 308–309.

[35]Coakley, "Anointing," 250.

[36]In antiquity alabaster was quarried only in Egypt, and so was a luxury item, as was perfume. See J. L. McKenzie, "Alabaster," *Dictionary of the Bible* (New York: MacMillan, 1965) 19.

[37]See Moshe Meiselman, *Jewish Woman in Jewish Law* (New York: KTAV Publication House, 1978) 84–95 for information on inheritance by women in rabbinic tradition. He also demonstrates Jewish women's financial independence by entering into contracts to acquire and dispose of property (pp. 81–83).

[38]Jane Gardner, *Women in Roman Law and Society* (Bloomington & Indianapolis: Indiana University Press, 1986) 233–255.

who anoints Jesus with a pound of costly ointment of pure nard in John 12:1-8.[39]

Even the action of pouring out the ointment from the alabaster flask has been interpreted as the action of a prostitute who disposes of a tool of her trade now that she has been forgiven. Kenneth Bailey, for example, notes that women were known to wear a flask with perfume around the neck that hung down below the breast, used to sweeten the breath and perfume the person. He then remarks that "it does not take much imagination to understand how important such a flask would be to a prostitute."[40] If one is predisposed to see this woman as a prostitute, then he is right, one's imagination would not have to be pressed far.

But if one were predisposed to see in a female figure a potential disciple, or one who could prefigure the Christ, it is possible to envision the symbolic action in another direction. Her pouring out of the expensive ointment out of love prefigures Jesus' pouring out of his precious life-blood on behalf of those whom he loves (22:20). There are further thematic connections between her story and the account of the death of Jesus.[41] This woman is assured salvation (7:50), just as is the repentant criminal in 23:41-42; her tears stand in contrast to those of Peter, who weeps bitterly after denying Jesus (22:62); her kisses contrast to the betraying kiss of Judas (22:47); and her position at Jesus' feet is the stance of a servant. At the Last Supper Jesus instructs the disciples to "let the greatest among you be as the youngest, and the leader as the servant" (22:26), underscoring for them, "I am among you as the one who serves" (22:27).

Choosing the better part, then, is to see the woman in 7:36-50 as one who exemplifies proper response to Jesus and whose actions mirror his own. The key question her story poses, not only to Simon, but to the modern reader is, "Do you see this woman?"

[39]Nor do commentators ever speak of erotic overtones in these three parallel stories as they do when discussing 7:36-50. A similarly intimate gesture by Jesus when he washes the disciples' feet in John 13:1-20 is never thought to be erotic.

[40]Kenneth E. Bailey, *Poet & Peasant and Through Peasant Eyes*, 2 vols. in 1 (Grand Rapids: Eerdmans, 1976) 2.8.

[41]Corley, *Private Women*, 128.

In the narrative, Simon's ability to perceive Jesus correctly rested on his ability to change how he saw the woman. Jesus invites him to move from seeing her as a sinner to seeing her as a woman who loves greatly. The story is open-ended: there is yet hope that Simon's vision can be corrected. The same invitation lies open to contemporary believers. This story challenges the modern reader to look again and to be converted from our misperceptions, prejudgments, and stereotyped views of women that can blind us to the full identity of Jesus. It is when we can see women, as well as men, as fully embodying the Christ that the way is open for the identity of Christ to be rightly perceived.

In Luke's day it may have been that Christian women were being labeled ''sinners'' because they were known to eat with men when the community gathered to celebrate the Lord's Supper. This story would serve to challenge such misperceptions of women believers and to vindicate their practice. Although today the presence of women at the Eucharistic celebration is not questioned, the access of women to all the ministerial roles at the banquet is yet a matter to be reexamined.

Chapter 9

Mary Magdalene, Joanna, and Susanna: Ministering Galilean Women

LUKE 8:1-3

[1]Afterward he journeyed from one town and village to another, preaching and proclaiming the good news of the kingdom of God. Accompanying him were the Twelve [2]and some women who had been cured of evil spirits and infirmities, Mary, called Magdalene, from whom seven demons had gone out, [3]Joanna, the wife of Herod's steward Chuza, Susanna, and many others who provided for them out of their resources.

With these brief lines, unique to Luke,[1] we have the first reference to women who accompanied Jesus and partook in his mission. Unlike "the Twelve" (Luke 6:12-16; 9:1-6), there is no narrative of the women's call to become disciples nor of their being sent on mission. There is no record of how they first came

[1]These verses were composed by Luke, as is evident from the abundance of vocabulary typical to him (See Fitzmyer, *The Gospel According to Luke*, 695). Although the names of the women differ, it is possible that Luke was influenced by Mark 15:40-41: "There were also women looking on from a distance. Among them were Mary Magdalene, and Mary the mother of the younger James and of Joses, and Salome. These women had followed him when he was in Galilee and ministered to him. There were also many other women who had come up with him to Jerusalem."

to know Jesus. All that is preserved is that some of them have been healed of evil spirits and infirmities, presumably by Jesus, which leads them to support his mission.

Mary Magdalene appears in every one of the Gospels as one of the Galilean women who watched Jesus' crucifixion, saw where he was buried, and returned to the tomb on the first day of the week.[2] With the exception of John 19:25 she is always the first mentioned, indicating her leadership among the women.[3] Mary Magdalene has been confused in Western tradition with several other anonymous women: the woman who wept over Jesus' feet, demonstrating her great love (Luke 7:36-50); the woman who anointed Jesus for burial (Mark 14:3-9; Matt 26:6-13); and the woman caught in adultery (John 7:53-8:11).[4] The idea that she was a prostitute has no basis in the New Testament.[5] Nor is there any indication that she was a sinner.[6]

[2]Matt 27:56, 61; 28:1-10; Mark 15:40, 47; 16:1-11; Luke 24:1-12; John 19:25; 20:1-18.

[3]Elisabeth Schüssler Fiorenza, *In Memory of Her: A Feminist Theological Reconstruction of Christian Origins* (New York: Crossroad, 1983) 139.

[4]See, for example, V. McNabb (*St. Mary Magdalen* [London: Burns Oates & Washbourne, 1942] 1), who identifies Mary Magdalen as: (1) the sister of Lazarus and Martha; (2) a publicly known sinner; (3) the woman who washed the feet and anointed the head of Jesus; (4) one of the women present on Calvary; (5) one who went to anoint Jesus' body on Easter morning; (6) the first to whom Jesus showed himself after the resurrection. A more current example of such confusion combined with fanciful invention is found in Carsten and Sylvi Johnsen, *The Writing in the Sand: The Part of the Story That You Were Never Told about Mary Magdalene* (New York: Vantage Press, 1984). See also Carolyn M. and Joseph A. Grassi, *Mary Magdalene and the Women in Jesus' Life* (Kansas City, Mo.: Sheed & Ward, 1986) who suggest first (p. 62) that Mary Magdalene is the woman with the hemorrhage (Mark 5:25-34; Luke 8:43-48) but then identify her with the woman who wept over and anointed Jesus' feet in Luke 7:36-50 (pp. 65-67).

[5]The belief that Mary Magdalene was a prostitute stems from confusing her with the woman in 7:36-50, who has commonly been thought to have been a prostitute. However, it is not entirely clear that that woman was a prostitute either. See above on 7:36-50. See also J. Schaberg, "How Mary Magdalene Became a Whore," *BibRev* 8 (1992) 30-37, 51-52; "Thinking Back Through the Magdalene," *Continuum* 2 (1991) 71-90.

[6]Nonetheless, this is a frequent presumption. See, for example, J. Grassi, *The Hidden Heroes of the Gospels: Female Counterparts of Jesus* (Col-

What Luke 8:2 asserts is that seven demons had gone out of her. "Seven" is a symbolic number for fullness or completeness. The ancients, not having the benefit of modern medical knowledge, attributed many illnesses to demon possession. What Luke states, then, is that Mary Magdalene had been very seriously ill, and that she had been healed.[7] Luke, in underscoring the gravity of Mary's illness, is more intent on highlighting the greatness of Jesus' power of healing than he is on telling us something about Mary. Rather than speculate on how ill she had been, we would choose the better part by focusing on how completely (indicated by the number seven) she had experienced the liberating power of the realm of God.[8] This results in her impressive presence and leadership among Jesus' faithful followers.

Next in the list is Joanna, the wife of Chuza, Herod's steward. Like most biblical women, she is identified by her relationship to a man. As the wife of Herod's steward, Joanna enjoyed a certain degree of wealth, status, and influence. She is named again in Luke 24:10 as one of the women with Mary Magdalene at the empty tomb. Susanna is mentioned only here and we have no other information about her. Her name recalls the beautiful, God-fearing woman who was the object of lust and false accusations of two elders, recounted in the book of Susanna. With Mary, Joanna, and Susanna are many other women,[9] who remain nameless.

There are many unanswered questions about these Galilean women. What was their marital status? In what did their service consist? If it was financial support from where did the money come? What were the social ramifications of their traveling with Jesus and the Twelve? What is their relationship to the other disciples?

The above questions are all interrelated. To try to answer one depends on the response to another. We will begin with what is

---

legeville, Minn.: The Liturgical Press, 1989) 86, who states that "seven demons" hints that Mary Magdalene was a "very lively sinner."

[7] Elisabeth Moltmann-Wendell (*The Women Around Jesus* [New York: Crossroad, 1987] 68) assumes that Mary suffered from a serious mental illness.

[8] Schüssler Fiorenza, *Memory*, 123–124.

[9] The Greek *heterai pollai* is feminine, which is not clear in the English translation "many others."

the crux of the matter: what were these women doing? In verse 3 the phrase "provided for them out of their resources"[10] *(diēkonoun autois ek tōn hyparchontōn autais)* contains the second Lukan instance of the verb *diakonein*. The interpretation of 8:1-3 hinges on the meaning of this verb.

Some scholars believe that here *diakonein* connotes making meals or clothes, domestic service in general. Accordingly, the Galilean women did not abandon their traditional roles, but rather these were given new significance and importance in that they were now performed for Jesus.[11] Along with the presupposition that *diakonein* always means table service, there is a further assumption underlying this interpretation: that women did not have financial means at their disposal. Therefore "resources" must mean time, talent, domestic service. However, as we have seen in the analysis of Luke 4:39, *diakonein* has a wide range of meanings. A problem with interpreting it as domestic service is that the situation envisioned in Luke 8:1-3 is not within the confines of a home; it takes place in open space during missionary travel. Moreover, it cannot be assumed that women disciples would have taken charge of the domestic chores for the group. Surprisingly, in several gospel incidents that occur during the missionary journeys, it is Jesus and the male disciples who are responsible for supplying the food (Mark 6:30-44; 8:1-9 and pars.; John 4:27-38).[12]

Alternatively, many scholars today understand the women's ministry to be that of financial support.[13] The word *hyparchontōn*, "resources," always means possessions, property, money, or goods in Luke and Acts.[14] This kind of support would be crucial since it seems that Jesus did not work for money once he began

---

[10]This is the translation of the *NAB, NJB,* and *NRSV.*

[11]E.g., Ben Witherington III, "On the Road with Mary Magdalene, Joanna, Susanna, and Other Disciples—Luke 8:1-3," *ZNW* 70 (1979) 243-248; *Women in the Ministry of Jesus* (Cambridge: Cambridge University Press, 1984) 116-118; *Women and the Genesis of Christianity* (New York: Cambridge University Press, 1984) 110-112; Carolyn M. Grassi and Joseph A. Grassi, *Mary Magdalene,* 5.

[12]David Sim, "The Women Followers of Jesus: The Implications of Luke 8:1-3," *HeyJ* 30 (1989) 58.

[13]Ibid., 51–62.

[14]Luke 11:21; 12:15, 33, 44; 14:33; 16:1; 19:8; Acts 4:32.

his ministry of proclaiming the gospel. And those disciples who left behind their occupations to follow Jesus (e.g., Peter, James, and John in 5:11) would need monetary aid. In addition, having rejected him in Nazareth (Luke 4:16-30), it is unlikely that Jesus' family and neighbors would have provided for his support.[15]

Some interpreters dispute this meaning on the grounds that in Jesus' day women did not have access to money. While it is true that the patriarchal system ensured that women would be economically dependent on men, there were some women who had money and had control of it. Under some circumstances women could inherit money and property (e.g., Num 27:8).[16] Many women earned money by working, as did Lydia (Acts 16:14), who appears to have been either single or widowed and running her own business. Prisca shared her husband's work of tentmaking (Acts 18:3).[17] The parable of the woman who loses one of her ten coins in Luke 15:8-10 presumes that she has charge of the family finances.[18] Inscriptions from Jewish women who were donors to synagogues show that at least some women had money or property and the power to donate it.[19]

[15]Sim, "Women Followers," 52. A slightly different interpretation is that of Robert Karris ("Women and Discipleship in Luke," *CBQ* 41 [1979] 1-20). He translates the last phrase of 8:3, "women who use their resources in going on mission for him." He accepts the textual variant *autọ̄*, "him," attested in ℵ, A, L, Tertullian, Cyprian, etc., instead of *autois*, "them," found in B D K W Δ Θ, etc. However, the greater likelihood is that the singular is a later Christocentric correction in line with Mark 15:41 and Matt 27:55 (Bruce Metzger, *A Textual Commentary on the Greek New Testament*, 3d ed. [London, New York: United Bible Societies, 1971] 144). As attractive as Karris' suggestion is, he does not postulate what exactly these female go-betweens were doing, nor does he answer the question he himself raises (p. 9) as to whether there is evidence from social research that the phenomenon of female messengers was possible.

[16]See Moshe Meiselman, *Jewish Woman in Jewish Law* (New York: KTAV, 1978) 84-95 for information on inheritance by women in rabbinic tradition. He also demonstrates Jewish women's financial independence by entering into contracts to acquire and dispose of property (pp. 81-83).

[17]See above p. 121 for a list of women's occupations in Greco-Roman times.

[18]A similar situation is reflected in Pliny the Younger's approving comment that his wife is sensible and careful with their money (*Letters* 4, 19.2-4).

[19]B. Brooten, *Women Leaders in the Ancient Synagogue: Inscriptional Evidence and Background Issues,* Brown Judaic Studies 36 (Chico, Calif.: Schol-

A frequent speculation is that the Galilean women were former prostitutes. This is based on the assumption that the only way for women in antiquity to earn money and to have the kind of independence envisioned in Luke 8:1-3 was through prostitution. This hypothesis is also linked with the saying in Matthew 21:31-32 about tax collectors and prostitutes believing John the Baptist. As discussed above in 7:36-50, this saying is a warning to the Jewish religious leaders, not necessarily a historical recollection on the composition of Jesus' group of followers. Whether or not prostitutes did, in fact, travel in Jesus' company, we simply do not know. And although prostitution was a thriving business in antiquity, women were engaged in many other types of work as well.

Some scholars propose that Mary, Joanna, Susanna, and the other women were not using their own money, but were administering the common fund.[20] Acts 2:44-45 and 4:32–5:11 tell of how the early Christians held all things in common and distributed to each according to their need. And John 12:6 makes reference to a common purse of Jesus and his disciples. However, John 12:6 says that Judas was the one who kept the common purse. More importantly, the possessive pronoun "their," *autais,* in Luke 8:3 is feminine plural and can only mean that the resources belonged to the women.

Luke presents Mary, Joanna, Susanna, and the other women as wealthy patrons of the mission.[21] They are part of a host of well-to-do believers in Luke and Acts: Levi (Luke 5:27-32); Zac-

---

ars Press, 1982) 143–144. Brooten has studied forty-three such inscriptions. See also Matthew S. Collins, "Money, Sex, and Power: An Examination of the Role of Women as Patrons of the Ancient Synagogue," *Recovering the Role of Women: Power and Authority in Rabbinic Jewish Society,* ed. Peter J. Haas, South Florida Studies in the History of Judaism 59 (Atlanta: Scholars Press, 1992) 5–22. See Richard Atwood (*Mary Magdalene in the New Testament Gospels and Early Tradition,* European University Studies, Series 23 Band 457 [Bern: Peter Lang, 1993] 17, n. 23) for examples of women who gave monetary aid and property to rabbis. Witherington, "On the Road," 244, n. 9 lists rabbinic texts that refer to women offering support to rabbis and their disciples in the form of money, property, or foodstuffs.

[20]E.g., Sim, "Women Followers," 53.

[21]Kathleen Corley, *Private Women, Public Meals* (Peabody, Mass.: Hendrickson, 1993) 111. See also Richard Pervo, *Profit with Delight: The Liter-*

chaeus, the chief tax collector (Luke 19:1-10); Barnabas, a property owner (Acts 4:36-37); an Ethiopian eunuch, who was a court official in charge of the entire treasury of the queen of the Ethiopians (Acts 8:27); Mary, whose house was a gathering place of the disciples in Jerusalem (Acts 12:12); Lydia, a dealer in purple cloth, a luxury good (Acts 16:14); prominent women in Thessalonica (Acts 17:4); influential Greek men and women in Beroea (Acts 17:12); Prisca and Aquila, who hosted Paul in Corinth (Acts 18:1-11) and who had the means to travel with him to Ephesus and establish a new mission base there (Acts 18:18-28).

The use of material possessions as related to discipleship is a constant Lukan theme, but there is no one model presented for disciples in Luke and Acts. There are repeated warnings in Jesus' sayings and parables of the danger of riches.[22] There are exemplary stories of the faithful poor (Luke 21:1-4) and accounts of those who leave everything behind to follow Jesus (Luke 5:1-11, 27-28). But there are also narratives involving wealthy disciples, whose way of following involves not relinquishing all their goods, but opening their homes and sharing their possessions with the community. In Acts, sharing everything in common becomes a hallmark of the early Christians (Acts 2:42-47; 4:32-37).[23] In Luke's works then, wealth and discipleship are not mutually exclusive. The decisive factor is how a follower uses his or her possessions. The Galilean women put their faith into action by paying the expenses of the apostolic mission.

Many commentators believe that these Galilean women were single or widowed.[24] They would have enjoyed greater personal and economic independence and would be freer to join Jesus'

---

ary Genre of the Acts of the Apostles (Philadelphia: Fortress Press, 1987) 40, 77ff., 106, on Luke's interest in portraying a movement with adherents that are more highly placed.

[22]Luke 1:53; 6:24; 8:14; 12:16-21, 33-34; 14:12-24; 16:1-14, 19-31; 18:18-30.

[23]See further L. T. Johnson, *The Literary Function of Possessions in Luke-Acts,* SBLDS 39 (Missoula, Mont.: Scholars Press, 1977); A. O'Leary, "The Role of Possessions in the Journey Narrative of Luke 9:51–19:27," *MillStud* 28 (1991) 41–60; J. S. Galligan, "The Tension Between Poverty and Possessions in the Gospel of Luke," *SpToday* 37 (1985) 4–12; J. Gillman, *Possessions and the Life of Faith: A Reading of Luke-Acts,* Zacchaeus Studies: New Testament (Collegeville, Minn.: The Liturgical Press, 1991).

[24]Sim, "Women Followers," 53.

itinerant movement. Married women were under the financial control of their husbands and they would be subject to greater social stigma for leaving their families. It is not possible, however, to determine from the scant information we have what was the marital status of these women. Mary, unlike most other women in the gospel, is identified in relation to a city, not a man. Luke 8:3 identifies Joanna as the wife of Herod's steward Chuza. Some scholars believe she has left him to follow Jesus because in 24:10 she is named as a witness at the empty tomb without reference to Chuza. Another explanation is that having once identified her as Chuza's wife, Luke does not repeat that information.

In trying to understand what these women did from day to day and how they interacted with the male disciples, Luke 8:1-3 tells us very little. That women traveling with an itinerant preacher was an unprecedented practice, we cannot say with certainty. Women did travel for feasts, as Luke says Mary did with her family each year for Passover (2:41). Women also traveled to visit family, as Mary did when hearing of Elizabeth's pregnancy (1:39-45). Business women, like Lydia (Acts 16:14), also traveled. But to say that it was unheard of for women to accompany a traveling preacher presumes that we know much more about the practices of religious leaders of Jesus' time than we do. All that can be said with certainty is that this is the only recorded instance of this phenomenon in that time and place.[25] Jane Schaberg proposes that, in light of the smallness of the geographic area, the women may have only gone out on day trips, and returned to their own homes each evening. As to the supposed scandal involved, she observes that if the practice were so shameful, it is curious that there is no mention or explicit defense of it in the traditions.[26] Malina and Rohrbaugh see the scandal averted if these were widows who now serve the surrogate family of Jesus' disciples in place of their biological family.[27]

[25]Ibid., 61, n. 3.

[26]Jane Schaberg, "Luke," *Women's Bible Commentary,* ed. Carol A. Newsom and Sharon H. Ringe (Louisville: Westminster/John Knox, 1992) 287.

[27]Bruce Malina and Richard Rohrbaugh, *Social-Science Commentary on the Synoptic Gospels* (Minneapolis: Fortress Press, 1992) 334. Similarly, Corley, *Private Women,* 118-119.

It is sometimes asserted that the list of the women followers in Luke 8:2-3 is intended as a Lukan pair to the list of the twelve male disciples called by Jesus in Luke 6:12-16 and commissioned in 9:1-6. Or it is said that the three women mirror the inner circle of the three men closest to Jesus: Peter, James, and John (5:1-11; 8:51; 9:28). The conclusion from this is that Luke intends equality for men and women disciples. However, this egalitarian interpretation is hard to sustain in view of the fact that there is no story in Luke in which a woman is either called or commissioned. Nor are women ever portrayed as sharing in the same mission as the male disciples. It is clear in 8:1-3 that both the twelve men and the women hear Jesus' proclaiming and preaching of the realm of God. And at the empty tomb the women's memory of the words Jesus had spoken in Galilee leads them to understand that he has risen (24:8). But, in contrast to their male counterparts, the women are not cast by Luke as engaged in any public ministry of the word. Luke is not attempting to portray men and women ministering together, as Paul does in Romans 16. Rather, Luke reinforces distinction.[28]

Some scholars point out that Luke's portrait of the Galilean women is very favorable in its literary context. Immediately following 8:1-3 is the parable of the sower and its explanation. Mary, Joanna, Susanna, and the other women exemplify the seed that falls on good ground and produces abundant fruit. Their service is rooted in attentiveness to Jesus' word.[29] But the text can also be read to say that the women's service is a way of reciprocating for their healing. Having been cured of evil spirits and infirmities, they give their monetary support to the movement out of gratitude, not from having heard the word.[30]

[28] Schaberg, "Luke," 287.

[29] Jane Kopas, "Jesus and Women: Luke's Gospel," *TToday* 43 (1986) 197; Witherington, "On the Road," 243.

[30] Schaberg ("Luke," 287) questions whether Luke portrays them as disciples at all. In the mind of Luke, she says, disciples are called to sell all and distribute alms to the poor (14:33; 18:22). These women, she observes, "are shown aiding the poor (disciples and Jesus), but as patrons from outside their ranks." However, as we have shown, there are rich disciples in Luke and Acts. The women's accompaniment of Jesus and the Twelve in 8:2-3 and their witness of the crucifixion and empty tomb places them inside the ranks of disciples.

In line with his program for women's roles, Luke portrays these rich patrons as providing silent, behind-the-scenes support. This passage is a summary statement, describing a prolonged or repeated situation.[31] The verb *diēkonoun*, "provided for," in the imperfect tense, also indicates that this was habitual or repeated action. Although Luke will not mention these women again until the crucifixion, their support of the mission is an ongoing one.

In the Church today women continue to minister out of their own resources: not only with their money but with their theological education and their aptitude and willingness to serve in all the ministerial roles. But there is a danger in women continuing to support a system that is not egalitarian. Such a system can persist in subordinating and exploiting women even as they themselves enable it to keep doing so.[32] Women are questioning whether, by choosing to remain within the Church and to support its mission, they are being co-opted into perpetuating a structure in which they can never have access to presbyteral ministry and decision-making power. Like the Galilean women, they continue to make it possible for the men to assume all the public ministries and leadership positions.

As is evident from Luke 23:44-49, 50-56; and 24:1-12 the Galilean women hold all the qualifications for leadership in the apostolic ministry that Luke lists in Acts 1:21-22, with the exception of gender. In today's Christian communities there are women who have all the necessary theological education, pastoral skills, and leadership capability to engage in every ministry. But the gender barrier still stands. When the social customs that dictated separation of women and men and distinguished their roles according to public and private spheres no longer hold, then such segregation of roles in ministry along gender lines must also be dissolved. Though Luke's story does not encourage this, Christian men and women today would be choosing the better part to do so.

While struggling for equal access for all the baptized to every ministry, it is important to remember that no mode of service is less important than any other (1 Cor 12:1-31). Advocating ad-

---

[31]Maria Anicia Co analyzes the function of such summaries in "The Major Summaries in Acts, Acts 2,42-47; 4,32-35; 5,12-16: Linguistic and Literary Relationships," *ETL* 68 (1992) 49-85.
[32]Schaberg, "Luke," 288.

mission of women to sacerdotal and leadership ministries does not in any way diminish the esteem for those women who have always performed behind-the-scenes, supportive service. Knowing the power of such tireless toil, one can speculate that the whole work of the Church would grind to a screeching halt if all women declared a moratorium on service to the Church for one day! The point is that women are also qualified and gifted for the ministries that have been traditionally entrusted to men.

This giftedness of women can be lost sight of when interpreters focus only on the illness, sinfulness, poverty, and oppression of women. It is curious how much attention commentators give to speculation about Mary Magdalene's illness or supposed sinfulness. By contrast, they never expostulate about the nature of Peter's sinfulness, even though Luke clearly stresses this in his call story (5:8).[33] Luke 8:1-3 can provide a corrective: both women and men are fallible followers of Jesus; both women and men have gifts and qualifications to be engaged in the mission.

One must be cautious about emphasizing Jesus' uniqueness in having women supporters. Such an assertion is historically questionable and can also lead to anti-Judaism. Accenting Jesus' supposed exceptional inclusion and liberation of women falsely pits him against other Jews. Alternatively, Luke 8:1-3 could be used today by groups of women and men journeying together in Christian mission to move toward egalitarian relationships as a result of both having heard the same message of Jesus. In their consequent expressions of service, both women and men would perform supportive ministries; both women and men would engage in leadership, according to the gifts of each, not determined by gender.

[33] Scholars always move instead to a discussion of the cross-influence of the traditions behind Luke 5:1-11 and John 21:1-11. It is only in Luke's call story that Peter says, "Depart from me, Lord, for I am a sinful man" (cf. Mark 1:16-20; Matt 4:18-22; John 1:35-42).

Chapter 10

Jairus' Daughter and a Woman with a Hemorrhage: Resuscitation and Bold Faith

LUKE 8:40-56

⁴⁰When Jesus returned, the crowd welcomed him, for they were all waiting for him. ⁴¹And a man named Jairus, an official of the synagogue, came forward. He fell at the feet of Jesus and begged him to come to his house, ⁴²because he had an only daughter, about twelve years old, and she was dying. As he went, the crowds almost crushed him. ⁴³And a woman afflicted with hemorrhages for twelve years, who [had spent her whole livelihood on doctors and] was unable to be cured by anyone, ⁴⁴came up behind him and touched the tassel on his cloak. Immediately her bleeding stopped. ⁴⁵Jesus then asked, "Who touched me?" While all were denying it, Peter said, "Master, the crowds are pushing and pressing in upon you." ⁴⁶But Jesus said, "Someone has touched me; for I know that power has gone out from me." ⁴⁷When the woman realized that she had not escaped notice, she came forward trembling. Falling down before him, she explained in the presence of all the people why she had touched him and how she had been healed immediately. ⁴⁸He said to her, "Daughter, your faith has saved you; go in peace."

⁴⁹While he was still speaking, someone from the synagogue official's house arrived and said, "Your daughter is dead; do not trouble the teacher any longer." ⁵⁰On hearing this, Jesus answered him, "Do not be afraid; just have faith and she will be saved." ⁵¹When he arrived at the house he allowed no one to enter with him except Peter and John and James, and the child's father and mother. ⁵²All were weeping and mourning for her, when he said, "Do not weep any longer, for she is not dead, but sleeping." ⁵³And they ridiculed him, because they knew that she was dead. ⁵⁴But he took her by the hand and called to her, "Child, arise!" ⁵⁵Her breath returned and she immediately arose. He then directed that she should be given something to eat. ⁵⁶Her parents were astounded, and he instructed them to tell no one what had happened.

The stories of Jairus' daughter and the woman with a hemorrhage have essentially been taken over by Luke (8:40-56) from Mark (5:21-43). The latter is well known for his literary technique of intercalating one story with another. The result is that each story enables better understanding of the other. The story at the center highlights a point that is to be understood about the other story that frames it. In this case the faith of the woman with a hemorrhage is a model of the sort of faith that Jairus would need for the healing of his daughter.[1] Further, the power that heals the bleeding woman (8:46) is to be understood as the same power by which Jairus' daughter is raised.[2] Catchwords link the two stories: both women are called "daughter" (Luke 8:42, 48), both mention "twelve years" (8:42, 43). In addition, the interruption of Jesus' journey to Jairus' house has the literary effect of prolonging the narrative time, allowing for the death of the child, so that the ensuing miracle will be a resuscitation.[3]

Both Mark and Luke locate the episode in Jesus' Galilean ministry, preceding his commissioning of the Twelve and following his

[1]A. Stock, *The Method and Message of Mark* (Wilmington: Glazier, 1989) 173.

[2]Joseph Fitzmyer, *The Gospel According to Luke,* AB 28 (Garden City, N.Y.: Doubleday, 1985) 744.

[3]Ibid., 743.

introductory teaching in parables, the calming of the storm at sea, and the healing of a possessed man in the Gerasene territory. Luke makes a number of editorial changes in the narratives, condensing and rearranging some elements, and employing different vocabulary.[4]

The story of the raising of Jairus' daughter mirrors the resuscitation of the widow's son at Nain (Luke 7:11-17). There a mother's only son is raised (7:12); here a father's only daughter (8:42). The story of the only son of the widow of Nain is found only in Luke. The detail of the girl being Jairus' *only* daughter is also unique to Luke (cf. Mark 5:23; Matt 9:18).[5] In a culture that prized sons far more than daughters, it is notable that when these two stories are read in tandem, an equal value is given by Jesus to the life of a daughter.

In the First Testament Isaac was an only son, and therefore most beloved (Gen 22:2, 12, 16; Heb 11:17). That an angel of God saved him from being sacrificed by his father stands in stark contrast to Jephthah's rendering up of his only child, his daughter, as a burnt offering (Judg 11:30-40). The Lukan Jesus rescues both an only son and an only daughter from death.[6] Their resuscitations prefigure the raising to life of Jesus by God,[7] and point forward to the resurrected life that will be enjoyed by both women and men who follow Jesus.

Inserted into the story of Jairus' daughter is the episode with the woman suffering from a hemorrhage. Although Luke shortens the story from the Markan tradition, the woman's desperate situation is clear. Her condition, ongoing for twelve years, has, undoubtedly, debilitated her physically. Although Luke eliminates the criticism that she had suffered much under many physicians,

---

[4] See ibid., 743-744 for details.

[5] The one other reference to an only child in the synoptic tradition also occurs in Luke. In 9:38 a man pleads with Jesus to heal his only son, who is possessed by a spirit. Again, it is clear that Luke has added the detail, since the Markan (9:17) and Matthean (17:15) accounts simply speak of a son.

[6] The only other instances of characters in the Scriptures who are said to be only children, *monogenēs,* are Sarah and Tobias in the book of Tobit (3:15; 6:10, 14; 8:17).

[7] In the Johannine tradition, it is Jesus who is the "only son" (John 1:14, 18; 3:16, 18; 1 John 4:9).

only to grow worse instead of better (cf. Mark 5:26),[8] he relates that she had spent her whole livelihood on doctors (8:43).[9] Luke provides no clue as to the source of her money. That she had money and had consulted professional physicians gives us a clue that she was probably a woman of elite status.[10] But we can taste the hopelessness of one left destitute without economic recourse. If her income was from her own work, how will she manage if she is ill and unable to work? If her money was inherited and it is now gone, what then? Who will support her if her husband or male kin have disowned her?

Furthermore, she would have been marginalized by other Jews, who, adhering to the regulations of Leviticus 15:25-31 would consider her unclean.

> When a woman is afflicted with a flow of blood for several days outside her menstrual period, or when her flow continues beyond the ordinary period, as long as she suffers this unclean flow she shall be unclean, just as during her menstrual period. Any bed on which she lies during such a flow becomes unclean, as it would during her menstruation, and any article of furniture on which she sits becomes unclean just as during her menstruation. Anyone who touches them becomes unclean; he shall wash his garments, bathe in water and be unclean until evening.
>
> If she becomes freed from her affliction, she shall wait seven days, and only then is she to be purified. On the eighth day she shall take two turtledoves or two pigeons and bring them

---

[8]It is thought by some that Luke the evangelist is to be identified with "Luke the beloved physician," mentioned in Colossians 4:14. This would explain why he tones down the negative remarks about doctors. However, H. J. Cadbury (*The Style and Literary Method of Luke*, HTS 6/1 [Cambridge, Mass.: Harvard University Press, 1920]) has shown that Luke's language and style shows no more evidence of medical training and interest than other Greco-Roman writers who were not physicians.

[9]Many early manuscripts omit the phrase *iatrois prosanalōsasa holon ton bion* ("had spent her whole livelihood on doctors"). However, it is found in some good manuscripts and is compatible with Luke's style. Because of the uncertainty about its originality, some modern translations, such as *NAB*, bracket this phrase.

[10]Bruce Malina and Richard Rohrbaugh, *Social Science Commentary on the Synoptic Gospels* (Minneapolis: Fortress Press, 1992) 338.

to the priest at the entrance to the meeting tent. The priest shall offer up one of them as a sin offering and the other as a holocaust. Thus shall the priest make atonement before the Lord for her unclean flow (Lev 15:25-31).

An audience that knew this law could well imagine the hemorrhaging woman's aloneness. If she were married she would not have been able to have relations with her husband or to carry out any of her domestic duties for him or her family without making them unclean. Everything she touched—furniture, cooking utensils, clothing—would be rendered unclean. If she had children, she would not have been able to cradle and fondle them without passing on to them her impurity. Her friends and associates would likewise keep their distance from her.

What sense of self is left for a woman who is so cut off from others? This question is especially important when one remembers that she belonged to a culture where one's very identity was derived from the communities in which one was embedded.[11] Likewise, how does she experience God when the law of her religious tradition defines her as unholy because of her flow of blood? Luke underscores the impossibility of her finding release from this desperate situation despite her incessant attempts to find someone to heal her (8:43).

Perhaps what gives her the boldness to touch the tassel of Jesus' cloak is that she has nothing more to lose. She is already depleted physically, economically, emotionally, and psychologically, and has been outcast socially and religiously. There can be no harm in risking worming her way through the crowd with the hopes of going unnoticed by those who would guard themselves from contact with her.

The impossibility of her situation and the immediacy of her cure (8:44) serve to underscore the power of Jesus that stands at the center of the story. Even as Jesus' power becomes the focus of the narrative, the character and the actions of the woman frame

[11]See Bruce Malina, *The New Testament World: Insights from Cultural Anthropology,* Rev. ed. (Louisville: Westminster/John Knox, 1993), especially, "The First-Century Personality: The Individual and the Group," pp. 63–89; "Clean and Unclean: Understanding Rules of Purity," pp. 149–183. See also Malina and Rohrbaugh, *Social-Science Commentary,* 318–320 on "Purity/Pollution."

the story so that she remains in strong relief. Her initiative in touching Jesus, without even a word of request, is unique among the gospel stories. Some interpret her surreptitious approach to Jesus and her subsequent fear as shame at breaking Jewish purity regulations, or shame at her disease or at having stolen power from Jesus without his authority.[12] Luke does not relate her good intentions as does Mark 5:28. It is only with Jesus' final statement in Luke 8:48 that it is clear that the woman is to be praised for her faith, not reprimanded for her potentially harmful touch. Furthermore, Jesus' power is not to be confused with magic; healing from him occurs only in the context of relationship with him. It is thus that he seeks her out, receives her homage and testimony, and speaks to her, affirming her faith and wholeness.

In the Markan account the woman speaks only to Jesus, telling him "the whole truth" (5:33). In Luke (8:47) her witness is public: "she declared *[apēngeilen]* in the presence of all the people." Luke specifies the content of what she proclaimed: "why she had touched him and how she had been healed immediately" (v. 47). The reaction of those who heard her faith witness is not related. Jesus' confirmation of her faith and wholeness in 8:48 stands against Peter's opposition or indifference to finding this witness (8:45). This woman's faith announcement prefigures that of Mary Magdalene, Joanna, and Mary, the mother of James in 24:1-12. In both stories the women truthfully announce *(apangellō)* their experience of the good news, but Peter and his companions think them unimportant or not to be believed (8:45; 24:10-12). Later Christian hearers of these stories know the women's witness to be true and they are vindicated.

With this interchange with Jesus, the woman's healing is complete. Although her flow of blood is said to have ceased in verse 44, it is only in verse 48 that Jesus says, "Daughter, your faith has saved you; go in peace." The verb *sesōken* has a double nuance: her faith has both "healed" her and "saved" her. She is healed not only of her physical malady, but is also brought back to full personhood and participation as "daughter,"[13] in the faith

---

[12]G. Theissen, *The Miracle Stories of the Early Christian Tradition* (Philadelphia: Fortress Press, 1983) 134.

[13]There is a verbal similarity with Luke 13:16 where Jesus asserts that because she is a "daughter of Abraham" the woman bent double ought to be loosed from her bond, even on the Sabbath.

community. Thus she can go in peace, in the full sense of *shalom:* complete well being and prosperity on every level.

The two interwoven stories comment on each other and reinforce the same message. Just as the cured "daughter" goes off with wholeness and peace in 8:48, a messenger comes from the synagogue leader's house with the news of his daughter's death (8:49). Jesus' assurance to him not to fear, only believe, and she would be healed/saved, echoes the hemorrhaging woman's story. The lot of the twelve-year-old girl, just coming of age as a woman, is the same as that of the woman whose flow has not stopped for twelve years. Whereas both were as good as dead, Jesus brings wholeness and salvation.[14]

It is often noted that Jesus' positive attitude toward the woman is not the expected reaction of a Jewish man who has just been rendered unclean by the touch of a menstruous woman. Marla Selvidge goes so far as to say that Jesus, by not reprimanding her for being in the middle of a crowd or for touching him, "subtly shatters the legal purity system and its restrictive social conditioning."[15] It is important, however, to remember that Jesus is portrayed in the Gospels as a healer who consistently touches persons who are "impure," as he also does when he takes the hand of Jairus' supposedly dead daughter in 8:54. Incurring ritual impurity by touching those who are ill is the lot of one engaged in a healing ministry.

To say that Jesus is attacking and undoing the whole levitical purity system runs counter to the tradition preserved in Luke 16:17, where Jesus states, "It is easier for heaven and earth to pass away than for the smallest part of a letter of the law to become invalid" (similarly, Matt 5:17). Jesus does not reject the

[14]One contrast between the two stories is that at the conclusion of the hemorrhaging woman's story, she publicly declares what had happened to her (8:47), whereas Jairus and his wife are commanded not to tell what had happened (8:56). The latter is a detail retained by Luke from Mark 5:43. In Mark's Gospel the theme of Jesus silencing all who experience his mighty deeds serves his literary purpose and allows Mark to make the theological point that only with Jesus' passion can one fully understand his identity and proclaim him (Mark 15:39). In the Third Gospel Jesus' identity is not kept secret, but in Luke 8:56 and elsewhere, Luke simply keeps this detail from his Markan source.

[15]M. Selvidge, "Mark 5:25-34 and Leviticus 14:19-20: A Reaction to Restrictive Purity Regulations," *JBL* 103 (1984) 622.

Jewish purity system, but rather demonstrates his interpretation of it to a synagogue leader. The purpose of the levitical laws was to ensure the holiness of the community by delineating boundaries between clean and unclean.[16] In this way Israel would be holy as its God is holy (Lev 11:45; 20:26; etc.). For Jesus the purpose of the law is to facilitate access to God, not impede it. His central concern is God's will, namely the wholeness and holiness of God's people; not the preservation of the purity system for its own sake.

It is true that later Christians would abandon the observance of the levitical purity regulations as a means to holiness. But we risk falling into a subtle yet insidious anti-Judaism if we envision Jesus as one who consciously undermined the Judaism of his day. Jesus was a Jew who attempted to reform and reinterpret Jewish laws and observance of them within Judaism. He was not intent on forming a new religion. Such a move would only happen well after his death, when the beliefs of Jewish Christians would diverge too greatly from those of other Jews.[17]

However positive the portrayal of this woman of faith, there is one important aspect of her story that is lost in the Lukan version. In Mark 5:25-34 there are three verbal links between her and Jesus that are removed in Lukan redaction. Mark introduces the woman as one who had "suffered much," *polla pathousa* (5:26). He uses the same expression to describe Jesus' predicted passion in Mark 8:31 and 9:12. Mark also says that the woman felt in her body that she was healed of her disease, *mastigos,* literally "scourge," (5:29, repeated in 5:34). In the third prediction of his passion, Jesus tells his disciples that the chief priests and scribes will scourge, *mastigōsousin,* him (10:34). Finally, the woman tells Jesus the whole truth, *alētheian,* (5:33). In Mark 12:14 some of the Pharisees assert that Jesus is truthful, *alēthēs.* Likewise, the scribe in 12:32 recognizes that Jesus speaks truthfully, *ep' alētheias.* Luke eliminates each of these three parallels between Jesus and the woman, and thus circumvents any identification of her suffering with that of Jesus.

[16]Malina, *New Testament World,* 149–183.
[17]See Judith Plaskow, "Feminist Anti-Judaism and the Christian God," *JFSR* 7 (1991) 95–134; "Christian Feminism and Anti-Judaism," *Crosscurrents* 28 (1978) 306–309.

Nonetheless, for contemporary women, the story of this bold woman can provide a paradigm of the kind of gutsy and persistent faith that does not relinquish hope even when all effort seems without result. Like her, many women today find they must overcome all kinds of obstacles, even from their own faith community, to gain access to the power that Jesus wants to compart with them; a power that brings healing and *shalom* to the whole community. The indifference and opposition of male leaders, exemplified by Peter in the narrative, is all too familiar to women believers who are well able to proclaim publicly and accurately the ways of God. Many women wait for the day when, like the woman of this story, their needless suffering will come to an end as the faith of daughters will be as fully valued as that of sons, bringing wholeness to the entire community.

To understand the story in this way, however, runs counter to Luke's intent, as he tames the woman's initial boldness with a final portrait of her trembling and prostrate before Jesus (8:47). Full incorporation into the religious and social community for women today is not achieved when women fall back into a submissive stance as "daughters" to dominant "fathers."[18] Rather, both women and men disciples choose the better part when both do obeisance to God, while taking bold new steps toward wholeness for the entire community. In such a community of *shalom* the gifts of both daughters and sons would be equally valued and utilized for every type of ministry.

---

[18]Mary Ann Tolbert, "Mark," *The Women's Bible Commentary*, ed. Carol A. Newsom and Sharon H. Ringe (Louisville: Westminster/John Knox, 1992) 268.

Chapter 11

Pitting Mary Against Martha

LUKE 10:38-42

[38]As they continued their journey he entered a village where a woman whose name was Martha welcomed him. [39]She had a sister named Mary [who] sat beside the Lord at his feet listening to him speak. [40]Martha, burdened with much serving, came to him and said, "Lord, do you not care that my sister has left me by myself to do the serving? Tell her to help me." [41]The Lord said to her in reply, "Martha, Martha, you are anxious and worried about many things. [42]There is need of only one thing. Mary has chosen the better part and it will not be taken from her."

The tensions imbedded in this story raise more questions and interpretive problems than any other Lukan text involving women. Although these two sisters appear in John 11:1-44; 12:1-11, the better-known scene is this one, unique to Luke. The most popular interpretation of Luke 10:38-42 is that Mary and Martha represent contemplation and action, respectfully. They are said to exemplify the tension in the life of each disciple who tries to balance the two. In the experience of most Christians, it is the contemplative side that gets short shrift. Accordingly, the message of Luke 10:38-42 is said to be that one who serves actively can only do so after having listened to the word at the feet of Jesus.

Although this is a true lesson for Christian life, is that the message Luke intends to convey? Why, if the Christian ideal is to integrate contemplation and action, are the two cast dualistically in this text, with the one choice approved, and the other denigrated? A host of other questions arises: Why, in a gospel where serving, *diakonein,* epitomizes the very mission of Jesus (22:27), does he reprimand Martha for doing such? Why is only hearing the word valued in this instance, when all through the Gospel there is a constant refrain that discipleship consists in both hearing and doing the word (e.g., 6:47; 8:15, 21; 11:28)? And why, if Mary is so good at listening, doesn't she hear Martha's plight? Why doesn't Jesus, who is so compassionate toward those who feel downtrodden, sympathize with Martha? A further question: Is this a true representation of an incident from the life of the historical Jesus? Or does it reflect, rather, a tension in Luke's community? A number of variants in the Greek manuscripts also contribute to the difficulties of interpreting this text.

To complicate matters, most women identify with Martha. Like her, they desperately try to juggle all the household demands, usually in addition to working outside the home, while at the same time managing to be a charming hostess, wife, mother, companion. From such a stance, there is no good news from a Jesus who not only seems indifferent to the burden of the unrealistic demands, but even reproaches one who pours out her life in service. Since Jesus is not supposed to be unfair, the resentment that one feels from the position of Martha is directed at those sisters who are approved for luxuriating in contemplative sitting.[1] Consequently, interpretations abound that try to rescue the text, or rescue Jesus from being unfairly critical of hard-working women.

One such approach is to focus on Martha's attitude. There are several variations of this line of interpretation. Some propose that Jesus disapproves of Martha's feeling burdened (v. 40) and her anxiety and worry (*merimnas* and *thorybazē* in v. 41), not of her service. In Luke 8:14 anxiety is one of the things that chokes off growth of the word.[2] In Luke 12:11, 22, 25 there are assurances to the disciples not to worry. And in Luke 21:34 Jesus warns his disciples against the "anxieties of daily life" that can prevent them

---

[1] Elisabeth Schüssler Fiorenza, *But She Said: Feminist Practices of Biblical Interpretation* (Boston: Beacon, 1992) 56.

[2] J. R. Donahue, *The Gospel in Parable* (Philadelphia: Fortress Press, 1988) 136.

from being vigilant. Accordingly, Jesus exalts Mary as exemplary for her calm ability to focus on him. From this stance comes the proper attitude in serving.

A similar approach is to see Jesus' displeasure with Martha as caused by her occupation with "many things" (v. 41) as opposed to the "one thing" required (v. 42). It is Martha's distraction (the *NRSV* translates *periespato* in v. 40 as "distracted" rather than "burdened") that is the problem and that is contrasted with Mary's attentiveness.[3] More pointedly, some interpret the "many things" as many dishes for the meal. Jesus' distress with Martha is that he wants only one dish, a simple meal, so that she does not spend all her energy in the kitchen and can join him in the theological discussions. The "one thing needed" is then understood to take on a deeper nuance, namely, the spiritual nourishment of listening to the word. One other psychologizing approach is to see Mary and Martha locked in competition for Jesus' attention. Some suggest that it is sexual jealousy that underlies their strife.[4]

There are a number of difficulties with these interpretations. Most importantly, they do not take seriously the tensions that are in the text. They try to smooth over the stark contrasts of the two women and the clear exaltation by Jesus of the one over the other. By trying to reconcile hearing of the word and doing it, they miss what the text actually says. There is no mention of how Mary will act on the word that she hears. Only the dimension of hearing is emphasized. The approaches that engage in psychological analysis of characters falter because they attribute to an ancient writer intentions that would be quite unfamiliar to his world. Furthermore, Martha's anxiety should not be equated with that denounced in other Lukan texts. In Luke 8:14 it is anxiety about riches and pleasures of life that chokes the growth of the word. In 12:11, it is worry about what a disciple would say when brought before synagogues, rulers, and authorities that is allayed. In 12:22 and 21:34 the admonition focuses on worries about daily life: what to eat and what to wear. In 10:40 Martha's preoccupation is not

---

[3] E.g., Joseph Fitzmyer, *The Gospel According to Luke,* AB 28A (Garden City, N.Y.: Doubleday, 1985) 892.

[4] Rachel Conrad Wahlberg, *Jesus According to a Woman* (New York: Paulist Press, 1976) 79.

about these kinds of worries; it concerns much serving. Contrary to the Lukan Jesus, Paul speaks approvingly of an unmarried woman or virgin who is "anxious about the things of the Lord" (1 Cor 7:34).

Those who understand the conflict to be about the number of courses for the meal presume that "serving" (*diakonia* and *diakonein* in v. 40) means table service and that "part" (*meris*, v. 42) is a portion of food. It is true that *meris* is used this way in the Septuagint in Genesis 43:34; Deuteronomy 18:8; 1 Samuel 1:4. However, this meaning is not demanded. In Psalm 16:5, for example, we find God addressed, "O LORD, my allotted portion [*meris*] and my cup" (similarly Ps 119:57). Nor is the meaning of *diakonein* restricted to serving a meal, as we have seen above. This verb refers to service of any sort on behalf of another. In the Christian communities of Luke's day, it designated a wide variety of ministries. Actually, there is no clear indication that a meal is involved in this text. Translations that render *diakonia* in verse 40 as "details of hospitality" (1970 edition of *NAB*) or "her many tasks" *(NRSV)* and *diakonein* as "all the work" *(NRSV)* only exacerbate the problem.

So intent have scholars become on trying to rescue both listening to the word and serving that even those who have recognized that 10:38-42 upholds only one position resolve the issue by reading it in tandem with 10:25-37. Thus, the good Samaritan illustrates Christian service, while Mary exemplifies the hearing of the word on which service is based.[5] There is, however, no indication that the two pericopes were so intimately connected in the transmission of the tradition. Episodes involving the same two sisters appear in John 11:17-44 and 12:1-11 and may have drawn on a similar tradition to that of Luke 10:38-42. Echoes of a com-

---

[5]E.g., Donahue, *Gospel in Parable*, 134–139; Walter Grundmann, *Das Evangelium nach Lukas*, 2d ed., THKNT (Berlin: Evangelische Verlagsanstalt, 1961) 225; I. Howard Marshall, *Commentary on Luke*, NIGTC (Grand Rapids: Eerdmans, 1978) 450–451. Following C. F. Evans ("The Central Section of St. Luke's Gospel," *Studies in the Gospels*, ed. D. E. Nineham [London: Blackwell, 1955] 37–53), Robert W. Wall ("Martha and Mary [Luke 10:38-42] in the Context of a Christian Deuteronomy," *JSNT* 35 [1989] 19–35) argues that Luke's connection of the episodes is patterned after Deuteronomy 5:1–8:3.

mon tradition can be seen in John 11:20, where Martha goes out to meet Jesus while Mary "sat at home" and in Martha's reproachful complaint to Jesus, "Lord, if you had been here, my brother would not have died" (John 11:21). And Martha is said to serve the dinner for Jesus after Lazarus was raised (John 12:2). In the Fourth Gospel there is no Good Samaritan incident connected to the stories involving Mary and Martha. Nor is there any convincing evidence that Luke so clearly intended the two passages to be read together.[6]

It is further argued that this is "an instance of Luke's practice of juxtaposing two narratives where a woman or a man is the principal protagonist in each narrative."[7] However, in each of those instances, the point of the story is the same, repeated with a female character after being exemplified by a male. The proposed juxtaposition of the Good Samaritan with Mary and Martha has each episode illustrating different and complementary points. It has also been argued that because Martha is introduced by the same formula, *gynē tis* (a certain woman), as the traveler in 10:29, *anthrōpos tis* (a certain man)[8] Luke intends to link them. This formula for introducing characters occurs very frequently throughout Luke and Acts; it does not prove any particular connection.[9] Certainly in liturgical proclamation each of these texts is considered individually. It is still necessary to attend to the tensions within 10:38-42 itself.

The difficulties with the absoluteness of this text go back to its earliest days of transmission. Changes made by copyists reflect the problems they encountered with its interpretation. There are several major variants in the textual tradition of verse 42.

[6] Turid Karlsen Seim (*The Double Message: Patterns of Gender in Luke-Acts* [Nashville: Abingdon, 1994] 14) agrees that there is insufficient reason to consider these a pair.

[7] Donahue (*Gospel in Parable,* 134–135) compares this pairing to that of the annunciations to Zechariah and to Mary (1:8-23, 26-38); the hymns of praise of Mary (1:46-55) and of Zechariah (1:67-79); the cures of the centurion's slave and the widow's son (7:1-17) and the twin parables of 13:18-21; 15:4-10; and 18:1-14.

[8] Ibid., 135.

[9] The phrase *anēr tis* occurs in Luke 8:27; 19:2; Acts 3:2; 5:1; 8:9; 10:1; 13:6; 14:8; 16:9; 19:35; 25:14; *gynē tis* in Luke 7:37; 8:2; 10:38; 15:8; 24:22; Acts 16:14.

"There is need of only one thing" is the best reading, as attested by the oldest manuscript of the Gospel, P[75]. Other manuscripts soften the saying by replacing "one thing" *(henos)* with "a few things" *(oligōn)*. Some manuscripts combine the two, which results in nonsense: "but of a few things there is need, or of one" *(oligōn de estin chreia ē henos).*[10] Finally, some copyists omitted the whole phrase, probably due to its incomprehensibility.[11] These attempts at alteration of the text mute the sharp criticism of Martha, with the result that her choice is not totally ruled out, but Mary's is presented as preferable.

Another approach that some feminists take is to point to Jesus' approval of Mary as a great stride for upholding theological education for women. They see Jesus as approving Mary's abandonment of the traditional domestic roles of women as she assumes the position of a disciple. She is like Paul, who was educated in the Law at the feet of Gamaliel (Acts 22:3), or like the Gerasene man who, after being exorcised of many demons, sits at Jesus' feet (Luke 8:35). Often it is asserted that Jesus is revolutionary in encouraging women to engage in theological discourse. Some also see his speaking alone with women or his eating with them as daring moves, crossing the boundaries of social custom.

There are problems with this approach as well. Although it exalts women's theological education in the character of Mary, it does so at the expense of Martha's service. In fact, some who take this approach go so far as to insist that Jesus is not devaluing Martha's efforts, nor is he abolishing women's traditional roles. He is simply defending Mary's right to learn from him as a disciple.[12] Such an interpretation completely ignores Martha and what is said of and to her in the text. And the issue of women's

[10]Gordon Fee (" 'One Thing Is Needful?' Luke 10:42," *New Testament Textual Criticism: Its Significance for Exegesis. Essays in Honour of Bruce M. Metzger,* ed. E. J. Epp and G. D. Fee [Oxford: Clarendon, 1981] 61–75) has argued for this reading on the basis that the more difficult reading is the more likely to be original. So also Kathleen Corley, *Private Women, Public Meals* (Peabody, Mass.: Hendrickson, 1993) 139–140.

[11]See Bruce Metzger, *A Textual Commentary on the Greek New Testament,* 3d ed. (London, New York: United Bible Societies, 1971) 153–154.

[12]See Ben Witherington *Women in the Ministry of Jesus: A Study of Jesus' Attitudes to Women and their Roles as Reflected in His Earthly Life,* SNTSMS 51 (Cambridge: Cambridge University Press, 1984) 101.

traditional roles only comes into play if *diakonia* is taken to refer to domestic service.

Further questions must be raised about whether Jesus was being so revolutionary by talking to, eating with, or instructing women. Such observations reflect stereotyped notions that social practices were uniform and universally observed. Our sources show, however, that though certain social mores were generally accepted, their observance was not uniform.[13] Moreover, customs were changing in the Hellenistic world of the first century. With regard to men speaking to women, it is generally thought that Jewish men did not speak to women in public, as reflected in the disciples' amazement over Jesus talking to the Samaritan woman in John 4:27. In the private sphere of the household, as well, the space of women and men was separated.[14] But the notion that these boundaries were never crossed or that Jesus was the first to do so cannot be substantiated. In scenes very similar to that of John 4, for example, the patriarchs or their male servants approach a woman as a prospective bride at a well (e.g., Gen 24:10-49; 29:4-14; Exod 2:15-22). It is never hinted that their ensuing conversation is disapproved.

There is no other incident in the New Testament in which commentators express such astonishment at conversation between Jesus and a woman. There are numerous gospel episodes in which Jesus addresses a woman directly, in both public and private contexts. Jesus speaks to the widow at Nain as they are carrying out her dead son (7:13); to the woman in Simon's home (7:48, 50); to the woman cured of hemorrhages while en route to Jairus' home (8:48); to the bent woman in the synagogue (13:12); to the "daughters of Jerusalem" who lamented him as he carried his cross through Jerusalem (23:28-31). It is curious that in no other gospel stories in which Jesus speaks with women do scholars highlight this supposedly "revolutionary" move of Jesus.[15]

[13]See Bernadette Brooten, "Jewish Women's History in the Roman Period: A Task for Christian Theology," *HTR* 79 (1986) 22–30.

[14]See Bruce Malina and Richard Rohrbaugh, *Social Science Commentary on the Synoptic Gospels* (Minneapolis: Fortress Press, 1992) 348–349.

[15]That the rabbis did still consider it improper for men to speak to women in public is reflected in *Pirqe' Abot* 1.5; *b.'Erub.* 53b. But in Acts 16:13, for example, there is no hint that Paul and his missionary companions are

Some commentators remark on how "liberated" Jesus was to engage in discussion alone with women. However, it is not entirely clear that Luke envisions such a situation. At the beginning of verse 38 Jesus is accompanied by others "As they continued their journey." When the second half of the verse shifts to the singular, "he entered a village . . . welcomed him," are we to imagine that the rest of his companions waited outside the village? A preferable solution is that in changing to the singular Luke is simply highlighting the interaction of Jesus with Mary and Martha.[16]

As for Jesus being unique in advocating women's theological education, recent studies have shown that in the Hellenistic period formal education of women began to be more acceptable, especially among elite Roman families.[17] Martial, a first-century Roman, for example, described the ideal woman as not only rich, noble, and chaste, but also erudite (*Epigrams* 12.97). Juvenal's exasperation with the woman who discourses on poets and poetry as soon as she sits down to dinner and his biting criticism of women who can quote all the rules of grammar, never making mistakes, is evidence that in certain circles women did eat with men and were educated and able to converse intelligently.[18] Musonius Rufus advocated advanced education of women in his essay, "That Women Too Should Study Philosophy."[19] Pliny the Younger says of his wife: "Because of her love for me, she has even gone so far as to take an interest in literature; she possesses

---

acting scandalously when they speak with Lydia and the women they find near the river in Philippi.

[16] Adele Reinhartz, "From Narrative to History: The Resurrection of Mary and Martha," *"Women Like This": New Perspectives on Jewish Women in the Greco-Roman World,* ed. Amy-Jill Levine, SBL Early Judaism and its Literature 1 (Atlanta: Scholars Press, 1991) 165.

[17] For evidence on women's education in the Greco-Roman world and in Jewish and Christian circles see Ross S. Kraemer, "Women's Authorship of Jewish and Christian Literature in the Greco-Roman Period," *"Women Like This",* 221–242.

[18] See Sarah B. Pomeroy, *Goddesses, Whores, Wives, and Slaves: Women in Classical Antiquity* (New York: Dorset, 1975) 172, for a translation of Juvenal, *Satire* 6.434-456.

[19] See Cora E. Lutz, "Musonius Rufus, 'The Roman Socrates,'" *Yale Classical Studies* 10 (1947) 38–43 for text and translation.

copies of my writings, reads them repeatedly and even memorizes them'' (*Letters* 4, 19.2-4). There are examples of epigrams, poems, historical memoirs, rhetorical letters, and philosophical treatises written by educated Hellenistic women.[20] Although early marriage curtailed advanced study for many women, some did pursue philosophy and rhetoric.

As for theological education for Jewish women, Rabbi Eliezer's opinion is often quoted, ''If any man gives his daughter a knowledge of the Law it is as though he taught her lechery'' (*m. Soṭa* 3:4). And ''Better to burn the Torah than place it in the mouth of a woman'' (*t. Soṭa* 21b). This is used to illustrate that Jewish women were prohibited from theological study and that Jesus deliberately broke with such restrictions in teaching Mary. There are a number of problems with this approach. Foremost are that it presents a skewed picture of Jewish tradition and fuels anti-Judaism. In this line of thinking, Jesus is not seen as a Jew and his teaching is pitted against that of Judaism. The result is that Christian liberation is won through vilification of the Jews. Rather, it should be remembered that Jesus was a Jew and his teaching and practice advocated liberative possibilities *within* Judaism.[21]

Another important factor is that the final redaction of the Mishnah, from which the quote of Rabbi Eliezer is taken, dates to around the year 200 C.E., some 175 years after Jesus' ministry. We cannot say with certainty that these rabbinic materials reflect the situation of Jesus' day. Much of what is found in the Mishnah may have been developed only after the destruction of the Temple in 70 C.E. It would be more accurate to compare early Christian patristic writings to those of the rabbis. If we were to do this, we would have to admit that many of the early Church fathers were every bit as misogynistic as the rabbis are thought to be.

[20]See Mary Lefkowitz, ''Did Ancient Women Write Novels?'' *''Women Like This''*, 208-211.

[21]See Katharina von Kellenbach, *Anti-Judaism in Feminist Religious Writings,* AAR Cultural Criticism Series 1 (Atlanta: Scholars Press, 1994); Judith Plaskow, ''Blaming the Jews for the Birth of Patriarchy,'' *Nice Jewish Girls,* ed. E. Torton Beck (Watertown, Mass.: Persephone, 1982) 250-254; ''Christian Feminism and Anti-Judaism,'' *Crosscurrents* 28 (1978) 306-309; ''Feminist Anti-Judaism and the Christian God,'' *JFSR* 7 (1991) 95-134.

It is also important to recognize that one is being very selective if only rabbi Eliezer is quoted. In the same tractate of the Mishnah (*m. Soṭa* 3:4) is also found the opinion of Ben Azzai who says, "A man ought to give his daughter a knowledge of the Law." Another such text is *m. Ned.* 4:3 which declares it a religious duty to educate sons and daughters. The Tosephta *Berakot* 2:12, which was compiled in Palestine approximately a century after the Mishnah, gives explicit permission to menstruating women to study religious texts. It follows that women not menstruating must have been engaged in theological study. Although there are a number of reasons why women were exempt from studying Torah, there are no legal injunctions against such in Judaism.

The first-century Jewish philosopher Philo of Alexandria describes women ascetics, the *Therapeutides,* who dedicated their lives to the study of Torah.[22]

That some Jewish women were educated in Torah is also apparent from epigraphical evidence for Jewish women leaders of synagogues.[23] They bore titles such as "head of the synagogue," "leader," "elder," "mother of the synagogue," and "priestess." Like their male counterparts, their duties would have included financial administration and oversight of the instruction and worship of the congregation. Education in Torah would be a requisite for such a position. It is not, then, an innovation of the Christian community that women were engaged in theological education.

It is also notable that in other instances in Luke where Jesus is educating disciples, the teaching is done through dialogue.[24] It is evident from the Mishnah and the Gemara that this was also the method used later by the rabbis. Rabbinic disciples did not simply listen to their teachers, but learned by engaging in discus-

---

[22]Philo, *Vit. Cont.* 68.

[23]Bernadette Brooten, *Women Leaders in the Ancient Synagogue: Inscriptional Evidence and Background Issues,* Brown Judaic Studies 36 (Chico, Calif.: Scholars Press, 1982), analyzes evidence from nineteen inscriptions that date from the first century B.C.E. through the sixth century C.E. from Italy to Asia Minor, Egypt, and Palestine.

[24]Jane Schaberg, "Luke," *Women's Bible Commentary,* ed. Carol A. Newsom and Sharon H. Ringe (Louisville: Westminster/John Knox, 1992) 289. E.g., 5:8-10; 8:9-10; 9:10-11, 46-48, 54-56; 18:26-30; 22:24-30; 24:13-35.

sion with them.[25] In Luke 10:39 Mary is more a silent audience than a disciple being educated.

The real crux of disagreement, both in the early Church and today, is not the question of whether women can study theology, but rather the question of what ministries they may perform as a result of their theological education. It is around Martha that the controversies swirl, not Mary. Recently, Elisabeth Schüssler Fiorenza has proposed that in Luke 10:38-42 we have a story that reflects a struggle in Luke's day over the proper ministerial roles for women, not one that records precisely an incident from the life of Jesus.[26] A clue to its setting in the life of the early Church and not that of the earthly Jesus is the use of the title "Lord," *kyrie* and *kyrios,* in verses 40-41, which reflects a post-resurrection context.

The conflict represented in the story is one that revolves around *diakonia,* ministerial service (v. 40), performed by women Christians. As we have seen above, this term, by the time of Luke's writing, connotes all manner of ministries, including ecclesial leadership. That there were women exercising a wide variety of ministries, including apostolic work, public proclamation, and leadership, is clear from a number of New Testament texts. Women like Phoebe, who led the Church at Cenchreae, bore the title *diakonos* (Rom 16:1). Paul says that she had been "a benefactor [*prostatis*] to many and to me as well" (16:2). Her financial position was probably a factor in her rise to ministerial leadership in this community. 1 Timothy 3:11 lists other qualifications for women deacons. In Romans 16:7 Paul greets Junia, a prominent woman apostle. Others of his female co-workers include Mary (Rom 16:6), Tryphaena, Tryphosa, Persis (Rom 16:12), and Prisca (Rom 16:3). In Philippians 4:2-3 Paul urges Euodia and Syntyche to resolve their misunderstandings. He says "they have

[25]Adele Reinhartz, "From Narrative to History: The Resurrection of Mary and Martha," *"Women Like This": New Perspectives on Jewish Women in the Greco-Roman World,* ed. Amy-Jill Levine (Atlanta: Scholars Press, 1991) 161–184.

[26]Elisabeth Schüssler Fiorenza, "A Feminist Critical Interpretation For Liberation: Martha and Mary: Lk. 10:38-42," *Rel & Int Life* 3 (1986) 21–36. The substance of this article also appears in *But She Said: Feminist Practices of Biblical Interpretation* (Boston: Beacon, 1992) 57–76.

struggled at my side in promoting the gospel, along with Clement and my other co-workers'' (4:3). It is apparent that these two women have been significant in the ministry of evangelization. Most probably their dispute is of a theological nature and Paul's appeal for a resolution is so urgent because of their influence on the Church at Philippi.

It is also quite clear that the early Church was not of one mind with regard to the propriety of such ministries being exercised by women. In the same letter in which Paul approves of both women and men praying and prophesying in the liturgical assembly (1 Cor 11:4-5) a later copyist has inserted the admonition that women keep silent in the churches and ''be subordinate, as even the law says'' (1 Cor 14:34). He further insists that if women want to learn anything they should ask their husbands at home (1 Cor 14:35).[27] Women teachers such as Prisca were well known (Rom 16:3-5; 1 Cor 16:19; 2 Tim 4:19) and applauded by Paul. However, the author of the Pastoral letters, written later in the first century by a Christian using Paul's name, insists that women not ''teach or have authority over a man'' (1 Tim 2:12). He blatantly disagrees with Paul's practice of allowing a woman like Prisca to take aside a prominent preacher and teacher like Apollos and presume to explain to him the Christian way more accurately (Acts 18:24-28). For him, a woman who receives instruction is to do so ''silently and under complete control'' (1 Tim 2:11). The teaching ministry of women elders is to be exercised only in training younger women (Titus 2:3-4). That there were similar divisions in Luke's churches over the exercise of ministry by women is evident in the Martha and Mary passage. Just as the copyist of 1 Corinthians 14:34-35 and the author of 1 Timothy 2:11-12 were intent on silencing women, so too was the third evangelist, who places on the lips of Jesus a resounding approval of the silent woman in Luke 10:42.

There is also an effort to obscure Martha's role as head of a house church in Luke 10:38. A number of important manuscripts read ''Martha welcomed him *into her home.*''[28] To end verse 38

---

[27]See Jerome Murphy-O'Connor, ''Interpolations in 1 Corinthians,'' *CBQ* 48 (1986) 81–94; W. O. Walker, ''1 Corinthians and Paul's Views Regarding Women,'' *JBL* 94 (1975) 94–110.

[28]Some manuscripts (P³ ℵ* C*) read *eis tēn oikian,* ''into the house''; L

with "welcomed him" (as the *NAB* translation above) is abrupt and incomplete. It is most likely that the clause "into her home" originally completed it. There is no apparent motive[29] for deleting "into her home" if it were originally in the text—none, except that of downplaying Martha's role as host of a house church. Other such women leaders of house churches were Lydia (Acts 16:40); Nympha (Col 4:14); Phoebe (Rom 16:1); and Prisca along with her husband Aquila (Acts 18:24-28; 1 Cor 16:19). Martha's very name, the feminine form *(Mār[ē]tā')* of the Aramaic word *(mārê')* for "lord," signifies her ministry and authority.

Another significant term in verse 38 is the verb *hypedexato*, "welcomed him." It is a compound form of the verb *dechomai*, "to receive," denoting hospitality, a crucial value everywhere in the ancient world. It takes on an even greater significance as a Christian ministry to those engaged in the apostolic work of traveling evangelists (Luke 9:5, 48; 10:8, 10; Acts 17:7).[30] The importance Luke attaches to the ministry of hospitality is evident in that this verb occurs almost as often in his two volumes (twenty-one times) as in the whole rest of the New Testament (twenty-four times). The first one to "receive" Jesus in the Third Gospel is Simeon (2:28). The Samaritans "did not receive him, because his face was set toward Jerusalem" (9:53). In contrast, the two gospel characters who do receive Jesus are Zacchaeus (19:6) and Martha (10:38).

Dechomai is used not only to refer to welcoming a person, but also to speak of receiving, hearing, or understanding the word. In the explanation of the parable of the sower and the seed, those on the rocky ground are said to be the ones who "when they hear, receive *[dechomai]* the word with joy, but they have no root" (8:13). In other instructions to his disciples Jesus says "whoever

and *Ξ* add *autēs*, reading "into her house"; A D K P W and *Δ* read *eis ton oikon autēs*, "into her house." The phrase is omitted in P[45,75], B, and the Sahidic version. The *NRSV* translation includes the phrase "into her home"; the *NJB* reads "into her house."

[29]Metzger, *Textual Commentary*, 153. See also Corley, *Private Women*, 134–135.

[30]See John Koenig, *New Testament Hospitality: Partnership with Strangers as Promise and Mission*, Overtures to Biblical Theology (Philadelphia: Fortress Press, 1989) esp. 85–123.

does not accept *[dechomai]* the kingdom of God like a child will not enter it'' (18:17). The Acts of the Apostles tells how Samaria (8:14), the Gentiles (11:1), and the Jews of Beroea (17:11) all ''welcomed the word.'' To welcome Jesus, the word, and the reign of God are all equivalent expressions for faith. Against this backdrop, Martha's welcoming of Jesus in 10:38 speaks of her reception of him as an act of faith, matching Mary's ''listening to him speak'' (v. 39). In the first two verses, then, there is no opposition between the two sisters. It is not that one contemplates Jesus' word and the other neglects this. Each receives Jesus and his word. The tension arises over how their acceptance of the word takes expression in ministry.

Read in light of the disputes in Luke's day over women's involvement in certain ministries, Martha's complaint to Jesus is not about having too much work to do, but rather that she is being denied her role in ministerial service. In the phrase *periespato peri pollēn diakonian* (''burdened with much serving'')[31] the preposition *peri* has the sense ''about'' or ''concerning.'' Martha is burdened *about* or *with reference to* her numerous ministerial works, not *by* or *with* them. Her distress *about* them is generated by the opposition of those who think she should be leaving them to men. A further possibility arises with closer examination of the verb *perispaō*. Although one of its meanings is ''to become distracted, quite busy, overburdened,'' its primary definition is ''to be pulled or dragged away.''[32] In other instances where the verb has this meaning it occurs with the preposition *eis* (''pulled toward'') or *apo* (''pulled from'');[33] in Luke 10:40 the word alludes to Martha's being pulled away from her diaconal ministry by those who disapprove.

To make matters worse, Martha bemoans the fact that her sister does not take her part. When Martha appeals to Jesus she does

---

[31]The phrase *periespato peri pollēn diakonian* has been translated various ways: ''burdened with much serving'' *(NAB)*; ''distracted by her many tasks'' *(NRSV)*; ''busy with all the details of hospitality'' (1970 edition of the *NAB*). These translations result from the presupposition that the situation concerns kitchen preparations.

[32]BAGD, 650.

[33]See BAGD, ''*perispaō*,'' 650, for examples. It occurs only here in the New Testament.

not make her complaint about Mary by name, but rather calls her "my sister" *(adelphē)*. "Sister" was the term Christians commonly used among themselves to refer to female members. But it also carries, at times, a further connotation of one engaged in the ministry as her primary occupation (e.g., Rom 16:1; Phlm 2).[34] It is possible that part of Martha's anguish is that her sisters, former companions in ministry, have been persuaded that silent listening is the proper role for women disciples, and have left her alone in the more visible ministries.

In the ensuing verse, Luke portrays Jesus authoritatively siding against Martha in this dispute. The double "Martha, Martha" chides her.[35] And in his reproach the word *diakonia* no longer appears. Whereas Martha had expressed concern about *pollēn diakonian*, her "much service," Luke's formulation of Jesus' response, "you are anxious and worried about much" in itself obliterates her diaconal ministry. It is the silent, passive Mary who has "chosen the better part."

Another indication that the "worry" involves a more public matter is the use of *thorybazō* in verse 41. This verb, meaning "be troubled" or "worried," occurs only here in the New Testament.[36] The cognates *thorybeō* and *thorybos* occur eleven times, always in the context of a disturbance made by a crowd.[37] This word suggests a troubledness that goes beyond an individual worry; the conflict is something that has the whole community in an uproar.[38]

---

[34] E. E. Ellis ("Paul and His Co-Workers," *NTS* 17 [1970/71] 437–452, especially pp. 446–447) includes *aldelphoi* in his analysis of different terms used of New Testament ministers. Mary Rose D'Angelo ("Women Partners in the New Testament," *JFSR* 6 [1990] 65–86) also sees *adelphē* as a missionary title and views Mary and Martha as a missionary pair.

[35] See also Luke 22:31; Acts 9:4; 22:7; 26:14.

[36] A number of manuscripts have replaced it with *tyrbazō*, which has the same meaning. *Thorybazō*, the better reading, is found in P³ P⁴⁵ P⁷⁵ ℵ B C D L W, etc. *Tyrbazō* occurs in A K P Δ, Π, Ψ, etc.

[37] *Thorybeō* occurs in Mark 5:39 and its parallel, Matthew 9:23. The Lukan redaction (8:52) eliminates the word. It also occurs in Acts 17:5; 20:10. *Thorybos* is found in Matthew 26:5; 27:24; Mark 5:38; 14:2; Acts 20:1; 21:34; 24:18.

[38] Corley, *Private Women*, 140.

A much different picture emerges from the way that the Fourth Evangelist has shaped the traditions about these two sisters.[39] In John 11:1-44 Martha plays a central role in the drama of the raising of Lazarus. This resuscitation will be the final straw for the Jewish leaders, who from that point on plan to kill Jesus (John 11:45-54). Martha is introduced thus: "Now Jesus loved Martha and her sister and Lazarus" (11:5). It is significant that she is named first and that in the Gospel that features the "Beloved Disciple" (John 13:23-26; 18:15-16; 19:25-27; 20:2-10; 21:7, 20-24) as the model disciple, Martha is also introduced as "beloved."

As the episode progresses, Lazarus dies and Jesus and his disciples journey to Bethany, the village of Martha and Mary. When Jesus arrives, Lazarus has already been in the tomb four days. Martha, upon hearing that Jesus was coming, went to meet him while Mary stayed at home (11:20). The ensuing exchange between Jesus and Martha is of the utmost importance. Martha greets Jesus with a declaration of faith, even in the face of her brother's death, "Lord, if you had been here, my brother would not have died. [But] even now I know that whatever you ask of God, God will give you" (11:21-22). Jesus and Martha then engage in a theological discussion about resurrection, which terminates with Jesus' revelation to Martha, " 'I am the resurrection and the life; whoever believes in me, even if he dies, will live, and everyone who lives and believes in me will never die. Do you believe this?' She said to him, 'Yes, Lord, I have come to believe that you are the Messiah, the Son of God, the one who is coming into the world' " (11:25-27). These are the same words the evangelist uses to describe his entire purpose in writing the Gospel: "that you may [come to] believe that Jesus is the Messiah, the Son of God, and that through this belief you may have life in his name" (20:31). Martha, then, is a model believer.

What is remarkable is that in the Gospel of John this full profession of faith comes from Martha. In the Synoptic Gospels we find it on the lips of Peter, "You are the Messiah, the Son of the liv-

---

[39]Though most scholars believe that there was no direct literary contact between the Gospels of Luke and John, their numerous similarities point to cross-influence from similar traditions at the stage of oral transmission. See further R. E. Brown, *The Gospel According to John I–XII*, AB 29 (New York: Doubleday, 1966) xlvi–xlvii.

ing God" (Matt 16:16; similarly Mark 8:29; Luke 9:20). Further-more, Martha makes this pronouncement before Jesus raises her brother from the dead. She exemplifies one who believes on the basis of Jesus' word, without seeing signs (John 20:29). The next chapter illustrates how Martha's belief in Jesus' word leads to the ministry of service, *diakonia* (12:2). At the dinner party given by Martha and Mary for Jesus after he raised Lazarus from the dead (John 12:1-8), Martha served *(diēkonei)*. In the Fourth Gospel there is no tension over women's diaconal service. In this Gospel is also found the story of the Samaritan woman as the first missionary (John 4:4-42), and that of Mary Magdalene as the first to see the risen Christ and whom he commissions to pro-claim the news to the rest of the disciples (John 20:1-18). The Fourth Gospel profiles strong women characters who engage in theological discussions with Jesus, profess their profound faith, and preach publicly and convincingly. Unlike the Gospel of Luke, there is no attempt to silence women or to restrict them to quiet, behind-the-scenes, homebound ministries. It is evident that the Johannine communities interpreted Jesus' words and deeds dif-ferently from Luke. They understood Jesus to commission all Christians, women as well as men, to express their faith in the performance of all manner of deaconal ministries.[40]

In proclaiming the story of Martha and Mary today, one must be cognizant of the many difficulties the Lukan version presents. The temptation is very strong to either rescue Jesus or to redeem the text so as to blunt its absolute approval of Mary and repri-mand of Martha. Our instincts are correct when they tell us that something is wrong with this picture; but to try to make it into something that it is not is equally problematic. The best approach is to recognize the historical situation reflected in this text and analyze both the similarities and differences from that of our day. It is important to know that the Lukan approval of silent, pas-sive women is only one side of an early Christian debate; the Johannine portrait upholds vocal, publicly-ministering women.

That later Christians rejected the Lukan disapproval of Martha is evident from art and literature. Medieval paintings of Martha often cast her in a pose akin to that of St. George—killing a

[40]See Sandra Schneiders, "Women in the Fourth Gospel and the Role of Women in the Contemporary Church," *BTB* 12 (1982) 35-45.

dragon![41] This image of Martha flourished particularly in France, Switzerland, Italy, and southern Germany, from the fourteenth through the sixteenth centuries. A most remarkable painting by Fra Angelico (1387–1455) depicts Martha and Mary present at Gethsemane. The three disciples are asleep, and Mary is absorbed in a book, while Martha's pose imitates that of Jesus. Both are alert, and praying with uplifted hands. Martha's mature faith and service is shown to endure all the way to Jesus' passion. In another painting, Fra Angelico shows her alongside Veronica at the foot of the cross. Meister Eckhart (c. 1260–1327), a Dominican monk and mystic, preached that Martha was the one who had already reached the stage of integrating contemplation and action. Mary, on the other hand, represents the novice in the contemplative life. Martha's plea is for Mary not to get stuck in the tranquil resting, indifferent to the needs around her.[42] Martha became the patron saint of innumerable women's communities who adopted her as their model in their active ministries.

If we were to follow this direction of creative revisioning of Luke 10:38-42, what might the ending of the story be if we were to rewrite the second half? How might the story be told if there were no polarization of "hearing" and "doing"? How would the episode end if there were no tensions over vocal, public ministries for women? What would happen if Mary, Martha, and Jesus interacted in an equal triad, not with Jesus in the center and the two sisters using him as a go-between? What if Mary and Martha, instead of being pitted one against the other, were portrayed as mutually supportive of each other, as in the visitation scene with Mary and Elizabeth (Luke 1:39-45)?

Would not such a portrait challenge rivalries or hostilities that are sometimes evident between women who advocate that the place for all women is in the home and those who assume public leadership positions? What would it mean for our day to "choose the better part?" What would be the "one thing needed" today? Would it be different for each person and each community and

41 See Elisabeth Moltmann-Wendel, *The Women Around Jesus* (New York: Crossroad, 1987) 14–48, for this and the following examples.

42 A contemporary scholar who adopts this interpretation is Mary O'Driscoll, "Dominican Spirituality: Contemplative Involvement in the World," *Justice and Truth Shall Meet* (Sinsinawa, Wis.: Parable, 1984) 135–136.

each age? If this last question is answered affirmatively, then we might begin to act out of a vision that allows for the rich diversity of gifts in the community to be used in service without regard to gender distinctions. Both women and men called to contemplative listening and women and men called to all forms of ministry would together hear Jesus' approval of their having "chosen the better part."

Chapter 12

Bent No More and Glorifying God!

LUKE 13:10-17

[10]He was teaching in a synagogue on the sabbath. [11]And a woman was there who for eighteen years had been crippled by a spirit; she was bent over, completely incapable of standing erect. [12]When Jesus saw her, he called to her and said, "Woman, you are set free of your infirmity." [13]He laid his hands on her, and she at once stood up straight and glorified God. [14]But the leader of the synagogue, indignant that Jesus had cured on the sabbath, said to the crowd in reply, "There are six days when work should be done. Come on those days to be cured, not on the sabbath day." [15]The Lord said to him in reply, "Hypocrites! Does not each one of you on the sabbath untie his ox or his ass from the manger and lead it out for watering? [16]This daughter of Abraham, whom Satan has bound for eighteen years now, ought she not to have been set free on the sabbath day from this bondage?" [17]When he said this, all his adversaries were humiliated; and the whole crowd rejoiced at all the splendid deeds done by him.

In recent years this story has become a paradigm for women's liberation from all that bends them double and holds them in bondage. This woman's eighteen years of suffering have become symbolic of the more than eighteen centuries of patriarchal burdens that women have carried. The number of years of this woman's bondage recalls two lengthy periods of servitude in Israel's history. As Israel was freed after eighteen years of bondage to Moab (Judg 3:14) and eighteen years of affliction from the Philistines and the Ammonites (Judg 10:8), so this story can speak of freedom that is possible within the Jesus tradition.

The passage, unique to Luke, weaves together a miracle story with a controversy story.[1] In the former (vv. 10-13), the woman occupies the center. The seriousness of her disability is emphasized: both the extreme physical effects and the satanic forces to which the ancients attributed it. The gravity of her illness serves to highlight the healing power of Jesus. Upon seeing her, Jesus interrupts his teaching, calls to her, affirms that she has been set free, and lays his hands on her. Her response is immediate: she stands upright[2] and continues to glorify God.[3]

Commentators often speculate on the woman's condition before encountering Jesus. Some postulate that her illness was *spondylitis ankylopoietica*,[4] a deformation resulting from fusion of the spinal joints. Some presuppose that she was regarded a sinner or unclean. The text, however, makes no mention of such. A malady that many modern day women suffer from is osteoporosis, a weakening of the bones, that can lead to a stooped posture. Sometimes this occurs as a direct result of women subordinating their own nutritional needs to those of their husbands and children.

Alternatively, we might focus on the faith of this woman who, though weighed down with her disability, has come to the syna-

---

[1] Joel B. Green, "Jesus and a Daughter of Abraham (Luke 13:10-27): Test Case for a Lucan Perspective on Jesus' Miracles," *CBQ* 51 (1989) 643-654, demonstrates the unity of the passage. Elisabeth Schüssler Fiorenza, "Lk 13:10-17: Interpretation for Liberation and Transformation," *TD* 36 (1989) 304, argues that the two be read separately.

[2] See D. Hamm, "The Freeing of the Bent Woman and the Restoration of Israel: Luke 13:10-17 as Narrative Theology," *JSNT* 31 (1987) 28 for instances in which *anorthoō*, "to set up, make erect," occurs in the Septuagint to refer to the restorative action of God. Hamm proposes that Luke uses this word in 13:13 with these connotations in mind.

[3] To glorify God is a common Lukan response to Jesus' words and deeds. See Luke 2:20; 5:25-26; 7:16; 17:15; 18:43; 23:47.

[4] J. Wilkinson, "The Case of the Bent Woman in Lk 13:10-17," *EvQ* 49 (1979) 195-205.

gogue on a Sabbath, presumably to offer praise to God. It is clear from this text that the assumption that women were not allowed into the synagogue is incorrect.[5] The incident is explicitly presented as happening in the synagogue, where Jesus was teaching.

In this first half of the story Jesus and his mission are almost incidental. The woman has come to worship God and continues to do so (the imperfect verb *edoxazen,* "glorified," in v. 13 carries the connotation of continued action). Whether bent or straight, her intent is to praise God. Jesus' words to the woman, *apolelysai,* "you have been freed," are expressed in the perfect passive form of the verb. Her freedom has already been accomplished by God before Jesus' intervention.[6] This formulation is similar to Luke 5:20 and 7:47, where forgiveness on the lips of Jesus is articulated in the perfect passive tense. The effect in those instances, as here, is the assertion that it is God who frees one. That God's freeing power is understood to be mediated by Jesus becomes clear from the ensuing controversies.

The second part of the story (vv. 14-17) is a controversy. The reaction of the synagogue official stands in stark contrast to the woman's praise (v. 13) and the crowd's acclamation (v. 17). A play on the word *dei,* "it is necessary," in verses 14 and 16 underscores the conflict. The synagogue official argues from the necessity of working on the six other days (v. 14); Jesus insists on the necessity of God's saving plan being realized (v. 16). Jesus criticizes the hypocrisy of his opponents,[7] and argues from the lesser to the greater: if an animal, who is bound only a few hours, can be loosed on the Sabbath, how much more this daughter of Abraham, fettered for eighteen years? Another word play strengthens the ironic contrast: one loosens *(luein)* an ox or ass (v. 15); so must the woman be loosened *(luein,* v. 16).

---

[5]See, e.g., Eduard Schweizer, *The Good News According to Luke* (Atlanta: John Knox, 1984) 222. See Bernadette Brooten (*Women Leaders in the Ancient Synagogue: Inscriptional Evidence and Background Issues,* Brown Judaic Studies 36 [Chico, Calif.: Scholars Press, 1982]), who shows from inscriptional evidence not only the presence of women in the ancient synagogue, but also their various leadership positions.

[6]Elisabeth Schüssler Fiorenza, *But She Said: Feminist Practices of Biblical Interpretation* (Boston: Beacon, 1992) 199.

[7]See also Luke 6:42; 12:1, 12:56.

In the second half of the narrative the straightened woman recedes from the center as Jesus and his objectionable action becomes the focus.[8] Whereas the freeing action had been attributed to God, now the dialogue ascribes it to Jesus. The identification of Jesus' works with God's is underscored by the use of the term *endoxois,* "mighty deeds," in verse 17. This same word is used in Deuteronomy 10:21 and Exodus 34:10 for what God has done for Israel.[9]

This is a two-edged story, depending on how one reads. As a paradigm for liberation for women it has freeing potential. But there are also pitfalls in this narrative. Once again we find a story that can be interpreted as freeing for women at the expense of Jews. Again a Jewish religious leader is cast as Jesus' opponent. From the remark in verse 17 about the humiliation of Jesus' adversaries, there seems little chance that this official was persuaded to adopt Jesus' perspective. In fact, this will be the last Lukan instance in which Jesus will teach in a synagogue. Henceforth the synagogue is always cast in opposition to the reign of God that Jesus brings. This often leads to the conclusion that Judaism held women bound whereas Jesus freed women. Such an interpretation is dangerous fuel for anti-Judaism.

Instead, Jesus should be seen as an observant Jew, one committed to keeping the Sabbath as prescribed in Exodus 20:8-11 and Deuteronomy 5:12-15. He does not arbitrarily disregard Sabbath observance, but he interprets it differently from his adversaries. Whereas the synagogue official relies on a narrow interpretation of the Law, Jesus reasons from commonly accepted exemptions that there are situations that take precedence. When the purpose of Sabbath rest is to be free to praise God, Jesus deems it necessary to free a bound woman so she can do precisely that.[10] Just as Jesus challenges the synagogue leader to focus on the intent of the Law, it would be well for those Christians who tend toward legalistic interpretations of Scripture and tradition

[8]Schüssler Fiorenza, *But She Said,* 208.

[9]See Hamm, "Freeing of the Bent Woman," 27.

[10]Elisabeth Schüssler Fiorenza, *In Memory of Her: A Feminist Theological Reconstruction of Christian Origins* (New York: Crossroad, 1983) 125–126.

to hear a similar summons. Instead of seeing a broken rule, can such a one see the broken person as of first importance?

Another danger in this story is that it casts a woman in the role of victim and the male Jesus as the one who brings healing. If the Christian reader identifies with the male Jesus, then Christian identity is established as male and women believers are either left out or have to read as if they were male. If Christian women identify with the woman as victim, the story can reinforce a dependency on males for well-being. Women who have suffered may also internalize the accusations of the synagogue leader. He blamed the woman for the broken Sabbath and interpreted her coming to the synagogue as deliberately looking for a cure that day (v. 14). In fact, the text does not say why the woman came. We have suggested that she came simply to praise God. It was Jesus who initiated the healing, not she (v. 12). For Christian men and women to work together to free the Church and society from bonds of sexism, they must resist the temptation to blame the victim. Moreover, women must take an active part in the work of liberation. They cannot wait for men with power to notice their burden and lift it.[11] Nor can they allow the work for equality to degenerate into a controversy by men over women, as happens in this text.

It is curious that this woman's liberation is so controversial for a people whose root metaphor is Exodus, liberation from oppressive bondage. The point at issue is not the liberating, it is the timing: no work of freeing is allowed on the Sabbath. It is true that in terms of enduring her disability, the woman could have waited one more day. But there is an urgency that *now* is the time of salvation. Repeatedly in Luke, there is a necessity about the present moment as the time to accept God's liberation (e.g., Luke 4:21; 19:9; 23:43). Moreover, the ability of the whole people of God to be holy and glorify God is at stake. While there is any brokenness in the community, to that extent the entire people is in need of healing. This woman is a "daughter of Abraham"[12] and Sarah, part of the people to whom God is bonded in covenant. "Daughter of Abraham" is a rare phrase. It occurs only

[11]Schüssler Fiorenza, *But She Said,* 199–200.
[12]See also Luke 1:54-55; 3:7-9; 8:48; 16:22-31; 19:1-10; Acts 13:26, which highlight the promises of God to Abraham's descendants.

here in the biblical tradition and rarely in rabbinic writings. In Luke 19:9 Jesus calls Zacchaeus a "son of Abraham" when he announces that salvation has come to him. In both instances Jesus has initiated an encounter with a marginal member of the community and insists that they belong as fully integrated members. This applies to both "daughters" and "sons."

Not unlike the synagogue official, there are many voices today that advocate patient endurance, assuring women that if they wait long enough the day of equality will come. Many women, like the woman bent double, have learned to live with the burdens of sexism. They have found a way to accommodate themselves to the system so that they can still hobble their way in to give praise to God. Although they know that the range of what can be seen from a bent over position is very limited, this is a familiar world, and one not readily relinquished. This text, however, can help us to choose the better part by moving us to realize the urgency of acting for liberation now. In it the voice of Christ can be heard to insist upon the necessity of setting free all the daughters of Abraham and Sarah today. In this way all God's people have fuller range of vision and glorify God standing erect. There will always be objections to the timing. Is there ever a convenient time for liberation?

Chapter 13

A Woman Mixing Dough

LUKE 13:20-21

[20]Again he said, "To what shall I compare the kingdom of God? [21]It is like yeast that a woman took and mixed [in] with three measures of wheat flour until the whole batch of dough was leavened."

This is the first of three Lukan parables that feature women protagonists. In the Synoptic Gospels, Jesus' teaching is most frequently expressed by means of parables. Using images from the everyday life of his audience, Jesus would capture peoples' attention with familiar-sounding situations such as farmers sowing (Luke 8:4-8); bringing in an unexpectedly abundant harvest (12:16-21); the inequities of rich and poor (16:19-31). But Jesus' parables were not pleasant tales that reinforced the status quo. Rather, they were puzzling stories that could turn a person's world upside down. There is always an unexpected twist in the story that invites the listener to imagine God and the realm of God in a radically different fashion than before. The parables are open-ended, without neat conclusions. They demand that the hearer work out what the story means and what their response to it will be.

The parables invite a person to identify with a particular character or to take up a specific point of view within the story. In three Lukan parables the hearers are to take the perspective of a woman character. The majority of gospel parables and narratives reflect the experience of men and revolve around male characters, so that women who listen to them have to read as if they were men. Here the reverse is true. Two of these parables are unique to Luke: a woman who searches for a lost coin (15:8-10), and a widow demanding justice (18:1-8). The story of a woman mixing dough (Luke 13:20-21) also appears in Matthew (13:33) and in the *Gospel of Thomas* (§96).[1]

> [33]He spoke to them another parable. "The kingdom of heaven is like yeast that a woman took and mixed with three measures of wheat flour until the whole batch was leavened" (Matt 13:33).

> "The kingdom of the Father is like a woman; she took a bit of leaven, hid it in dough, [and] made it into big loaves. Let him who has ears hear" (*Gos. Thom.* §96).

The wording in Matthew and Luke is almost identical, except for the introduction. Taking the saying from the Q source,[2] each tailored the opening in his own fashion. Matthew begins with a statement; Luke with a rhetorical question, as if searching for the most apt image for the reign of God. Luke used this same technique to begin the preceding parable of the mustard seed (13:18-19).

As with all parables, this one is open to many possible interpretations. It is important to remember that the parables bear no titles in the Greek text, and that those provided by translators and commentators may prejudice the interpretive process. We will explore several possible meanings of Luke 13:20-21, and then propose ways in which it might be most powerfully used today.

Luke's introduction tells that this parable gives an image of the reign of God *(basileia tou theou)*.[3] It is difficult to capture well

---

[1]The Gospel of Thomas is part of the Nag Hammadi Library discovered in Egypt in 1945, and is dated to approximately the second century C.E.

[2]Most New Testament scholars believe that the approximately 230 sayings of Jesus found in Luke and Matthew but absent from Mark came to them from a written source, called "Q," short for *Quelle,* the German word for "source."

[3]Matthew's version says "the kingdom of heaven" *(basileia tōn ouranōn)* rather than "kingdom of God" *(basileia tou theou)*. Like pious Jews who refrain from using the name of "God," Matthew substitutes "heaven" as a circumlocution.

in English the meaning of the Greek expression *basileia tou theou*. Most frequently it is translated "the kingdom of God." This English phrase conjures up the notion of a place, usually thought of as belonging to another sphere of time and locale (e.g., "up in heaven" and "the next life") in which God dwells and rules as monarch. But such images of God and the divine realm do not entirely cohere with those attached to this symbolic phrase in the synoptic sayings.[4] By translating *basileia tou theou* as "the reign of God" or "the realm of God," we avoid reinforcing some of the male-centered monarchical imagery that "kingdom of God" evokes and further allow the parables to take our imaginations into the rich meanings attached to the symbol *basileia*.

The most common interpretation of the parable in Luke 13:20-21 focuses on the small amount of yeast that one would mix with flour to produce a loaf of bread. The point is said to be the astonishing growth of something small into something that permeates a large entity. In this interpretation, the leaven is thought to be Jesus' preaching, or the word of God, which grows phenomenally in its efficacy throughout time and history.[5] In the version of the saying found in the Gospel of Thomas there is such a contrast, between the "bit of leaven" used and the "big loaves" it made. However, there is no reference in the Lukan or Matthean versions of the parable to the amounts involved.[6]

A parable that does emphasize a contrast between small beginnings and a large outcome is the Markan parable of the mustard seed. It compares the reign of God to "a mustard seed that, when it is sown in the ground, is the smallest of all the seeds on the earth. But once it is sown, it springs up and becomes the largest of plants and puts forth large branches, so that the birds of the sky can dwell in its shade" (Mark 4:30-32). Matthew's rendition (13:31-32) also has this contrast, but Luke's (13:18-19) omits it.

---

[4]Sallie McFague, *Models of God: Theology for an Ecological, Nuclear Age* (Philadelphia: Fortress Press, 1987), especially pp. 63–69, shows the inadequacies of the monarchical metaphor for God.

[5]E.g., Joachim Jeremias, *Rediscovering the Parables* (New York: Charles Scribner's Sons, 1966) 116–117.

[6]Knowledge of Paul's proverbial statement, "A little yeast leavens the whole batch of dough" (Gal 5:9; similarly 1 Cor 5:6), may also influence one to read a contrast of amounts into the parable.

Because the parable of the mustard seed immediately precedes that of the leaven in Matthew and in Luke, the interpretation of the former has influenced that of the latter. However, in the Gospel of Thomas the two parables are not connected. Mark's Gospel does not have the parable of the leaven. Thus, at one stage of the tradition, the two stories circulated separately and do not necessarily have the same point.[7] This is especially true for the Lukan versions: neither story has a small-large contrast in the text.

Important to the meaning of the parable is the fact that in every other instance in Scripture in which leaven occurs, it represents evil or corruption. In Exodus 12:15-20, 34 the Passover ritual prescribes that unleavened bread be eaten for seven days. This recalls the Israelites' hasty departure from Egypt, with no time to wait for dough to be leavened. Eating unleavened bread becomes a sign of membership in God's holy people. Grain offerings are to be unleavened (Lev 2:11), equating unleavened with sacred. In Mark 8:15 (similarly Matt 16:6, 11, 12) Jesus cautions his disciples, "Watch out, guard against the leaven of the Pharisees and the leaven of Herod." In his version of this saying Luke (12:1) defines the leaven of the Pharisees as "hypocrisy." Twice Paul uses leaven as a symbol for corruption. He admonishes the Corinthians, "Do you not know that a little yeast leavens all the dough? Clear out the old yeast, so that you may become a fresh batch of dough, inasmuch as you are unleavened. For our paschal lamb, Christ, has been sacrificed" (1 Cor 5:6-7). To the Galatians he quotes the proverb, "A little yeast leavens the whole batch of dough" (5:9), warning them not to be misled by those preaching a different message from his own.[8]

For some interpreters such a singular positive use of leaven in Jesus' parable is the unexpected twist in the story. However, if leaven is meant to connote corruption, the startling message is that the reign of God is like a batch of dough that has been permeated by what societal standards would consider a "corruptive yeast." In other words, Jesus' story presents an image of God's realm as one that reverses previous notions of holiness: no longer

[7]Bernard Brandon Scott, *Hear Then the Parable* (Minneapolis: Fortress Press, 1991) 323.

[8]In other Greek writers, e.g., Plutarch, *Mor.* 289 E-F and 659 B, leaven also connotes corruption.

unleavened, but leavened is the locus of the sacred. It proclaims that God's realm thoroughly incorporates persons who would have been considered corrupt, unclean, or sinners according to prevailing interpretations of the Jewish purity regulations.

To understand the parable this way accords well with Jesus' other teachings and actions, particularly in the Gospel of Luke, in which Jesus continually extends himself to people who are poor, outcast, or marginalized. The challenge of the parable for those who are on the fringes is to begin to see themselves as "leaven," a vital component of the believing community. For those who are privileged, it is a summons to change their attitude toward those they consider "corrupt" and to see them as the very ones who provide the active ingredient for the growth of the community of God's people.[9]

As Luke's predominantly Gentile community retold the story in their day, they may have been thinking of how Gentile Christians, who began as a hidden minority mixed into the batch of predominantly Jewish Christian communities, were now beginning to permeate the whole. To Jewish Christians, this "corrupting" influence would have had a disturbing effect on their prevailing theology and praxis. Having let a few Gentiles mix in, these now were changing the character of the whole community! For believers today, the message may be a challenge to discard attempts at keeping the faith community a flat, "unleavened" mass of homogenous people, and to enthusiastically embrace an image of God's reign that includes persons of diverse races, ethnic origin, class, gender, age, sexual orientation, differing physical and mental abilities, who energize and transform the whole.

Focusing on the hiddenness of the leaven, some scholars understand the point to be that the reign of God, like leaven, works silently, imperceptibly within, surely bringing about transformation.[10] This interpretation is not far removed from that of the

---

[9]See e.g., R. W. Funk, "Beyond Criticism in Quest of Literacy: The Parable of the Leaven," *Int* 25 (1971) 149–170; S. Praeder, *The Word in Women's Worlds: Four Parables,* Zacchaeus Studies, New Testament (Wilmington: Glazier, 1988) 32; Scott, *Hear Then the Parable,* 329.

[10]E.g., C. H. Dodd, *The Parables of the Kingdom,* rev. ed. (New York: Charles Scribner's Sons, 1961) 155–156; Joseph Fitzmyer, *The Gospel According to Luke,* AB 28A (Garden City, N.Y.: Doubleday, 1985) 1019.

small-to-large contrast. But there is something more to be explored in this detail. The parable says that the woman "took and hid *([en]ekrypsen)*" leaven in three measures of flour. The verb *(en)kryptō* is nowhere else attested in a recipe for "mixing" dough.[11]

There are, however, other instances in Luke in which forms of the verb *kryptō* ("to hide") occur. In Luke 10:21 "[Jesus] rejoiced in the Holy Spirit and said, 'I thank you, Father, Lord of heaven and earth, because you have hidden *[apekrypsas]* these things from the wise and the intelligent and have revealed them to infants; yes, Father, for such was your gracious will.' " In 18:34 the Twelve do not grasp what Jesus says to them about his coming passion: "what he said was hidden *[kekrymmenon]* from them." In 19:42, Jesus laments over Jerusalem, saying, "If you, even you, had only recognized on this day the things that make for peace! But now they are hidden *[ekrybē]* from your eyes."

In each of these instances full understanding of some aspect of the mystery of the divine realm is concealed by God (the passive voice of the verb *kryptō* in 18:34 and 19:42 is a theological passive, that is, God is understood to be the subject).[12] These examples provide further clues to the meaning of the parable in Luke 13:20-21. In this instance also, there is something hidden in the reign of God and the one who does the concealing is God. Two things are startling in this image: that God is portrayed as a woman, and that she conceals, rather than reveals.

The latter point most likely reflects the struggle of the early Christian communities to explain the paradoxes that framed their

[11]Praeder, *Women's Worlds,* 35. Elizabeth Waller, "The Parable of the Leaven: A Sectarian Teaching and the Inclusion of Women," *USQR* 35 (1979-1980) 99-109, proposes that the verb *enkryptō,* "to hide," came into the leaven parable by its similar sound to the noun *enkrypsias,* "cakes," found in Genesis 18:6 (LXX). Waller asserts that the story in Genesis 18:1-10 stands behind the leaven parable. Both concern a woman who mixes three measures of dough for an epiphany.

[12]Similar uses of *kryptō* occur in Matthew: "I will open my mouth to speak in parables; I will proclaim what has been hidden *[kekrymmena]* from the foundation of the world" (13:35); and "The kingdom of heaven is like a treasure buried *[kekrymmenō]* in a field, which a person finds and hides *[ekrypsen]* again, and out of joy goes and sells all that he has and buys that field" (Matt 13:44).

faith. They declared that a crucified criminal was the Messiah (Acts 2:36), that death was the way to life (Acts 17:3), and that suffering was the path to glory (Luke 24:26). For people who readily attributed all things to God, the incomprehensibility of these seeming contradictions could be explained in terms of God concealing their full meaning until the propitious time of revelation.

The image of God as a woman is perhaps as great a stumbling block for believers today as in the time of Jesus. Although there are other feminine images of God in the Scriptures, male images and language predominate. Jesus was not the first to tell stories that presented God as a woman. In the Hebrew Scriptures there are several examples of God portrayed as a birthing mother. In Deuteronomy 32:18 Moses reminds the Israelites not to forget "the God who gave you birth." The prophet Isaiah compares God's anguish over Israel to that of "a woman in labor" (Isa 42:14). Isaiah also consoles Israel, "Can a woman forget her infant, be without tenderness for the child of her womb? Even should she forget, yet I will never forget you" (Isa 49:15). And, "As a mother comforts her son, so I will comfort you; in Jerusalem you shall find your comfort" (Isa 66:13). The psalmist describes reliance on God "like a weaned child on its mother's lap" (Ps 131:2).

Job shows the creator as both father and mother: "Has the rain a father, or who has begotten the drops of dew? Out of whose womb comes the ice, and who gives the hoarfrost its birth in the skies?" (38:28-29). In a non-human maternal metaphor, God is likened to a mother eagle who incites her nestlings forth by hovering over her brood, spreading her wings to receive them, bearing them up on her pinions and giving them refuge under her wings (Deut 32:11-12; Ps 91:4). Jesus uses this same image to express his care for Jerusalem in Luke 13:34.

The prophet Isaiah and the psalmist both portray God as a midwife: "Yet you drew me forth from the womb, made me safe at my mother's breast. Upon you I was thrust from the womb; since birth you are my God" (Ps 22:10-11). In Isaiah 66:9 God says to Zion, "Shall I bring a mother to the point of birth, and yet not let her child be born? says the LORD; or shall I who allow her to conceive, yet close her womb? says your God."

The parables of the woman mixing dough (13:20-21) and of the woman who searches for a lost coin (15:8-10) are two of the clearest instances in which Jesus invites believers to envision God as a woman.[13] Although God does not have a gender, when we picture a personal God, our human experience of persons being either male or female enters into our imagination. All language about God is metaphorical; no image adequately expresses who God is.[14] God is like a woman hiding leaven in bread dough, a woman searching for a lost coin, a shepherd going after a lost sheep, but God *is* not any of these. But the language and images we use for God are extremely important because they work in two directions: what we say about God reflects what we believe about human beings made in God's image. Genesis 1:27 asserts that male and female are made in God's image. But when we use predominantly male metaphors for God, then being male is equated with being god-like. Consequently, women are not thought to be like God, and are regarded as less holy than men. Jesus' teaching and praxis contradicts such a notion and invites believers to envision God in such a way that women and men are both seen to reflect God's image equally. When the parable of the woman mixing bread dough is paired with that of the man who sowed mustard seed in his garden (Luke 13:18-19; Matt 13:31-32), it shows that women and men both act in the divine image to bring about the realm of God.

One other startling element in the story is the grandiose amount of flour, three measures—approximately fifty pounds! The woman is preparing bread for a feast fit for a manifestation of God. In fact, the very same amount of flour is used by Sarah when she bakes for Abraham's three heavenly visitors (Gen 18:6). Gideon uses this amount, too, when preparing for an angel of God (Judg 6:19), as does Hannah when making the offering for the presentation of Samuel in the Temple at Shiloh (1 Sam 1:24). In each

[13]Interestingly, in the version of the parable in the *Gospel of Thomas*, the focus of the story clearly shifts away from the leaven to the woman. Waller ("Leaven," 102–103) believes that Thomas' version of the introduction is earlier than that of Matthew or Luke. Her arguments for such are not convincing. Her desire to make the figure of the woman central to the story can be achieved without resorting to an earlier date for the version of Thomas.

[14]See Elizabeth Johnson, *She Who Is: The Mystery of God in Feminist Theological Discourse* (New York: Crossroad, 1992); Sandra Schneiders, "God is More Than Two Men and a Bird," *U.S. Catholic,* (May, 1990) 20–27; *Women and the Word* (New York: Paulist Press, 1986).

of these instances, the large-scale baking prepares for an epiphany. So too, the parable in Luke 13:20-21 portrays the work of a woman as a vehicle for God's revelation.

The role that the bakerwoman plays is a traditional one, presumably carried out in the confines of her home.[15] To use the parable to reinforce the value of women's bake sales and other such traditional endeavors for contributing to the building up of the reign of God, or to uphold the "hiddenness" of women's ministries behind the scenes, is not helpful for a Church that strains toward equality among men and women disciples. While such traditional endeavors are not to be denigrated,[16] today women's roles in working for the reign of God cannot be restricted to the domestic sphere.

A liberative approach capitalizes on the image of women's ministry as leaven, the critical ingredient for vitality and transformative action in the life of the Church and the reign of God. In areas of ministry that have traditionally been closed to women, the agitating action of introducing the leaven of women's work will appear to some to be the ruination of the unleavened cakes. Others will thrill with the fermentation that causes the whole loaf to rise and be transformed into fulfilling fare for the whole community of believers. For women not only to bake the bread, but then to preside at the table as the bread is broken and given out, completes the process of preparing the way for God's repeated manifestation in our midst.

Finally, we might query how it was that leaven, a good thing, which brings taste and texture to the loaf, came to be used exclusively as a symbol of corruption and evil. Similarly, we may ask how it was that women's leadership in ministry, so vital to the Church's early life, came to be regarded as a corrosive element

[15]See further Praeder, *Women's Worlds,* 11-35. Her study shows that domestic bread production was carried out by freeborn women, freedwomen, and slaves of both sexes. Commercial baking was done by men. Praeder postulates that the woman of the parable is a domestic worker of modest means.

[16]See Susan Starr Sered, *Women as Ritual Experts: The Religious Lives of Elderly Jewish Women in Jerusalem* (New York: Oxford University Press, 1992) particularly chapter five, "Sacralizing the Feminine: Food Preparation as Religious Activity," who shows how the rituals of food preparation imbue with holiness the everyday domestic work of the Middle Eastern women.

to what became men's exclusive domain. To have leavened bread is what is normal. It was the crisis situation of having to flee hastily from Egypt, with no time to wait for bread to be leavened (Exod 12:15-20, 34) that gave rise to the Jewish custom of eating unleavened bread in remembrance at Passover. Likewise, the restriction of women from the ministry of the breaking of the bread might be considered to have arisen from a crisis situation in the first Christian decades, where for the survival of the fledgling communities in a patriarchal and imperial world, these roles were taken over by men. Today, choosing the better part would be to return to a situation of leavened bread, where the mix of women with men in the same ministerial roles is considered "normal."

Chapter 14

A Woman Searching for a Lost Coin

LUKE 15:8-10

[8]"Or what woman having ten coins and losing one would not light a lamp and sweep the house, searching carefully until she finds it? [9]And when she does find it, she calls together her friends and neighbors and says to them, 'Rejoice with me because I have found the coin that I lost.' [10]In just the same way, I tell you, there will be rejoicing among the angels of God over one sinner who repents."

This parable, unique to Luke, is sandwiched between the parables of the lost sheep (Luke 15:3-7) and the lost sons (15:11-32).[1] The key to understanding all three parables lies in the opening verses of the chapter: "The tax collectors and sinners were all drawing near to listen to him, but the Pharisees and scribes began to complain, saying, 'This man welcomes sinners and eats with them.' So to them he addressed this parable" (15:1-3). This introduction comes from Luke's hand. It clarifies that the three parables are meant to vindicate Jesus' practice of receiving sinners and eating with them. At the same time they level a criticism against the Pharisees for not seeking out the lost.

[1]The parable of the lost sheep appears also in Matthew 18:10-14. The parable of the lost sons (15:11-32) is unique to Luke.

179

Before examining the parable of the lost coin, it is important to understand the charge directed against Jesus. We will deal first with Pharisaism and Jewish notions of sinfulness and table practice in the historical setting of Jesus' day, then with the level of Luke's literary presentation.

The popular notion that the Pharisees were rigid, legalistic, hypocritical, and the dominant force among the Jewish religious leaders of Jesus' day is incorrect. The Pharisees were one group among the many diverse sects of Jews at the time of Jesus. Pharisaism was a lay movement noted for its oral and accurate interpretations of the Jewish law. They were less accommodating toward Hellenization than the Sadducees, but were not separatists like the Essenes.[2] Disputes over theological interpretations and practices would have been common among all the various Jewish sects. The Pharisees were not the prevailing religious force in Jesus' day;[3] this became so only after the destruction of the Jerusalem Temple in 70 C.E., and it is this situation that the Gospels reflect.

Luke's literary presentation of the Pharisees does not entirely match the historical reality of Jesus' day.[4] As characters in Luke's narrative, they serve as a foil to Jesus. Their understanding of the reign of God is set in contrast to that of Jesus. Their increasingly hostile response to Jesus is meant to provoke the opposite reaction in Luke's readers.[5]

[2]See Jacob Neusner, *Judaism in the Beginning of Christianity* (Philadelphia: Fortress Press, 1984) 45–61.

[3]According to Josephus (*Ant.* 17.42) there were six thousand Pharisees in Palestine in Jesus' day. This would make them only about one percent of the Jewish population.

[4]See J. T. Carroll, "Luke's Portrayal of the Pharisees," *CBQ* 50 (1988) 604–621.

[5]From their first appearance in Luke 5:17–6:11 the Pharisees evolve into increasingly hostile opponents of Jesus. Although Jesus dines with them (7:36–50; 11:37-54; 14:1-24) the table discussion always ends in conflict. The Pharisees' warning to Jesus about Herod in 13:31-33 does not cast them in a positive light, but further illustrates their misapprehension of Jesus' mission. The conflict between Jesus and the Pharisees escalates as Jesus approaches Jerusalem (11:37-54; 12:1; 14:1-24; 15:1-32; 16:14-31; 17:20-21; 18:9-14; 19:37-40) to complete his mission. Curiously, the Pharisees are absent from Luke's passion narrative. In Acts, Pharisees no longer appear as

The idea that Jesus' table practice of eating with "tax collectors and sinners" was a mission to free the common people from the oppressive Pharisaic purity regulations surrounding meals is also incorrect. The Jewish purity laws did not, for the most part, affect table companionship; they prescribed the process for cleansing before entering the Temple. There were certain Jews, *haberim,* who voluntarily took on themselves stricter ritual observance and more rigid tithes on food. This resulted in their shunning table companionship with those outside their group. Their concern was not about the morality of such persons, but the avoidance of eating untithed food. The *haberim* represented a very small percentage of the Jewish population. Though some Pharisees belonged to this group, it is doubtful that they should be entirely identified with them.

The charge that Jesus received sinners and ate with them had to do, then, with his attitude toward sinners, not with his failure to avoid association at table with people who did not observe strict purity regulations. E. P. Sanders argues that what offended other Jews was that Jesus offered to sinners[6] forgiveness and admission into his community without making the normal demand of restitution and commitment to the law. He shows that Jesus' offer of forgiveness was not novel: in Judaism one could always turn to God, repent, and be saved (e.g., Isa 45:22). Nor was Jesus' offense that he offered forgiveness to sinners before they performed acts of restoration and amended their way of life rather than vice versa. If Jesus were bringing people to repentance and a life conformable to the law, this theological distinction would not be such an offense as to evoke mortal hostility from other

---

antagonists to the Christian message. Gamaliel persuades the Sanhedrin to let Christianity run its course (5:34-42); some Pharisees had become believers (15:5), and Paul, himself a Pharisee, is implicitly defended by the Pharisees (23:1-10). In Acts the Pharisees serve to confirm Christianity as a legitimate expression of Jewish faith.

[6]E. P. Sanders, *Jesus and Judaism* (Philadelphia: Fortress Press, 1985) 174-211. See J. R. Donahue, "Tax Collectors and Sinners: An Attempt at Identification," *CBQ* 33 (1971) 39-61, for various definitions of "sinners." He concludes that the reason that toll collectors were regarded as sinners was because of their dishonesty. See also David A. Neale, *None But the Sinners: Religious Categories in the Gospel of Luke,* JSNTSup 58 (Sheffield: JSOT, 1991).

Jews. Sanders proposes that the novelty and offense of Jesus' message was that sinners who heeded him would be included in the reign of God even though they did not repent by making restitution, sacrifice, and turning to obedience to the law. Jesus' companionship with such people was a sign that God would save them, and, moreover, implied a claim to know whom God would include.

If such were the historical reality, Luke's portrayal of Jesus' mission deliberately puts repentance back into the picture. He alters Mark's conclusion of the call of Levi, so that Jesus declares as his mission, "I have not come to call the righteous to repentance but sinners" (Luke 5:32).[7] The Lukan parable of the lost sheep ends with a saying about heavenly joy over sinners who repent (15:7), whereas there is no mention of repentance in the Matthean parallel (18:14). Warnings about repentance appear in other passages unique to Luke: 13:3, 5; 16:30. In Luke 17:3-4, unlike the corresponding sayings in Matthew 18:15, 21-22, repentance is a condition for forgiveness of one's brother or sister.[8] Finally, the concluding instruction of the Lukan Jesus to his disciples as he is about to ascend is to proclaim "repentance, and for forgiveness of sins" (Luke 24:47). This evidence leads to the conclusion that repentance is a particular theme of the Third Evangelist, which he inserts into the tradition wherever forgiveness appears.

It is probable that Luke is not so concerned with what constituted Jesus' offensive table practice in the eyes of other Jews of his day. Rather, Luke has in mind the tensions of his own day surrounding table companionship. As a Gentile Christian, writing for communities that were a mix of Gentile and Jewish Christians with Gentiles increasingly becoming the majority, his concern is to help settle struggles between the two components. In his second volume, in Acts 15, he recounts some of the difficulties in the early Church over dietary regulations and how they came to be resolved. In Luke's communities the parables that

---

[7]The Markan version (2:17) does not mention repentance. The only time that repentance appears on Jesus' lips in Mark's Gospel is at the initial declaration of his mission, "Repent, and believe in the gospel" (1:15).

[8]There are two instances in which repentance appears in both the Lukan and Matthean renditions of Q material: Luke 10:13 = Matt 11:21 and Luke 11:32 = Matt 12:41.

vindicated Jesus' practice of eating with sinners would have been understood as justification for Jewish Christians eating with Gentile Christians who did not adopt the dietary practices of Judaism.[9]

The first parable of the three, that of the shepherd and the lost sheep (Luke 15:4-7), is readily understandable as a metaphor for God who seeks out and restores sinners.[10] But it is not a gentle story. The opening line would have been jarring to Pharisees and scribes. By asking, "What man among you . . . ?" Jesus would have the Pharisees and scribes imagine themselves as the shepherd who loses the sheep. Although "shepherd" was a familiar metaphor for God (e.g., Psalm 23), and for religious leaders (e.g., Ezekiel 34), real shepherds were disdained. They were thought to be dishonest and thieving, leading their herds onto other people's land and pilfering the produce of the herd.[11] It is a shock for respected religious leaders to be asked to think of themselves as lowly shepherds. Yet a disdained shepherd illustrates God's search for the lost better than do the religious leaders who thought themselves upright. The parable challenges religious leaders to ac-

[9]From a Jewish point of view, Gentiles, because they did not live according to the Law, were synonymous with sinners (see K. Rengstorf, *"hamartōlos,"* *TDNT* 1 [1964] 325-328). As more and more Gentiles became Christians, there was a variety of positions held by Jewish Christians: (1) those who insisted on circumcision and the full observance of the law for both Jewish and Gentile Christians, e.g., the "circumcised believers" in Acts 11:2 and the "false brothers" in Galatians 2:4; (2) those who did not demand that Gentile converts be circumcised, but only keep a few Jewish observances, e.g., James and Peter in Acts 15; (3) those who demanded neither circumcision nor any Jewish observances of Gentile converts, e.g., Paul; (4) those who abandoned all Jewish observances and came to manifest an overtly hostile attitude toward Jewish practices, e.g., the Hellenists in Acts 6. That the issue of Jewish association with Gentiles was still a lively one for Luke's community is also evident in the struggle of Peter in Acts 10. There, a vision from God resolves the difficulty. In Luke 15 legitimation is derived from Jesus' practice.

[10]See K. E. Bailey, "Psalm 23 and Luke 15: A Vision Expanded," *IBS* 12 (1990) 54-71, who shows how Luke 15 uses themes from Psalm 23, Ezek 26:22-26; Hosea 11:4; 14:4; Isa 43:3-4 to show that it is God who brings back the lost one and that "repentance" means acceptance of being found.

[11]Joachim Jeremias, *Jerusalem in the Time of Jesus* (Philadelphia: Fortress Press, 1969) 303-305, 310, cites examples from the Mishnah that list herdsmen among the despised trades.

tively seek out the "lost sheep," such as tax collectors and sinners, and bring them back to the fold.

The parable of the lost coin (15:8-10) has the same structure as that of the lost sheep.[12] In each story the main character loses, searches (15:4, 8), and finds the lost object (15:5, 9), and then calls friends together to rejoice (15:6, 9). Both conclude with a saying about the heavenly joy over "one sinner who repents" (15:7, 10). The point of the parable of the lost coin is identical to that of the lost sheep: Jesus' disciples, particularly the leaders among them, are to be like God, who actively seeks out the lost until they are found. She then calls together the whole community to share in the ensuing joy.

It is often remarked that the parable of the woman searching for the lost coin makes a contrast between a poor woman who goes to great length over one *drachma* (one day's wage) and a rich shepherd with a sizeable herd.[13] However, it is not clear that

---

[12]S. Durber, "The Female Reader of the Parables of the Lost," *JSNT* 45 (1992) 59-78, sees subtle but significant differences from the parable of the lost sheep. The shepherd's rejoicing is compared with "greater joy in heaven" (v. 7) while the woman's with "joy among the angels of God" (v. 10). For her this circumlocution signals that the woman is less easily compared with God. The address in verse 4 is, "If one of you . . ." whereas in verse 8 it is, "if a woman . . . ." She sees the reader invited to take the position of the shepherd, but not that of the woman. The woman is just a woman, someone different from the reader. On this point, Kenneth Bailey (*Finding the Lost: Cultural Keys to Luke 15,* Concordia Scholarship Today [St. Louis: Concordia, 1992] 93-94) also recognizes the difference between the addressees in verses 4 and 8, but remarks that in a patriarchal Middle Eastern culture a speaker cannot compare a male audience to a woman without giving offense. But is that any more offensive than comparing religious leaders to shepherds? Durber concludes that women discover that they must either read as men or admit that they are excluded. Her cautions are well taken. However, I propose that there is a third option: recognizing the masculine perspective of the text, women can read against its intent, and unleash its liberating potential for inclusivity.

[13]Praeder (*The Word in Women's Worlds: Four Parables,* Zacchaeus Studies, New Testament [Wilmington: Glazier, 1988] 42) remarks that she is a woman of relative poverty because the rich would not be troubled over a mere *drachma.* Joseph Fitzmyer, *The Gospel According to Luke,* AB 28A (Garden City, N.Y.: Doubleday, 1985) 1080, suggests that Luke may intend to depict her as miserly.

the shepherd owns all one hundred sheep himself. He may be tending a herd with sheep that belong to several members of the clan. As for the woman, an audience of first-century Palestinian peasants who lived at a subsistence level under precarious economic conditions[14] would see her as rather well-off if she had one-third of a month's salary at hand. A rich-poor contrast weakens the impact of the parable.[15] The point is that both a male character[16] and a female one equally represent the manner in which God acts.

Another frequent speculation is that the lost coin was part of a set of decorative coins on a bridal headdress or a necklace. Such a theory makes the coin valuable because it is part of the woman's dowry, or because the whole necklace loses its value if it is missing one coin. As attractive to the imagination as such suggestions are, it must be noted that what they describe is a modern practice of nomadic Bedouin women, not Jewish women of the first century. More importantly, this line of thinking assumes that there must be a special motive for the woman's search. The simple point of the story is that the woman has lost a valuable coin and she expends a great deal of effort to find it, just as a shepherd who loses a valuable sheep, and the father whose precious sons are lost.

Some modern commentators decry Luke's portrait of the woman's action as trivial, and important only to women (the friends, *philas,* and neighbors, *geitonas,* with whom she celebrates in v. 9 are feminine). But in a first-century Mediterranean world a woman exercised power and status by maintaining orderly household management. The woman in the parable has control over the private sphere of the home and derives support from female networks. She is entrusted with the household finances and has the power to restore honor and order to the home.[17] The point

[14]See Douglas E. Oakman, *Jesus and the Economic Questions of His Day,* Studies in the Bible and Early Christianity 8 (Lewiston/Queenston: Edwin Mellen, 1986).

[15]See Bailey, *Cultural Keys,* 102.

[16]It is also common for girls and women to engage in shepherding. However the masculine verb endings in verses 4-6 imply that the shepherd is male.

[17]Carol Schersten LaHurd, "Rediscovering the Lost Women in Luke 15," *BTB* 24 (1994) 70–72, records that these observations still hold for contemporary Arab Christian women in northern Yemen.

is that the ancient reader would have regarded her successful search for the coin with high esteem. For contemporary readers, choosing the better part is not to use this parable to relegate women to the private sphere of household management, but rather, to accord esteem and value to the work of women in all spheres.

All three parables of Luke 15 emphasize the lengths to which the shepherd, the woman, and the father go to recover what was lost. The shepherd must traverse the rugged land until he finds the sheep (v. 4). And when he does he must carry the heavy animal back on his shoulders (v. 5).[18] The woman pays a high price to find the coin. She uses precious oil to light a lamp and expends much energy in sweeping the house and searching carefully in the cracks and corners.[19] The father endures insult and distress over the disloyal actions and attitudes of both his sons. He goes out to meet each while he is yet lost. All three characters go to the expense of entertaining friends and neighbors to celebrate their find. Notably, it is the woman, in the center of the three, whose search is described with the verb *zēteō* (v. 8), as is Jesus' seeking of the lost in order to save them (19:10).

Perhaps the most challenging part of this story is that, like the parable of the woman mixing dough (13:20-21), it portrays God as a woman.[20] Though today the shock value of asking religious leaders to identify themselves with God in the figure of a shep-

---

[18]Bailey, *Cultural Keys,* 75-76, notes that sheep can weigh up to 70 pounds—a very heavy burden. He points out that frequently in early Christian depictions of the good shepherd the sheep is disproportionately large, highlighting the great price that the shepherd pays for the sheep.

[19]First-century Palestinian houses were dark, with small, high windows. Floors were usually of packed dirt. Some were paved with stones, between which were cracks where a coin could easily lodge.

[20]LaHurd, "Rediscovering," 66-67, reports, however, that in reading the parable with Arab Christian women in northern Yemen they "showed little interest in Jesus' apparent use of a female as an image for God and focused instead on the act of searching and reasons for the intensity of the search. They assumed that this woman's role was to guard the money 'earned by men' and to 'keep everything in order.' The woman's desire to recover the coin seemed more a function of such cultural expectations and of the desire to restore the set of coins to completeness than of any intrinsic monetary value of the coin itself."

herd has diminished, such is not the case when God is portrayed as a woman. Many Christians yet resist shifting from the prevailing image of God as "loving father." Far more familiar and comfortable than the parable of the woman searching for the coin is the ensuing story of the father seeking out his lost sons (15:11-32).

Because the Gospels present Jesus as speaking of and to God as his father (e.g., Mark 14:36; Matt 11:25; Luke 23:34; John 17:1), and teaching his disciples to do likewise (Matt 6:9-13; Luke 11:1-4) many Christians believe "father" to be the exclusive revelation of God through Jesus. But the address of God as "father" was not unique to Jesus. It also occurs in the Hebrew Scriptures, several Qumran texts, Philo, Josephus, and rabbinic literature.[21] In fact, it is not possible to determine with certitude that Jesus himself used this address for God. From the Gospels and Romans 8:15 and Galatians 4:6 we know that "father" was an important term for God for the early Christians. But that it derived directly from Jesus is not provable.[22] The Gospels preserve not only Jesus' words, but also his followers' understanding of his message.

It is also important to realize that where "father" appears as a title for God in the ancient Jewish and Christian literature, it is always in a context of a petitioner seeking refuge from affliction or looking for assurance of forgiveness. It is God's *power* as "father" that is invoked, not intimacy and tenderness.[23] In the context of Roman imperial rule, where the emperor claimed the title of *pater patriae* and ruled the empire as the head of a patriarchal family, the application of "father" to God by Jews and Christians presented a challenge to imperial authority: God, not

[21]E.g., Sir 23:1, 4; Wis 2:16-20; 14:3; 3 Macc 6:3-4, 7-8; Tobit 13:4; 4Q372 1.16; 4Q460; fragment 2 of the *Apocalypse of Ezekiel;* Jos. *Ant.* 2.6.8 §152; Philo, *Op. mund.* 10, 21, 72-75; *m. Yoma* 8:9; *b. Ta'an.* 25b. These examples are given by Mary Rose D'Angelo, "*ABBA* and 'Father': Imperial Theology and the Jesus Traditions," *JBL* 111/4 (1992) 611–630. Remarks that follow are also based on this work.

[22]Some would say that because *'Abba* is an Aramaic word it must be an authentic word of Jesus. However, Jesus' first disciples also spoke Aramaic. D'Angelo (*"ABBA,"* 615) notes that no one attributes the Aramaic expression *Maranatha* (Rev 22:20) to Jesus.

[23]See James Barr " *'Abba* Isn't Daddy," *JTS* n.s. 39 (1988) 28–47 and "*'Abba* and the Familiarity of Jesus' Speech," *Theology* 91 (1988) 173–179.

the emperor, is the supreme power. For Christians today, invoking God exclusively as "father" does not have this kind of subversive effect. It does not challenge a patriarchal world view, but rather absolutizes it, transferring male dominance from earth to heaven.[24]

However much Christian tradition has enshrined the image of God as father, it must not be forgotten that all language about God is metaphorical and no one image ever captures the whole of the divine reality. The parables of the woman mixing bread dough (Luke 13:20-21) and the woman searching for the lost coin (Luke 15:8-10) provide at least two instances in which Jesus' teaching presents a feminine image of God. Moreover, it is Jesus himself who is the supreme revelation of God, not the metaphor "father." The Gospels portray Jesus as acting with power and authority such as a "father" God would have, but Jesus also speaks of himself in "motherly" terms. When he laments over Jerusalem, he likens himself to a mother hen trying to gather her unruly brood under her wings (Luke 13:34; similarly Matt 23:37). This saying equates Jesus' role with that of God, who is likened to a mother eagle in Deuteronomy 32:11-12 and Psalm 91:4. Perhaps the most strikingly feminine portrait of Jesus is found in the Gospel of John, where there are strong parallels between Jesus and Lady Wisdom.[25]

By entering into the figurative world of the parable of the woman searching for the lost coin, believers are able to expand their repertoire of God images and more fully apprehend the divine mystery. Choosing the better part is to see the woman seeking the coin as a metaphor that is equally apt for speaking of God as is "father." Just as the Pharisees and scribes are asked to imag-

[24]To argue that the father in Luke 15:11-32 is very "unpatriarchal" in his "motherly" tenderness is to miss this point. It also falsely stereotypes "feminine" and "masculine" traits. See further Phyllis Trible, "God the Father," *TToday* 37 (1980) 118; Elizabeth Johnson, *She Who Is: The Mystery of God in Feminist Theological Discourse* (New York: Crossroad, 1992) 18-19, 33-41.

[25]See Raymond E. Brown, *The Gospel According to John I-XII*, AB 29 (Garden City, N.J.: Doubleday, 1966) CXXII-CXXV; Elizabeth Johnson, "Jesus the Wisdom of God: A Biblical Basis for Non-Androcentric Christology," *ETL* 61 (1985) 261-294; Martin Scott, *Sophia and the Johannine Jesus*, JSNTSup 71 (Sheffield: JSOT, 1992).

ine themselves as this woman, current believers, male and female,[26] are challenged to do the same: to imitate her godly action of diligently seeking out and restoring the lost.

---

[26]It is not the case that the parable of the lost coin is only for women; all three parables in Luke 15 are for all believers.

Chapter 15

The Persistent Widow

LUKE 18:1-8

¹Then he told them a parable about the necessity for them to pray always without becoming weary. He said, ²"There was a judge in a certain town who neither feared God nor respected any human being. ³And a widow in that town used to come to him and say, 'Render a just decision for me against my adversary.' ⁴For a long time the judge was unwilling, but eventually he thought, 'While it is true that I neither fear God nor respect any human being, ⁵because this widow keeps bothering me I shall deliver a just decision for her lest she finally come and strike me.'" ⁶The Lord said, "Pay attention to what the dishonest judge says. ⁷Will not God then secure the rights of his chosen ones who call out to him day and night? Will he be slow to answer them? ⁸I tell you, he will see to it that justice is done for them speedily. But when the Son of Man comes, will he find faith on earth?"

The final story in the trilogy of parables with women casts the characters of the widow and the judge in ways that overturn biblical stereotypes. The judge is moved neither by fear of God, nor by human codes of honor and shame. He does not match the portrait established in 2 Chronicles 19:6-7, where judges are to be God-fearing, judging on behalf of God, just, impartial, and immune to bribes. Nor does the widow correspond to the pervasive biblical image of one who is poor, oppressed, and helpless. A number of biblical prescriptions make widows the objects of special care. Along with orphans and aliens, they were to be allowed to glean the left-overs of the harvest. Their clothing was not to be taken as a pledge (Deut 24:17-22). Cursed was anyone who violated the rights of a widow (Deut 27:19; Isa 10:2; Luke 20:47). But the widow of Luke 18:1-8 is not powerless. She repeatedly faces the impervious judge, voicing her demands until she achieves justice on her own behalf.

To Jesus' first audience, the notion of a woman arguing her own case before the judge would have been startling. Adjudication was the domain of men. At the death of her husband, the widow's nearest male relative would have taken responsibility for her. We suspect that her complaint is against the very man who should have been her protector!

The story makes it clear that the just decision comes about only after a long period of time has elapsed (v. 4), in which the judge's intransigence is finally overcome by the widow's coming again and again. He has not been converted. He simply wants to be rid of her bothersome presence. Moreover, he fears that she may "blacken his eye" (v. 5b). The verb *hypōpiazō* is a boxing term[1] that literally means "to strike under the eye." It also has a figurative sense, meaning "to slander," "to besmirch one's character."[2] Because verses 2 and 4 insist that this judge cares nothing about his reputation before God or human beings, this metaphorical sense for *hypōpiazō* is ruled out. The judge fears that the widow will do him physical harm.[3]

The picture of the judge being fearful that the widow will resort to physical violence is almost ludicrous. As such, it conveys

[1] See also 1 Cor 9:26-27.

[2] *BAGD*, 848 also suggests that in Luke 18:5 it may be taken in a weakened sense, "annoy greatly, wear out" (so the *NRSV* translation). But this is the only example where *hypōpiazō* is thought to have this nuance. To propose this connotation dilutes the irony of the literal "strike," which is part of the twist of the story.

[3] D. Daube, "Shame Culture in Luke," in *Paul and Paulinism: Essays in Honour of C. K. Barrett,* ed. M. D. Hooker and S. G. Wilson (London: SPCK, 1982) 361-362, notes that a blow in the face is the archetypal shaming insult among Hebrews (see also Isa 50:6), Greeks, and Romans. He thinks it more likely that the literal sense is intended in Luke 18:5.

a message about the absurdity of trying to right wrongs with violence. Instead it presents a model for achieving justice by persistent presence and by articulating its demands repeatedly.

Most scholars recognize verses 2-5 as the core of Jesus' original parable, with interpretations attached to it in verses 1,6-8. Luke's introduction first construes this as a parable about praying always without becoming weary.[4] But the parable proper does not specifically speak of prayer, rather it exemplifies persistence in demanding justice. Moreover, there are serious theological difficulties if this is seen as a parable illustrating persistent prayer. If the widow is an exemplar of persistent prayer, then the judge would represent God. But the judge is specifically said to be unjust and dishonorable. He is not moved by the pleas of the widow. This is totally contrary to what Sirach 35:14-19 says of God: "He is not deaf to the wail of the orphan nor to the widow when she pours out her complaint . . . the Most High responds, judges justly and affirms the right. God indeed will not delay." Furthermore, this interpretation presents a theology of prayer that says if one badgers God long enough the request will be answered. How can such an image of God be reconciled with that of a gracious God looking to give good gifts to all who ask (Luke 11:9-13)?

If, however, like the previous two parables, the woman represents God, then an entirely different message emerges. Here is an unexpected twist in the parable. That God would be relentlessly pursuing justice is not a new image of the divine (e.g., Sir 35:14-19). But that God is more akin to a victimized widow than a powerful judge is startling. She embodies godly power in the midst of apparent powerlessness. This is a message that achieves its full flowering in the passion, death, and resurrection of Jesus. His seeming helplessness in the face of his executioners is transformed into the very defeat of the powers of sin and death. Followers of Jesus are invited to take up this same stance: to draw on the power of weakness to overcome death-dealing powers.

Verses 6-8 provide other secondary explanations. Verse 8b seems unrelated to the parable, a transplant from the discussion in chapter 17 on the coming of the Son of Humanity. The link to verses 6-8a is the notion of delay. Behind verse 8b one can hear the con-

___

[4]See above, pp. 35–38, on the prominence of the theme of prayer in Luke and Acts.

cern of Luke's community over the delay in the second coming. This is attached to the question of God delaying in answering the chosen ones who call out day and night. Verses 6-8a give reassurance to those growing weary in the pursuit of justice. They affirm that God rewards unflagging petition, day and night, with speedy justice.

The widow of this parable is not unique in her assertive action for justice. The stories of Ruth and Tamar before her, widows who take critical action for the salvation of their people, shatter the stereotype of widows as poor and helpless.[5] In fact, a widow enjoys greater freedom from the restraints of care of husband and children, allowing her to move from the domestic sphere into more public ministerial roles. Like the widowed Anna, who spent her days in the Temple prophesying to all who were awaiting redemption (2:36-38), so this widow appears before the judge day after day, relentlessly speaking out for justice.[6] With widowhood comes the opportunity to cross the gender divisions that assign passive endurance to women and decisive action to men.[7]

The widow's story is repeated in that of countless women throughout the ages. She is like the widows and mothers of Argentina, who, for almost twenty years, have continued their weekly march in the Plaza de Mayo in Buenos Aires. They have uncovered the fate of about one-third of their nine thousand disappeared husbands and sons. Her face is seen in the Jewish "Rose Street Women," who gathered on a Berlin street in 1943 where their husbands had been taken by the Nazis. They cried out repeatedly, "We want our men. Give us back our men!" until they succeeded in blocking their deportation. Neither the Argentinian nor

[5]Don C. Benjamin, "The Persistent Widow," *TBT* 28 (1990) 213–219, shows parallels between Ruth and the widow of Luke 18. He also notes that OT widows are never involved in small claims. They defend the divine endowments of land and children.

[6]Susan Starr Sered (*Women as Ritual Experts: The Religious Lives of Elderly Jewish Women in Jerusalem* [New York: Oxford University Press, 1992]), in chapter 6, "The Liberation of Widowhood: From the Private to the Public," reports this same experience by modern Yemenite widows.

[7]Karen J. Torjesen, "In Praise of Noble Women: Gender and Honor in Ascetic Texts," *Semeia* 57 (1992) 41–64, shows the quest for honor as a male quest; whereas heroism for women consists in passive endurance, not decisive action.

the German women converted the repressive governments against which they protested. But they did achieve one small step for justice. Unlike the widow of the parable, they did not act alone, but found strength in numbers and dogged resistance.

Luke faithfully preserves a story told by Jesus which shatters stereotypes and highlights the power of the seeming powerless. With his introduction, however, Luke sidetracks the reader from this message. Since this kind of role is not what he would encourage for women, he softens the parable's impact by posing the widow as an example of persistent prayer, a docile and acceptable role. Contemporary believers, women and men alike, choose the better part when they hear this parable as a clarion to courageously face death-dealing powers and persistently demand justice. Such includes relentlessly confronting sexism until it is eradicated.

Chapter 16

The Widow Who Gives All

LUKE 21:1-4

[1]When he looked up he saw some wealthy people putting their offerings into the treasury [2]and he noticed a poor widow putting in two small coins. [3]He said, "I tell you truly, this poor widow put in more than all the rest; [4]for those others have all made offerings from their surplus wealth, but she, from her poverty, has offered her whole livelihood."

This widow has traditionally been held up as the epitome of generosity, giving from her want, and not from surplus. Contemporary Christian development campaigns often appeal to her as the model donor. In Luke's community her story would have presented a real challenge to the richer members: the large contributions of the wealthy have not the weight of the paltry two coins[1] of the poor.

The final verse has a double meaning. The Greek word *bios* means both "life itself" and "means of subsistence." There are two nuances, "She put in all the means she had to live on" and "she put in all the life she had." This latter connotation is highlighted by the literary context. This episode comes shortly before

---

[1]The two coins, *lepta duo,* were small copper coins, the smallest in use in Palestine at the time. They were worth about one-eighth of a cent each. In Luke 12:59 *leptos* is usually translated "penny."

the passion narrative. The widow who gives her whole life prefigures Jesus' own handing over of his very life on behalf of others.[2] She and the widow Anna (2:37) frame the gospel story with their pouring out of their very lives in the Temple. Her story invites the hearer to do the same.

Another interpretation questions whether her sacrifice is meant to be lauded and emulated. When read in tandem with Luke 20:45-47 another meaning altogether emerges. In this passage immediately preceding 21:1-4 Jesus denounces the scribes who desire honor and prestige, whose prayer is insincere, and who "devour the houses of widows."[3] The widow's sacrifice in 21:1-4 may be an illustration of how the scribes "devour the houses of widows." As such, Jesus is not praising the woman's generosity, but rather laments the religious system that takes advantage of her by prompting her to give her last cent.[4] Her misdirected support of a system that oppresses her is not unlike that of the woman with the hemorrhages who "spent all she had *[holon ton bion]* on physicians" (8:43) to no avail. Moreover, the verses immediately following the poor widow's action show that her gift to the Temple is a waste. Jesus asserts that "there will not be left a stone upon another stone that will not be thrown down" (21:6).

In the text of 21:1-4 there is nothing that reveals which way the story is to be taken. In verses 3-4 Jesus simply remarks on the amount that she puts into the treasury. We do not know whether it is with a tone of praise or lament. Moreover, there is no exhortation to imitate her.

---

[2]Elizabeth Struthers Malbon, "The Poor Widow in Mark and Her Poor Rich Readers," *CBQ* 53 (1991) 589-604.

[3]Joseph Fitzmyer, *The Gospel According to Luke,* AB 28A (Garden City, N.Y.: Doubleday, 1985) 1318, lists possible interpretations for how the scribes "devoured" widows' houses: (1) they accepted payment for legal aid to widows, even though such was forbidden; (2) they cheated widows of what was rightfully theirs; (3) they sponged on the hospitality of these women of limited means; (4) they mismanaged the widows' property; (5) they took large sums of money from credulous old women in return for promised prolonged prayer on their behalf; (6) they took the houses as pledges for debts that could not be paid.

[4]Addison G. Wright, "The Widow's Mites: Praise or Lament?—A Matter of Context," *CBQ* 44 (1982) 256-265.

If the audience for Jesus' remark is his disciples (20:45), then this story is most likely meant to issue a warning.[5] Jesus advises his followers to guard against acting like the scribes, who are portrayed negatively throughout the gospel. They team with the Pharisees, chief priests, and the elders in challenging Jesus[6] and in looking for a way to kill him.[7] The only favorable remark about scribes occurs in 20:39 where they admit that Jesus has answered well the Sadducees' question about resurrection. Recognizing how easy it would be for his followers to emulate the poor example of such religious authorities, Jesus' remarks point out to them the disastrous effects of such leadership. In 22:26-27 he offers a contrary model: the leader as the servant.

It is difficult, however, to see this passage only as a warning. Perhaps, like the parables, it is open-ended, and conveys a different meaning depending on where one stands. For those who would align themselves with the voracious scribes, it offers a challenge to reject all ways of feeding off the poorest, particularly under the guise of religion. For those who are oppressed and poor, it issues an invitation to reject giving support to those very systems that treat them unjustly. Finally, the action of the widow is a foretaste of Jesus' offering of his entire life, an offering made from poverty, not wealth. It invites one to enter into and emulate the same mystery that Paul describes in 2 Corinthians 8:9: "For you know the gracious act of our Lord Jesus Christ, that for your sake he became poor, so that by his poverty you might become rich." In each case, choosing the better part results in fullness of life for all.

---

[5]Eugene LaVerdiere, "The Widow's Mite," *Emmanuel* 92 (1986) 316–321, 341.

[6]Luke 5:21, 30; 6:7; 11:53; 15:2; 20:1.

[7]Luke 9:22; 19:47; 20:19; 22:2, 66; 23:10.

Chapter 17

The Galilean Women: Disbelieved Witnesses

LUKE 23:44-56

[44]"It was now about noon and darkness came over the whole land until three in the afternoon [45]because of an eclipse of the sun. Then the veil of the temple was torn down the middle. [46]Jesus cried out in a loud voice, "Father, into your hands I commend my spirit"; and when he had said this he breathed his last. [47]The centurion who witnessed what had happened glorified God and said, "This man was innocent beyond doubt." [48]When all the people who had gathered for this spectacle saw what had happened, they returned home beating their breasts; [49]but all his acquaintances stood at a distance, including the women who had followed him from Galilee and saw these events.

[50]Now there was a virtuous and righteous man named Joseph who, though he was a member of the council, [51]had not consented to their plan of action. He came from the Jewish town of Arimathea and was awaiting the kingdom of God. [52]He went to Pilate and asked for the body of Jesus. [53]After he had taken the body down, he wrapped it in a linen cloth and laid him in a rock-hewn tomb in which no one had yet been buried. [54]It was the day of preparation, and the sabbath was about to begin. [55]The women who had come from Galilee with him followed behind, and when they had seen the tomb and the way in which

his body was laid in it, ⁵⁶they returned and prepared spices and perfumed oils. Then they rested on the sabbath according to the commandment.

LUKE 24:1-12

¹But at daybreak on the first day of the week they took the spices they had prepared and went to the tomb. ²They found the stone rolled away from the tomb; ³but when they entered, they did not find the body of the Lord Jesus. ⁴While they were puzzling over this, behold, two men in dazzling garments appeared to them. ⁵They were terrified and bowed their faces to the ground. They said to them, "Why do you seek the living one among the dead? ⁶He is not here, but he has been raised. Remember what he said to you while he was still in Galilee, ⁷that the Son of Man must be handed over to sinners and be crucified, and rise on the third day." ⁸And they remembered his words. ⁹Then they returned from the tomb and announced all these things to the eleven and to all the others. ¹⁰The women were Mary Magdalene, Joanna, and Mary the mother of James; the others who accompanied them also told this to the apostles, ¹¹but their story seemed like nonsense and they did not believe them. ¹²But Peter got up and ran to the tomb, bent down, and saw the burial cloths alone; then he went home amazed at what had happened.

Having last appeared in 8:1-3, financing the mission of Jesus and the Twelve, the Galilean women now resurface as the Gospel reaches its climax. Luke's version contrasts considerably with that of Mark. In the latter these women appear for the first time in the passion narrative. In Mark all Jesus' male disciples had "left him and fled" at his arrest (14:50; see also Matt 26:56). It is at the crucifixion that Mark first introduces Mary Magdalene, Mary the mother of the younger James and of Joses, and Salome (15:40). Although Mark includes no narrative account of their ministry, he notes, "These women had followed him when he was in Galilee and ministered to him [diēkonoun autō]. There were also many other women who had come up with him to Jerusalem" (15:41). Again Mark names the women who witnessed Jesus' burial: "Mary Magdalene and Mary the mother of Joses watched where he was laid" (15:47). And in the next verse they are listed again: "Mary Magdalene, Mary, the mother of James, and Salome bought spices, so that they might go and anoint him" (16:1). It is the women witnesses who will provide the vital link for the Markan community.

In the parallel passages in Luke we find that the women are overshadowed by a host of other witnesses. In Luke the male disciples do not flee at Jesus' arrest. And so at the crucifixion Luke relates, "all his acquaintances stood at a distance, including the women who had followed him from Galilee and saw these events" (23:49). That Luke has added "all his acquaintances" to a tradition in which there were only women witnesses is evident from the verb "watching" *(horōsai)*, which is a feminine plural participle.[1] Unlike Mark 15:40 Luke neither names the women nor mentions their ministry at this point. Nor does Luke, in contrast to Mark, name the Galilean women who witness Jesus' burial and make preparations to anoint the body (Luke 23:56; Mark 15:47). It is only at the end of the empty tomb story (24:11) that Luke lists Mary Magdalene, Joanna, and Mary the mother of James, while the other women who accompanied them remain nameless.

As in all the Gospel accounts it is the Galilean women who discover the empty tomb.[2] But unlike Mark 16:7; Matthew 28:7, 10; and John 20:17, the Lukan women are not commissioned to tell the news to the other disciples. Rather, they are told, "Remember what he said to you while he was still in Galilee, that the Son of Man must be handed over to sinners and be crucified, and rise on the third day" (24:6-7). It is the men disciples who will be the proclaimers and witnesses.

When the Galilean women do announce everything to the eleven and the rest they are not believed: "their story seemed like nonsense" (24:11). Peter runs to the tomb (the location of which must have been communicated to him by the women, since he is not said to be present at the burial) and verifies that the body was not there (24:12). That he believes in the resurrection at this point

---

[1] Jane Schaberg, "Luke," *Women's Bible Commentary,* ed. Carol A. Newsom and Sharon H. Ringe (Louisville: Westminster/John Knox, 1992) 290.

[2] In Mark 16:1 the women are Mary Magdalene, Mary the mother of James, and Salome; in Matthew 28:1 Mary Magdalene and the other Mary; in John 20:1 Mary Magdalene alone.

is not at all evident; he simply goes home "amazed" (v. 12). Luke will insist, however, in the primacy of Peter's witness when he inserts an ancient tradition into his Emmaus account: "The Lord has truly been raised and has appeared to Simon!" (24:34). There is no narrative of this appearance, but this tradition affirms for Luke's community Peter's authority as first leader of the disciples. Paul's first letter to the Corinthians (15:5) echoes a similar tradition. As Paul passes on the kerygma he has received, he lists Kephas (Peter's name in Aramaic) as the first to whom the risen Christ appeared.

Unlike the other Gospels, there is no Lukan appearance of the resurrected Christ to the Galilean women. Although many believe that Cleopas' companion on the way to Emmaus was female, Luke never reveals this person's identity (24:13-35). Those to whom Jesus appeared in Jerusalem (24:36-49) are not specified. Presumably it is "the eleven and those with them" (24:33). If Luke envisions women as part of this group he does not say so. In his introduction to Acts, Luke recounts that Jesus had "presented himself alive" to the "apostles whom he had chosen" (Acts 1:2-3), an allusion to the twelve men called in Luke 6:13. By contrast, the Markan appendix (16:9); Matthew 28:9-10; and John 20:11-18 all relate that Mary Magdalene (and "the other Mary" in Matthew) was the first to encounter the risen Christ. In the latter two there is no hint that their testimony was doubted.

Luke's redaction of his traditions results in a definite diminishment of the role of the Galilean women at the crucial moments of Jesus' crucifixion, burial, and resurrection.[3] In other accounts, they are the sole witnesses, they are commissioned to tell the others, and they see the risen Christ. In Luke, they are not needed to testify; others have also seen. Should a woman nonetheless at-

---

[3] See Carolyn Osiek, "The Women at the Tomb: What Are They Doing There?" *Ex Auditu* 9 (1993) 97-107. Although many think (based on Josephus' statement in *Ant.* 4.219) that women were not able to serve as public witnesses, the Mishnah shows otherwise. Of course we cannot be sure that laws in the Mishnah were in effect in the first century. But there we find that women's testimony was solicited and accepted in matters relating to the private sphere, e.g., regarding family and domestic issues, and questions pertaining particularly to women. For matters pertaining to the public sphere, witness was needed by men. See Moshe Meiselman, *Jewish Women in Jewish Law* (New York: KTAV, 1978) 73-80.

tempt to proclaim, Luke's presentation encourages his readers to disregard her words as sheer nonsense. A woman reader of this Gospel internalizes the message that if she dares to speak she will never be believed or credited with faithful and true witness. In contrast to the story of the visitation with Elizabeth and Mary, this final episode of Lukan women causes women to doubt the authenticity of their own experience and their ability to interpret God's ways accurately to others. They can remember what they have heard, but it is for the men to interpret and proclaim. This is reinforced in Acts, where there is no mention of the empty tomb in the kerygma. Resurrection faith is based on the appearances to the male disciples, not the testimony of the women.[4]

The tension in the two strands of New Testament tradition over whether Mary Magdalene (so Matthew and John) or Peter (so Paul and Luke) was the first to see the risen Christ is also found in apocryphal gospels. The Gospel of Mary, preserved in a second-century Coptic manuscript from Nag Hammadi and in two fragmentary Greek manuscripts dating to the beginning of the third century, uses a resurrection appearance as a framework for gnostic teaching.[5] In the first part, the risen Christ gives instructions to Peter and then departs. The disciples are left "grieved and wept sore, saying, 'How shall we go to the heathen and preach the Gospel of the Kingdom of the Son of man? If he was not spared at all, how shall we be spared?' " Mary Magdalene then intervenes, comforting them and urging them forward, "Weep not, be not sorrowful, neither be ye undecided, for his grace will be with you all and will protect you. Let us rather praise his great-

---

[4]See Schaberg, "Luke," 289. Maria-Luisa Rigato, " 'Remember'. . . Then They Remembered": Luke 24:6-8," *Luke and Acts,* ed. G. O'Collins and G. Marconi (New York: Paulist Press, 1993) 93–102, emphasizes instead the importance of "remembering" in Luke and Acts and sees the women as vitally included at all the key moments. She misses, however, the mixed message about women that Luke conveys throughout.

[5]The translation that follows is that of Edgar Hennecke, *New Testament Apocrypha,* 2 vols., ed. W. Schneemelcher (Philadelphia: Westminster, 1963) 342. See also Karen L. King, "The Gospel of Mary Magdalene," *Searching the Scriptures: A Feminist Commentary,* vol. 2, ed. E. Schüssler Fiorenza (New York: Crossroad, 1994) 601–634.

ness, for he has made us ready, and made us to be men.''[6] She succeeds in turning "their mind to good, and they began to discuss the words of the [Saviour]."

In the second part Peter asks Mary to tell him and the other disciples about the separate revelations that she received from Christ, "who loved her above all other women." When Mary finishes relating the appearance and teaching she received, Andrew voices his disbelief. Peter joins in with incredulity, "Did he then speak privately with a woman rather than with us, and not openly? Shall we turn about and all hearken unto her? Has he preferred her over against us?" Mary is distressed and weeps that Peter does not believe her. She asks, "Do you believe that I imagined this myself in my heart, or that I would lie about the Savior?" Finally, Levi comes to Mary's defense. He addresses Peter, "Peter, you have ever been of a hasty temper. Now I see how you exercise yourself against the woman like the adversaries. But if the Savior has made her worthy, who then are you, that you reject her? Certainly the Savior knows her surely enough. Therefore did he love her more than us. Let us rather be ashamed, put on perfection as he charged us, and proclaim the Gospel, without requiring any further command or any further law beyond that which the Savior said."[7] And so the work concludes with them following Levi's exhortation to go off and preach.

It is clear from both the canonical and apocryphal traditions that the witness of Mary Magdalene and the other Galilean women is not preserved uniformly. Behind the diverse texts we can detect the struggles of the early Christians over the delineation of leadership in ministry along gender lines.[8] One canonical gospel

---

[6]Karen King, "The Gospel of Mary Magdalene," *Searching the Scriptures: A Feminist Commentary*, vol. 2, ed. E. Schüssler Fiorenza (New York: Crossroad, 1994) 611, translates, "made us true human beings." She interprets this as affirming Mary's full humanity, not as emphasizing her "now-reformed female defectiveness." See also Marvin Meyer, "Making Mary Male: The Categories 'Male' and 'Female' in the Gospel of Thomas," *NTS* 31 (1985) 554–570.

[7]Edgar Hennecke, *New Testament Apocrypha*, 2 vols., ed. W. Schneemelcher (Philadelphia: Westminster, 1963, 1964) 343.

[8]Gerald O'Collins and Daniel Kendall, "Mary Magdalene as Major Witness to Jesus' Resurrection," *TS* 48 (1987) 631–646, see complementarity,

reflects a community that resolved the questions differently from Luke. The women in the Fourth Gospel—the Samaritan woman, Martha and Mary of Bethany, and Mary Magdalene—enter into theological discussion with Jesus (John 4:7-26; 11:21-27; 20:14-17), make profound faith proclamations (John 4:29; 11:27; 20:18), and act as prophets and apostles (John 4:28-30, 39-41; 12:3-7; 20:18) over the objection of Jesus' male disciples (4:27; 12:5). Such stories would only have made sense in a community in which women acted as theologians, teachers, prophets, preachers, and apostles and were approved for doing so.[9] Luke considers such roles inappropriate for Christian women and shapes his stories to reinforce silent, receptive women as model believers.

Today our proclamation of Luke's version of the empty tomb story can serve to ritualize the grief that Christian women have experienced for twenty centuries when their faithful and true witness is dismissed as "nonsense." It can remind us of the deprivation imposed on the whole Christian community when its female members are silenced. It can move believers to choose the better part by taking actions to ensure that the faithful preaching of women be heard and accepted in our day.

---

rather than rivalry, between Mary Magdalene and Peter. However, in a patriarchally structured world, "complementarity" means subordination for women, never equality.

[9] See Sandra Schneiders, "Women in the Fourth Gospel and the Role of Women in the Contemporary Church," *BTB* 12 (1982) 35–45.

Chapter 18

Conclusions:
New Meaning from Ancient Texts

The purpose of this study has been to offer a direction for engaging the liberating potential of the stories of women in the Third Gospel. It is intended not so much as a book *about* the women in Luke as a book *for* women and men who seek to emulate the liberative praxis of Jesus toward transformation of Church and society.

It has employed historical, social, and literary critical methods, through a feminist approach. Recognizing that Luke's narrative casts women disciples in primarily silent, passive roles, it has attempted to unravel the patriarchal underpinnings of the text and ask fresh questions for a Church that struggles for gender equality. When the gender roles assigned according to private and public spheres of Luke's day no longer hold, we are faced with the need for new analyses and new meanings from the text. There are choices to be made. If one chooses to teach and preach Luke's stories uncritically, they continue to reinforce patriarchal role divisions. On the other hand, if one engages in the difficult task of reinterpreting the text from a feminist perspective, reading against Luke's intent, then the stories can be recontextualized to proclaim a message of good news for women and men called equally to share in the same discipleship and mission of Jesus. Each chapter has attempted to point a way that would lead to this second approach of "choosing the better part."

We have seen in the stories of Elizabeth, Mary, and Anna three strong, vocal, prophetic women. They hear God's word and respond by contemplating it, sharing it with others, and proclaiming it faithfully to friends, relatives, and all who will listen. They exhibit a profoundly incarnational theology, knowing God in bodiliness and as one who delights not in suffering, but in new life. They are Spirit-filled and exude blessing. As promising as is the portrait of these first three female characters, it becomes clear that Luke does not consider them the ideal for Christian women. They are like the powerful women prophets of the First Testament. But in this New Age Luke advocates silence and passivity for respectable Christian women.

The majority of Luke's stories with women characters present them as needy and restored by Jesus to wholeness. Beyond being nameless objects of compassion, each has further potential for discipleship. In the story of Simon's mother-in-law are traces of a call story of a woman who responded to Jesus with service that matches his own mission. The silence of the widow of Nain can be seen as a voiceless protest against death that ends with restoration of life. The forgiven woman who showed great love can convert us from misperceptions of women that blind us to the full identity of the Christ. The woman healed of hemorrhages prods us to gutsy faith that overcomes all obstacles to well-being. Her healing and that of Jairus' young daughter bring wholeness and health for all the sons and daughters of Abraham and Sarah. The woman released from eighteen years of bondage to Satan issues a call that now is the time for all who are bent under the weight of oppression to stand erect so that the whole people may glorify God.

There are the stories of the women who minister: Mary Magdalene, Joanna, Susanna, and the others who provided for the mission from their financial resources; Martha, who is reprimanded for her concern about serving; Mary Magdalene, Joanna, Mary the mother of James, and the others who announced the angels' words and were not believed. Each of these presents us with a mixed message. Each preserves traditions about the presence of women in various ministerial endeavors. But Lukan redaction renders the women silent, reinforcing behind-the-scenes, supportive roles for them. These stories confront us with the reliability, giftedness, and resources of women for mission and invite us to reevaluate any restrictions of access to ministry on the basis of gender alone.

The three parables—a woman mixing dough, a woman searching for a lost coin, and a persistent widow—offer feminine images of God that help believers more fully apprehend the divine mystery. The first invites us to see women's ministry like the work of leaven in baking bread: critical for the vitality and rising of the whole. The second underscores the godly action of a woman who diligently seeks out and restores the lost at great personal expense. The third overturns the stereotype of poor helpless widows, exemplifying instead the strength of weakness and the power of persistent pursuit of justice.

Finally, three of the women characters particularly exemplify the action of Jesus, who pours out his life on behalf of others. The woman who loved greatly pours out copious tears and her entire flask of expensive ointment in an act of self-emptying love. The woman searching for a lost coin expends every effort for the sake of the lost. The widow who gave her whole life with her Temple donation likewise exhibits the same profound action. These stories challenge us to see that in women, as well as men, Christ is fully embodied.

Although these positive directions can emerge from the Lukan stories of women, there are serious pitfalls as well. Each can still be used to undergird patriarchally constructed systems that relegate women to silent, passive, supportive roles. Each must continually be reinterpreted and recontextualized for every new age. This is a task particularly incumbent on preachers and teachers. Daily hearing and contemplating the Word anew, with a willingness to be converted and respond with liberative praxis, is the call to each disciple. The price of such an endeavor is great. It costs everything, changes everything, but by it both women and men have everything to gain. The better part awaits our choice.

Bibliography

Abba, R. "Name." *IDB* 3, 500–508.

Agnew, F. H. "The Parables of Divine Compassion." *TBT* 27 (1989) 35–40.

Ahern, Barnabas. "By the Grace of God." *The Way* 17 (1977) 3–11.

Archer, Leonie J. *Her Price Is Beyond Rubies: The Jewish Woman in Graeco-Roman Palestine.* Sheffield: JSOT Press, 1990.

Atwood, Richard. *Mary Magdalene in the New Testament Gospels and Early Tradition.* New York: Peter Lang, 1993.

Aune, David. *The New Testament in its Literary Environment.* Library of Early Christianity. Philadelphia: Westminster, 1987.

Bailey, Kenneth. *Finding the Lost: Cultural Keys to Luke 15.* Concordia Scholarship Today. St. Louis: Concordia, 1992.

_____. *Poet and Peasant and Through Peasant Eyes.* 2 vols. in 1. Grand Rapids: Eerdmans, 1976, 1980.

_____. "Psalm 23 and Luke 15: A Vision Expanded." *IBS* 12 (1990) 54–71.

Balsdon, J.P.V.D. *Roman Women, Their History and Habits.* New York: Barnes & Noble, 1983.

Barr, James. " '*Abba* and the Familiarity of Jesus' Speech." *Theology* 91 (1988) 173–179.

_____. " '*Abba* Isn't Daddy." *JTS* n.s. 39 (1988) 28–47.

Bauer, W., W. F. Arndt, F. W. Gingrich, and F. W. Danker. *A Greek Lexicon of the New Testament and Other Early Christian Literature.* 2d ed. Chicago/London: University of Chicago Press, 1979.

Bearsley, P. "Mary the Perfect Disciple: A Paradigm for Mariology." *TS* 41 (1980) 461–504.

Benjamin, Don C. "The Persistent Widow." *TBT* 28 (1990) 213–219.

Beydon, F. "A temps nouveau, nouvelles questions. Luc 10,38-42." *FoiVie* 88 (1989) 25–32.

Bird, Phyllis. "Images of Women in the Old Testament." *Religion and Sexism,* edited by R. R. Ruether, 62–63. New York: Simon and Schuster, 1974.

Black, M. *An Aramaic Approach to the Gospels and Acts.* 3d ed. Oxford: Clarendon, 1967.

Bock, D. *Proclamation from Prophecy and Pattern: Lucan Old Testament Christology.* Sheffield: JSOT, 1987.

Bouwman, G. "La pécheresse hospitalière (Lc., VII,36-50)." *ETL* 45 (1969) 172–179.

Brenner, Athalya. "Female Social Behavior: Two Descriptive Patterns Within the 'Birth of the Hero' Paradigm." *VT* 36 (1986) 257–273.

Brodie, Thomas L. "Luke 7:36-50 as an Internalization of 2 Kings 4:1-37: A Study in Luke's Use of Rhetorical Imitation." *Bib* 64 (1989) 457–485.

————. "Not Q but Elijah: The Saving of the Centurion's Servant (Luke 7:1-10) as an Internalization of the Saving of the Widow and her Child (1 Kgs 17:1-16)." *IBS* 14 (1992) 54–71.

————. "Towards Unravelling Luke's Use of the Old Testament: Luke 7:11-17 as an *Imitatio* of 1 Kings 17:17-24." *NTS* 32 (1986) 247–267.

Brooke, George J. "A Long-Lost Song of Miriam." *BAR* 20 (1994) 62–65.

Brooten, Bernadette. "Jewish Women's History in the Roman Period: A Task for Christian Theology." *HTR* 79 (1986) 22–30.

————. *Women Leaders in the Ancient Synagogue: Inscriptional Evidence and Background Issues.* Brown Judaic Studies 36. Chico, Calif.: Scholars Press, 1982.

Brown, Raymond E. "The Annunciation to Mary, the Visitation, and the Magnificat." *Worship* 62 (1988) 249–259.

————. "The Annunciation to Zechariah, the Birth of the Baptist, and the Benedictus (Luke 1:5-25, 57-80)." *Worship* 62 (1988) 482–496.

————. *The Birth of the Messiah.* Garden City, N.Y.: Doubleday, 1977.

————. *The Gospel According to John I–XII.* AB 29. Garden City, N.Y.: Doubleday, 1966.

————. "Gospel Infancy Narrative Research From 1976 to 1986: Part I (Matthew)." *CBQ* 48 (1986) 468–483.

_____. "Gospel Infancy Narrative Research From 1976 to 1986: Part II (Luke)." *CBQ* 48 (1986) 660–680.

_____. "Jesus and Elisha." *Perspective* 12 (1971) 84–104.

_____. "The Presentation of Jesus (Luke 2:22-40)." *Worship* 51 (1977) 2–11.

Brown, R. E., et al., eds. *Mary in the New Testament*. Philadelphia: Fortress Press, 1978.

Buckley, F. J. "Healing and Reconciliation in the Gospel According to Luke." *Emmanuel* 96 (1990) 74–80.

Burns, Rita J. *Has the Lord Indeed Spoken Only Through Moses? A Study of the Biblical Portrait of Miriam*. SBLDS 84. Atlanta: Scholars Press, 1987.

Burrus, Virginia. *Chastity as Autonomy: Women in the Stories of Apocryphal Acts*. Lewiston, N.Y.: Edwin Mellen Press, 1987.

Buth, R. "What Is the Priest Doing? Common Sense and Culture." *Jerusalem Perspective* 4 (1991) 12–13.

Cadbury, H. J. *The Style and Literary Method of Luke*. HTS 6/1. Cambridge, Mass.: Harvard University Press, 1920.

Cantarella, Eva. *Pandora's Daughters: The Role and Status of Women in Greek and Roman Antiquity*. Baltimore: Johns Hopkins University Press, 1987.

Carroll, J. T. "Luke's Portrayal of the Pharisees." *CBQ* 50 (1988) 604–621.

Chathanatt, J. "The Annunciation of Birth and the Birth of the Messiah." *CBQ* 47 (1985) 656–663.

Chestnutt, Randall D. "Revelatory Experiences Attributed to Biblical Women in Early Jewish Literature." *"Women Like This": New Perspectives on Jewish Women in the Greco-Roman World,* edited by Amy-Jill Levine, 107–125. SBL Early Judaism and Its Literature 1. Atlanta: Scholars Press, 1991.

Chittister, Joan. "Yesterday's Dangerous Vision: Christian Feminism in the Catholic Church." *Sojourners* (July 1987) 18–21.

Co, Maria Anicia. "The Major Summaries in Acts, Acts 2,42-47; 4,32-35; 5,12-16: Linguistic and Literary Relationships." *ETL* 68 (1992) 49–85.

Coakley, J. "The Anointing at Bethany and the Priority of John." *JBL* 107 (1988) 241–256.

Coleridge, Mark. *The Birth of the Lukan Narrative: Narrative as Christology in Luke 1-2*. JSNTSup 88. Sheffield: JSOT, 1993.

Collins, Adela Y., ed. *Feminist Perspectives on Biblical Scholarship*. Chico, Calif.: Scholars Press, 1985.

Collins, John N. *DIAKONIA. Re-interpreting the Ancient Sources*. New York: Oxford University Press, 1990.

Connolly, R. H., ed. *Didascalia Apostolorum*. Oxford: Clarendon, 1929.

Conrad, E. W. "The Annunciation of Birth and the Birth of the Messiah." *CBQ* 47 (1985) 656–663.

Conzelmann, Hans. *The Theology of St. Luke*. Philadelphia: Fortress Press, 1961.

Corley, Kathleen. *Private Women: Public Meals*. Peabody, Mass.: Hendrickson, 1993.

_____. "Were the Women Around Jesus Really Prostitutes? Women in the Context of Greco-Roman Meals." *SBL Seminar Papers*. Atlanta: Scholars Press, 1989. Pp. 487–521.

Cotter, W. J. "The Parables of the Mustard Seed and the Leaven: Their Function in the Earliest Stratum of Q." *Toronto Journal of Theology* 8 (1992) 38–51.

Craig, K. M., and M. A. Kristjansson. "Women Reading as Men/Women Reading as Women: A Structural Analysis for the Historical Project." *Semeia* 51 (1990) 119–136.

Cranfield, C.E.B. "The Parable of the Unjust Judge and the Eschatology of Luke-Acts." *SJT* 16 (1963) 297–301.

Culpepper, R. Alan. "Seeing the Kingdom of God: The Metaphor of Sight in the Gospel of Luke." *CurTM* 21 (1994) 434–443.

D'Angelo, Mary Rose. "*ABBA* and 'Father': Imperial Theology and the Jesus Traditions." *JBL* 111/4 (1992) 611–630.

_____. "Women in Luke-Acts: A Redactional View." *JBL* 109 (1990) 441–461.

_____. "Women Partners in the NT." *JFSR* 6 (1990) 65–86.

Darr, John A. *On Character Building: The Reader and the Rhetoric of Characterization in Luke-Acts*. Literary Currents in Biblical Interpretation. Louisville: Westminster/John Knox, 1992.

Daube, D. "Shame Culture in Luke." *Paul and Paulinism: Essays in Honour of C. K. Barrett,* edited by M. D. Hooker and S. G. Wilson, 355–372. London: SPCK, 1982.

Davidson, J. A. "Things to Be Understood and Things to Be Done." *ExpTim* 94 (1983) 306–307.

Davies, S. *The Revolt of the Widows: The Social World of the Apocryphal Acts*. Carbondale: Southern Illinois University Press, 1980.

Dawsey, James M. *The Literary Function of Point of View in Controlling Confusion and Irony in the Gospel of Luke*. Ann Arbor: University Microfilms, 1984.

_____. *The Lukan Voice: Confusion and Irony in the Gospel of Luke*. Macon: Mercer University Press, 1986.

_____. "What's in a Name? Characterization in Luke." *BTB* 16 (1986) 143–147.

Delobel, P. "Encore la pécheresse. Quelques réflexions critiques." *ETL* 45 (1969) 180–183.

_____. "L'onction par la pécheresse. La composition littéraire de Lc.: VII, 36-50." *ETL* 42 (1966) 415–475.

Derrett, J.D.M. "Fresh Light on the Lost Sheep and the Lost Coin." *NTS* 26 (1979) 41–42.

_____. "Law in the New Testament: The Parable of the Unjust Judge." *NTS* 18 (1972) 178–191.

_____. "Positive Perspectives on Two Lucan Miracles." *DRev* 104 (1986) 272–287.

Dodd, C. H. *The Parables of the Kingdom*. Rev. ed. New York: Charles Scribner's Sons, 1961.

Donahue, John R. *The Gospel in Parable*. Philadelphia: Fortress Press, 1988.

_____. "Tax Collectors and Sinners: An Attempt at Identification." *CBQ* 33 (1971) 39–61.

Donnelly, Doris, ed. *Mary, Woman of Nazareth: Biblical and Theological Perspectives*. New York: Paulist Press, 1989.

Drury, John. *Tradition and Design in Luke's Gospel: A Study of Early Christian Historiography*. London: Darton, Longman, and Todd, 1976.

Durber, Susan. "The Female Reader of the Parables of the Lost." *JSNT* 45 (1992) 59–78.

Edwards, Richard. *A Theology of Q. Eschatology, Prophecy and Wisdom*. Philadelphia: Fortress Press, 1976.

Elliott, J. K. "Anna's Age (Luke 2:36-37)." *NovT* 30 (1988) 100–102.

_____. "Household and Meals versus the Temple Purity System: Patterns of Replication in Luke-Acts." *BTB* 21 (1991) 102–108.

_____. "The Anointing of Jesus." *ExpTim* 85 (1974) 105.

Ellis, E. E. "Paul and His Co-Workers." *NTS* 17 (1970/71) 437–452.

Evans, C. F. "The Central Section of St. Luke's Gospel." *Studies in the Gospels,* edited by D. E. Nineham, 37–53. London: Blackwell, 1955.

Farmer, William R. *The Synoptic Problem: A Critical Analysis.* New York: Macmillan, 1964.

Fee, Gordon D. " 'One Thing is Needful'? Luke 10:42." *New Testament Text Criticism: Its Significance for Exegesis: Essays in Honour of Bruce M. Metzger,* edited by E. J. Epp and G. D. Fee, 61–75. Oxford: Clarendon, 1981.

Fensham, F. C. "Widow, Orphan, and the Poor in Ancient Literature." *JNES* 21 (1962) 129–139.

Ferry, B.-M. "La pécheresse pardonnée (Lc 7,36-50). Pourquoi verse-t-elle des pleurs?" *EspVie* 99 (1989) 174–176.

Fetterley, Judith. *The Resisting Reader: A Feminist Approach to American Fiction.* Bloomington & London: Indiana University Press, 1978.

Fitzmyer, Joseph. *The Gospel According to Luke.* AB 28, 28A. Garden City, N.Y.: Doubleday, 1981, 1985.

_____. *Luke the Theologian: Aspects of His Teaching.* Mahwah, N.J.: Paulist Press, 1989.

_____. "Pauline Theology." *New Jerome Biblical Commentary.* Ed. Raymond E. Brown, Joseph A. Fitzmyer, and Roland E. Murphy. Englewood Cliffs, N.J.: Prentice Hall, 1990. Article 82, paragraphs 101–107, pp. 1406–1407.

_____. "The Priority of Mark and the Q Source." *To Advance the Gospel: New Testament Studies.* New York: Crossroad, 1981. Pp. 3–40.

Flanagan, N. M. "The Position of Women in the Writings of St. Luke." *Mareanum* 40 (1978) 288–304.

Flynn, Elizabeth A., and Patrocinio P. Schweickart, eds. *Gender and Reading: Essays on Readers, Texts, and Contexts.* Baltimore and London: Johns Hopkins University Press, 1986.

Ford, J. M. "Zealotism and the Lukan Infancy Narratives." *NovT* 18 (1976) 280–292.

Freed, E. D. "The Parable of the Judge and the Widow (Luke 18.1-8)." *NTS* 33 (1987) 38–60.

Funk, Robert W. "Beyond Criticism in Quest of Literacy: The Parable of the Leaven." *Int* 25 (1971) 149–170.

Galligan, J. S. "The Tension Between Poverty and Possessions in the Gospel of Luke." *Sp Today* 37 (1985) 4–12.

Gardner, Jane, and Thomas Wiedemann. *The Roman Household: A Sourcebook.* New York: Routledge, 1991.

Gardner, Jane. *Women in Roman Law and Society*. Bloomington, Ind.: Indiana University Press, 1986.

Gebara, I., and M. C. Bingemer. *Mary, Mother of God, Mother of the Poor*. Maryknoll, N.Y.: Orbis, 1989.

Gillman, John. *Possessions and the Life of Faith: A Reading of Luke-Acts*. Zacchaeus Studies: New Testament Series. Collegeville, Minn.: The Liturgical Press, 1991.

Goulder, M. D. *Luke: A New Paradigm*. JSNTSup 20. Sheffield: JSOT, 1989.

Grassi, Joseph. *The Hidden Heroes of the Gospels: Female Counter-parts of Jesus*. Collegeville, Minn.: The Liturgical Press, 1989.

Grassi, Carolyn M., and Joseph A. Grassi. *Mary Magdalene and the Women in Jesus's Life*. Kansas City, Mo.: Sheed and Ward, 1986.

Green, Joel B. "Jesus and a Daughter of Abraham (Luke 13:10-27): Test Case for a Lucan Perspective on Jesus' Miracles." *CBQ* 51 (1989) 643–654.

_____. "The Social Status of Mary in Luke 1,5–2,52: A Plea for Methodological Integration." *Bib* 73 (1992) 457–472.

Grundmann, W. *Das Evangelium nach Lukas,* 2d ed., THKNT. Berlin: Evangelische Verlagsanstalt, 1961.

Haas, Peter, ed. *Recovering the Role of Women: Power and Authority in Rabbinic Jewish Society*. Atlanta: Scholars Press, 1992.

Haenchen, Ernst. *The Acts of the Apostles*. Philadelphia: Westminster, 1971.

Hamm, D. "The Freeing of the Bent Woman and the Restoration of Israel: Luke 13:10-17 as Narrative Theology." *JSNT* 31 (1987) 23–44.

_____. "Sight to the Blind: Vision as Metaphor in Luke." *Bib* 67 (1986) 457–477.

_____. "What the Samaritan Leper Sees: The Narrative Christology of Luke 17:11-19." *CBQ* 56 (1994) 273–287.

Harrington, Daniel J. *Interpreting the New Testament: A Practical Guide*. NTM 1. Wilmington: Glazier, 1979.

Haskins, Susan. *Mary Magdalen: Myth and Metaphor*. London: Harper Collins, 1993.

Heffner, Blake R. "Meister Eckhart and a Millenium with Mary and Martha." *LQ* 5 (1991) 171–185.

Hengel, Martin. "Maria Magdalena und die Frauen als Zeugen." *Abraham unser Vater,* edited by O. Betz, M. Hengel, and P. Schmid, 243–256. Leiden: Brill, 1963.

Hennecke, Edgar. *New Testament Apocrypha.* 2 vols. Ed. W. Schnee-melcher. Philadelphia: Westminster, 1963, 1964.

Hennessy, L. R. "*Diakonia* and *Diakonoi*: Early Christian Perspectives on Service and the Servants." *NTR* 4 (1991) 5–23.

Heschel, Susannah, ed. *On Being A Jewish Feminist: A Reader.* New York: Schocken Books, 1983.

Hickling, C.J.A. "A Tract on Jesus and the Pharisees? A Conjecture on the Redaction of Luke 15 and 16." *HeyJ* 16 (1975) 253–265.

Hofius, O. "Fusswaschung als Erweis der Liebe. Sprachliche und sachliche Anmerkungen zu Lk 7,44b." *ZNW* 81 (1990) 171–177.

Holst, R. "The One Anointing of Jesus: Another Application of the Form Critical Method." *JBL* 95 (1976) 435–446.

Horsley, Richard. *The Liberation of Christmas: The Infancy Narratives in Social Context.* New York: Crossroad, 1989.

Horsley, Richard, and John S. Hanson. *Bandits, Prophets, and Messiahs: Popular Movements at the Time of Jesus.* Minneapolis: Winston, 1985.

House, H. W. "Should a Woman Prophesy or Preach before Men?" *BibSac* 145 (1988) 141–161.

Irigoin, J. "La composition rythmique des cantiques de Luc." *RB* 98 (1991) 5–50.

Irvin, Dorothy. "The Ministry of Women in the Early Church: The Archaeological Evidence." *Duke Divinity School Review* 45 (1980) 76–86.

Janzen, J. Gerald. "Song of Moses, Song of Miriam: Who Is Seconding Whom?" *CBQ* 54 (1992) 211–220.

Jegen, Carol Frances. *Mary According to Women.* Kansas City, Mo.: Sheed & Ward, 1985.

Jensen, Richard A. "Telling Luke's Story: A Narrative Approach to Preaching on the Third Gospel." *CurTM* 21 (1994) 444–451.

Jeremias, Joachim. *Jerusalem in the Time of Jesus.* Philadelphia: Fortress Press, 1969.

_____. *Rediscovering the Parables.* New York: Charles Scribner's Sons, 1966.

Jervell, J. "The Daughters of Abraham: Women in Acts." *The Unknown Paul: Essays on Luke-Acts and Early Christian History.* Minneapolis: Augsburg, 1984. Pp. 146–157.

Johnsen, Carsten and Sylvi. *The Writing in the Sand: The Part of the Story That You Were Never Told about Mary Magdalene.* New York: Vantage, 1984.

Johnson, Elizabeth. "Feminist Hermeneutics." *Chicago Studies* 27 (1988) 123–135.

_____. "Jesus the Wisdom of God: A Biblical Basis for Non-Androcentric Christology." *ETL* 61 (1985) 261–294.

_____. *She Who Is: The Mystery of God in Feminist Theological Discourse.* New York: Crossroad, 1992.

Johnson, Luke T. *The Gospel of Luke.* Sacra Pagina 3. Collegeville, Minn.: The Liturgical Press, 1991.

_____. *The Literary Function of Possessions in Luke-Acts.* SBLDS 39. Missoula: Scholars Press, 1977.

_____. "On Finding the Lukan Community: A Cautious Cautionary Essay." *SBL Seminar 1979 Papers.* Vol. 1. 87–100. Missoula: Scholars Press, 1979.

Karris, R. "Luke 23:47 and the Lucan View of Jesus' Death." *JBL* 105 (1986) 65–74.

_____. "Missionary Communities: A New Paradigm for the Study of Luke-Acts." *CBQ* 41 (1979) 80–97.

_____. "Women and Discipleship in Luke." *CBQ* 56 (1994) 1–20.

Keegan, Terrence. *Interpreting the Bible: A Popular Introduction to Biblical Hermeneutics.* New York: Paulist Press, 1985.

Kiehl, E. H. " 'The Lost' Parables in Luke's Gospel Account." *ConcJ* 18 (1992) 244–258.

Kilgallen, J. "John the Baptist, the Sinful Woman, and the Pharisee." *JBL* 104 (1985) 675–679.

_____. "A Proposal for Interpreting Luke 7,36-50." *Bib* 72 (1991) 305–330.

_____. "A Suggestion regarding *gar* in Luke 10,42." *Bib* 73 (1992) 255–258.

Kilpatrick, G. D. "Luke 2,4-5 and Leviticus 25,10." *ZNW* 80 (1989) 264–265.

King, Karen L. "The Gospel of Mary Magdalene." *Searching the Scriptures: A Feminist Commentary.* Vol. 2. 601–634. Ed. E. Schüssler Fiorenza. New York: Crossroad, 1994.

Kingsbury, Jack Dean. *Conflict in Luke: Jesus, Authorities, Disciples.* Minneapolis: Fortress Press, 1991.

Kingston, M. J. "Martha Gives the 'Right' Answer." *ExpTim* 96 (1985) 181–182.

Kloppenborg, John. *The Formation of Q: Trajectories in Ancient Wisdom Collections.* Studies in Antiquity and Christianity. Philadelphia: Fortress Press, 1987.

Knight, David M. *Mary in an Adult Church: Beyond Devotion to Response*. Memphis: His Way Communications, 1988.

Koenig, John. *New Testament Hospitality: Partnership with Strangers as Promise and Mission*. Overtures to Biblical Theology. Philadelphia: Fortress Press, 1989.

Kopas, Jane. "Woman in Luke's Gospel." *ThT* 43 (1986) 192–202.

Kraemer, Ross S. "Women and the Religions of the Greco-Roman World." *RSRev* 9 (1983) 127–139.

_____. "Women's Authorship of Jewish and Christian Literature in the Greco-Roman Period." *"Women Like This": New Perspectives on Jewish Women in the Greco-Roman World*. Ed. Amy-Jill Levine. SBL Early Judaism and Its Literature 1. 221–242. Atlanta: Scholars Press, 1991.

Kurz, William S. *Reading Luke-Acts: Dynamics of Biblical Narrative*. Louisville: Westminster/John Knox, 1993.

Lacan, M.-F. "Une présence dont je puis jouir." *LumVie* 39 (1990) 63–80.

Lacey, W. K. *The Family in Classical Greece*. Ithaca: Cornell University Press, 1968.

LaFon, G. "Le repas chez Simon." *Études* 377 (1992) 651–660.

LaHurd, Carol Schersten. "Rediscovering the Lost Women in Luke 15." *BTB* 24 (1994) 66–76.

LaVerdiere, E. *Luke*. NTMS 5. Wilmington: Glazier, 1980.

_____. "The One Thing Required." *Emmanuel* (1983) 398–403.

_____. "The Widow's Mite." *Emmanuel* 92 (1986) 316–321, 341.

Lampe, G.W.H. "The Lucan Portrait of Christ." *NTS* 2 (1955/56) 160–175.

Lefkowitz, Mary. "Did Ancient Women Write Novels?" *"Women Like This": New Perspectives on Jewish Women in the Greco-Roman World*. 208–211. Atlanta: Scholars Press, 1991.

Lefkowitz, Mary R., and Maureen B. Fant. *Women's Life in Greece and Rome: A source book in translation*. Baltimore: Johns Hopkins University Press, 1982.

Legault, A. "An Application of the Form-Critique Method to the Anointings in Galilee (Lk. 7.36-50) and Bethany (Mt. 26.6-13; Mk. 4.3-9; John 12.1-8)." *CBQ* 16 (1954) 131–145.

Levine, Amy-Jill, ed. *"Women Like This": New Perspectives on Jewish Women in the Greco-Roman World*. Atlanta: Scholars Press, 1991.

Loades, Ann. *Searching for Lost Coins: Explorations in Christianity and Feminism*. Allison Park, Pa.: Pickwick, 1987.

Lutz, Cora. "Musonius Rufus, 'The Roman Socrates.' " *Yale Classical Studies* 10 (1947) 38–43.

MacDonald, Dennis. "Virgins, Widows, and Paul in Second-Century Asia Minor." *SBL 1979 Seminar Papers,* edited by Paul Achtemeier. 169–184. Missoula: Scholars Press, 1979.

MacMullen, Ramsay. *Changes in the Roman Empire: Essays in the Ordinary.* Princeton, N.J.: Princeton University Press, 1990.

Mainville, Odette. *L'esprit dans l'oeuvre de luc.* Héritage et Projet 45. Quebec: Fides, 1991.

Malbon, Elizabeth Struthers. "The Poor Widow in Mark and Her Poor Rich Readers." *CBQ* 53 (1991) 589–604.

Malina, Bruce J. *The New Testament World: Insights from Cultural Anthropology.* Rev. ed. Louisville: Westminster/John Knox, 1993.

Malina, Bruce, and Richard Rohrbaugh. *Social Science Commentary on the Synoptic Gospels.* Minneapolis: Fortress Press, 1992.

Maloney, Linda, and Elizabeth Smith. "The Year of Luke: A Feminist Perspective." *CurTM* 21 (1994) 415–423.

Mangan, C. "Mary in Scripture." *MillStud* 22 (1988) 41–44.

Marshall, I. Howard. *Commentary on Luke.* NIGTC. Grand Rapids: Eerdmans, 1978.

McCown, C. C. "Luke's Translation of Semitic into Hellenistic Custom." *JBL* 58 (1939) 213–220.

McFague, Sallie. *Models of God: Theology for an Ecological, Nuclear Age.* Philadelphia: Fortress Press, 1987.

McKenzie, J. L. *Dictionary of the Bible.* New York: MacMillan, 1965.

McNabb, V. *St. Mary Magdalen.* London: Burns Oates & Washbourne, 1942.

Meier, John P. "On the Veiling of Hermeneutics (1 Cor 11:2-16)." *CBQ* 40 (1978) 212–226.

Meiselman, Moshe. *Jewish Woman in Jewish Law.* New York: KTAV, 1978.

Menken, M.J.J. "The Position of *splagchnisesthai* and *splagchna* in the Gospel of Luke." *NovT* 30 (1988) 107–114.

Metzger, Bruce. *A Textual Commentary on the Greek New Testament.* 3d ed. London, New York: United Bible Societies, 1971.

Meyer, Marvin. "Making Mary Male: The Categories 'Male' and 'Female' in the Gospel of Thomas." *NTS* 31 (1985) 554–570.

Moessner, David P. *Lord of the Banquet: The Literary and Theological Significance of the Lukan Travel Narrative.* Minneapolis: Fortress Press, 1989.

Moloney, Frank J. *Woman First Among the Faithful.* Notre Dame: Ave Maria, 1986.

Moltmann-Wendel, Elisabeth. *The Women Around Jesus.* New York: Crossroad, 1987.

Murphy, Cullen. "Women and the Bible." *The Atlantic Monthly* (August 1993) 39–64.

Murphy-O'Connor, Jerome. "Sex and Logic in 1 Corinthians 11:2-16." *CBQ* 42 (1980) 482–500.

_____. "1 Cor 11:2-16 Once Again." *CBQ* 50 (1988) 265–274.

Mussies, G. "Vernoemen in de antieke wereld. De historische achtergrond van Luk. 1,59-63." *NedTheolTijd* 42 (1988) 114–125.

Neale, David A. *None But the Sinners: Religious Categories in the Gospel of Luke.* JSNTSup 58. Sheffield: JSOT, 1991.

Nelson, R. D. "David: A Model for Mary in Luke?" *BTB* 18 (1988) 138–142.

Neusner, Jacob. *Judaism in the Beginning of Christianity.* Philadelphia: Fortress Press, 1984.

Newsom, C. A. and S. H. Ringe, eds. *The Women's Bible Commentary.* Louisville: Westminster/John Knox, 1992.

Neyrey, Jerome H. "Jesus' Address to the Women of Jerusalem (Luke 23:27-31)—A Prophetic Judgment Oracle." *NTS* 29 (1983) 74–86.

_____, ed. *The Social World of Luke-Acts: Models for Interpretation.* Peabody, Mass.: Hendrickson, 1991.

O'Collins, G., and D. Kendall, "Mary Magdalene as Major Witness to Jesus' Resurrection." *TS* 48 (1987) 631–646.

O'Collins, G., and G. Marconi, eds. *Luke and Acts.* New York: Paulist Press, 1991.

O'Driscoll, Mary. "Dominican Spirituality: Contemplative Involvement in the World." 118–138. *Justice and Truth Shall Meet* (Sinsinawa, Wis.: Parable, 1984).

O'Leary, A. "The Role of Possessions in the Journey Narrative of Luke 9:51–19:27." *Mill Stud* 28 (1991) 41–60.

O'Toole, Robert F. "The Parallels Between Jesus and Moses." *BTB* 20 (1990) 22–29.

_____. "Some Exegetical Reflections on Luke 13,10-17," *Bib* 73 (1992) 84–107.

_____. *The Unity of Luke's Theology: An Analysis of Luke-Acts.* Good News Studies 9. Wilmington: Glazier, 1984.

Oakman, Douglas E. *Jesus and the Economic Questions of His Day.* Studies in the Bible and Early Christianity 8. Lewiston/Queenston: Edwin Mellen, 1986.

Osiek, C. *Beyond Anger: On Being A Feminist in the Church.* New York: Paulist Press, 1986.

_____. "The Feminist and the Bible: Hermeneutical Alternatives." *Feminist Perspectives on Biblical Scholarship.* Chico, Calif.: Scholars Press, 1985.

_____. "The Social Sciences and the Second Testament: Problems and Challenges." *BTB* 22 (1992) 88–95.

_____. *What Are They Saying About the Social Setting of the New Testament?* 2d ed. New York: Paulist Press, 1992.

_____. "Widow as Altar: Rise and Fall of a Symbol." *Second Century* 3 (1983) 159–169.

_____. "The Women at the Tomb: What Are They Doing There?" *Ex Auditu* 9 (1993) 97–107.

Padgett, A. "Paul on Women in the Church: The Contradictions of Coiffure in 1 Corinthians 11.2-16." *JSNT* 20 (1984) 69–86.

Parsons, Mikeal C., and Richard I. Pervo. *Rethinking the Unity of Luke and Acts.* Minneapolis: Fortress Press, 1993.

Parvey, Constance. "The Theology and Leadership of Women in the New Testament." *Religion and Sexism,* edited by Rosemary R. Ruether. 139–146. New York: Simon & Schuster, 1974.

Pervo, Richard. *Profit with Delight: The Literary Genre of the Acts of the Apostles.* Philadelphia: Fortress Press, 1987.

_____. "Social and Religious Aspects of the 'Western' Text." *The Living Text: Essays in Honor of Ernest W. Saunders,* edited by Dennis Groh and Robert Jewett. 229–241. New York: University Press of America, 1985.

Pilch, John J. "Sickness and Healing in Luke-Acts." *TBT* 27 (1989) 21–28.

_____. "Sickness and Healing in Luke-Acts." *The Social World of Luke-Acts,* edited by J. Neyrey. 181–209. Peabody, Mass.: Hendrickson, 1991.

Plaskow, Judith. "Blaming the Jews for the Birth of Patriarchy." *Nice Jewish Girls,* edited by E. Torton Beck. 250–254. Watertown, Mass.: Persephone, 1982.

_____. "Christian Feminism and Anti-Judaism." *Crosscurrents* 28 (1978) 306–309.

_____. "Feminist Anti-Judaism and the Christian God." *JFSR* 7 (1991) 95–134.

_____. *Standing Again at Sinai: Judaism from a Feminist Perspective.* San Francisco: Harper and Row, 1990.

Plevnik, J. "The Eyewitnesses of the Risen Jesus in Luke 24." *CBQ* 49 (1987) 90–103.

Plummer, Alfred. *The Gospel According to S. Luke.* 5th ed. ICC. Edinburgh: T. & T. Clark, 1981.

Pomeroy, Sarah B. *Goddesses, Whores, Wives and Slaves: Women in Classical Antiquity.* New York: Dorset, 1975.

Powell, Mark A. *What is Narrative Criticism?* Guides to Biblical Scholarship. Philadelphia: Fortress Press, 1990.

Powell, Mark A. *What are they Saying about Luke?* New York/Mahwah: Paulist Press, 1989.

Praeder, Susan. "Acts 17:1–28:16: Sea Voyages in Ancient Literature and the Theology of Luke-Acts." *CBQ* 46 (1984) 683–706.

————. *The Word in Women's Worlds: Four Parables.* Zacchaeus Studies: New Testament. Wilmington: Glazier, 1988.

Quesnell, Quentin. "The Women at Luke's Supper." *Political Issues in Luke-Acts,* edited by R. J. Cassidy and P. J. Scharper. Maryknoll: Orbis, 1983.

Ravens, D.A.S. "The Setting of Luke's Account of the Anointing: Luke 7.2–8.3." *NTS* 34 (1988) 282–292.

Reid, Barbara E. "The Ethics Luke." *TBT* 31 (1993) 283–287.

————. "Luke: The Gospel for Women?" *CurTM* 21 (1994) 405–414.

————. *The Transfiguration: A Source- and Redaction-Critical Study of Luke 9:28-36.* Cahiers de la Revue Biblique 32. Paris: Gabalda, 1993.

Reinhartz, A. "From Narrative to History: The Resurrection of Mary and Martha." *"Women Like This": New Perspectives on Jewish Women in the Greco-Roman World,* edited by Amy-Jill Levine. SBL Early Judaism and Its Literature 1. 161–184. Atlanta: Scholars, 1991.

Rengstorf, K. *"hamartōlos."* *TDNT* 1 (1964) 325–328.

Resseguie, J. L. "Luke 7:36-50." *Int* 46 (1992) 285–290.

Richard, Earl, ed. *New Views on Luke and Acts.* Collegeville, Minn.: The Liturgical Press, 1990.

Rigato, Maria-Luisa. " 'Remember' . . . Then They Remembered: Luke 24:6-8." *Luke and Acts,* edited by G. O'Collins and G. Marconi. 93–102. New York: Paulist Press, 1993.

Robbins, V. K. "By Land and Sea: The We-Passages and Ancient Sea Voyages." *Perspectives on Luke-Acts,* edited by C. H. Talbert. 215–242. Danville, Va.: Association of Baptist Professors of Religion, 1978.

_____. "The Woman Who Touched Jesus' Garment: Socio-Rhetorical Analysis of the Synoptic Accounts." *NTS* 33 (1987) 502–515.

Ruether, Rosemary Radford. *Mary—The Feminine Face of the Church*. Philadelphia: Westminster, 1977.

_____. *New Woman New Earth: Sexist Ideologies & Human Liberation*. New York: Crossroad, 1975.

_____. *Sexism and God-Talk: Toward A Feminist Theology*. Boston: Beacon, 1983.

Russell, L. M., ed. *Feminist Interpretation of the Bible*. Philadelphia: Westminster, 1985.

_____. *Human Liberation in a Feminist Perspective*. Philadelphia: Fortress Press, 1974.

Ryan, R. "The Women from Galilee and Discipleship in Luke." *BTB* 15 (1985) 56–59.

Sanders, E. P. *Jesus and Judaism*. Philadelphia: Fortress Press, 1985.

Schaberg, Jane. "How Mary Magdalene Became a Whore." *BibRev* 8 (1992) 30–37, 51–52.

_____. "Luke" *Women's Bible Commentary*, edited by Carol A. Newsom and Sharon H. Ringe. 275–292. Louisville: Westminster/John Knox, 1992.

_____. *The Illegitimacy of Jesus*. New York: Crossroad, 1990.

_____. "Thinking Back Through the Magdalene." *Continuum* 2 (1991) 71–90.

Schaps, David. *Economic Rights of Women in Ancient Greece*. Edinburgh: Univ. Library, 1979.

Schillebeeckx, Edward. *Ministry: Leadership in the Community of Jesus Christ*. New York: Crossroad, 1981.

_____. *The Church With a Human Face: A New Expanded Theology of Ministry*. New York: Crossroad, 1987.

Schillebeeckx, Edward, and Catharina Halkes. *Mary: Yesterday, Today, Tomorrow*. New York: Crossroad, 1993.

Schneiders, Sandra. "God is More Than Two Men and a Bird." *U.S. Catholic* (May 1990) 20–27.

_____. *The Revelatory Text: Interpreting the New Testament as Sacred Scripture*. San Francisco: HarperSanFrancisco, 1991.

_____. *Women and the Word*. New York: Paulist Press, 1986.

Schrock, J. H. " 'I Am Among You as One Who Serves': Jesus and Food in Luke's Gospel." *Daughters of Sarah* 19 (1993) 20–23.

Schüssler Fiorenza, Elisabeth. *Bread Not Stone: The Challenge of Feminist Biblical Interpretation*. Boston: Beacon, 1984.

————. *But She Said: Feminist Practices of Biblical Interpretation.* Boston: Beacon, 1992.

————. "A Feminist Critical Interpretation for Liberation: Martha and Mary: Lk. 10:38-42." *Rel & Int Life* 3 (1986) 21–36.

————. *In Memory of Her: A Feminist Theological Reconstruction of Christian Origins.* New York: Crossroad, 1983.

————. "Lk 13:10-17: Interpretation for liberation and transformation." *TD* 36 (1989) 303–319.

————, ed. *Searching the Scriptures.* 2 vols. New York: Crossroad, 1993, 1994.

————. " 'Waiting at Table': A Critical Feminist Theological Reflection on Diakonia." *Concilium 198. Diakonia: Church for the Others,* edited by N. Greinacher and N. Mette. 84–94. Edinburgh: T. & T. Clark, 1988.

————. "Women in the Pre-Pauline and Pauline Churches." *USQR* 33 (1978) 153–166.

Schweizer, Eduard. *The Good News According to Luke.* Atlanta: John Knox, 1984.

Scott, Bernard Brandon. *Hear Then the Parable.* Minneapolis: Fortress Press, 1991.

Scott, Martin. *Sophia and the Johannine Jesus.* JSNTSup 71. Sheffield: JSOT, 1992.

Seim, Turid Karlsen. *The Double Message: Patterns of Gender in Luke-Acts.* Nashville: Abingdon, 1994.

Selvidge, Marla J. *Daughters of Jerusalem.* Scottsdale, Penn.: Herald Press, 1987.

————. "Mark 5:25-34 and Leviticus 14:19-20: A Reaction to Restrictive Purity Regulations." *JBL* 103 (1984) 619–623.

Sered, Susan Starr. *Women as Ritual Experts: The Religious Lives of Elderly Jewish Women in Jerusalem.* New York: Oxford University Press, 1992.

Sheeley, Steven M. *Narrative Asides in Luke-Acts.* JSNTSup 72. Sheffield: JSOT, 1992.

Sim, D. C. "The Women Followers of Jesus: The Implications of Luke 8:1-3." *HeyJ* 30 (1989) 51–62.

Smith, D. E. "Table Fellowship as a Literary Motif in the Gospel of Luke." *JBL* 106 (1987) 613–638.

Snell, P. "The Women From Galilee." *Sisters Today* 60 (1989) 483–485.

Soards, M. L. "The Historical and Cultural Setting of Luke-Acts." *New Views on Luke and Acts,* edited by Earl Richard. 33–47. Collegeville, Minn.: The Liturgical Press, 1990.

_____. "Traditions, Composition, and Theology in Jesus' Speech to the 'Daughters of Jerusalem' (Luke 23:26-32)." *Bib* 68 (1987) 221–244.

Spencer, A. B. "Mary's Influence on Jesus' Message." *Daughters of Sarah* 14 (1988) 28–29.

Spicq, C. "La Parabole de la Veuve Obstinée et du Juge Inerte, aux Décisions Impromptues (Luc 18:1-8)." *RB* 68 (1961) 68–90.

Stagg, Evelyn, and Frank Stagg. *Woman in the World of Jesus.* Philadelphia: Westminster, 1978.

Stählin, Gustav. "Das Bild der Witwe." *Jahrbuch für Antike und Christentum* 17 (1974) 5–20.

Stock, A. *The Method and Message of Mark.* Wilmington: Glazier, 1989.

Strack, H., and P. Billerbeck. *Kommentar zum Neuen Testament.* 6 vols. Munich: Beck, 1922–1961.

Sugirtharajah, R. S. "The Widow's Mites Revalued." *ExpTim* 103 (1991) 42–43.

Sweetland, D. "The Good Samaritan and Martha and Mary." *TBT* 21 (1983) 325–329.

_____. "Following Jesus: Discipleship in Luke-Acts." *New Views on Luke and Acts,* edited by Earl Richard. 109–123. Collegeville, Minn.: The Liturgical Press, 1990.

_____. *Our Journey with Jesus: Discipleship According to Luke-Acts.* Good News Studies 23. Collegeville, Minn.: The Liturgical Press, 1990.

Swidler, L. *Biblical Affirmations of Women.* Philadelphia: Westminster, 1979.

_____. "Jesus Was a Feminist." *The Catholic World* 212 (1971) 177–183.

_____. *Women in Judaism.* Metuchen: Scarecrow, 1976.

Talbert, Charles H. "Discipleship in Luke-Acts." *Discipleship in the New Testament,* edited by Fernando F. Segovia. 62–75. Philadelphia: Fortress Press, 1985.

_____. *Literary Patterns, Theological Themes and the Genre of Luke-Acts.* SBLMS 20. Missoula: Scholars Press, 1974.

_____. "Luke 1:26-31." *Int* 39 (1985) 288–290.

_____. *Luke-Acts: New Perspectives from the Society of Biblical Literature Seminar.* New York: Crossroad, 1984.

_____. *Reading Luke: A Literary and Theological Commentary on the Third Gospel.* New York: Crossroad, 1982.

Tannehill, Robert C. *The Narrative Unity of Luke-Acts: A Literary Interpretation.* 2 vols. Foundations and Facets: New Testament. Philadelphia: Fortress Press, 1986, 1990.

————. "Should We Love Simon the Pharisee? Hermeneutical Reflections on the Pharisees in Luke." *CurTM* 21 (1994) 424–433.

Taussig, H. "The Sexual Politics of Luke's Mary and Martha Account: An Evaluation of the Historicity of Luke 10:38-42." *Forum* 7 (1991) 317–319.

Theissen, Gerd. *The Miracle Stories of the Early Christian Tradition.* Philadelphia: Fortress Press, 1983.

Thibeaux, Evelyn. " 'Known to be a Sinner': The Narrative Rhetoric of Luke 7:36-50." *BTB* 23 (1993) 151–160.

Thompson, C. "Hairstyles, Head-coverings, and St. Paul." *BA* 51 (1988) 99–115.

Thrall, M. E. *Greek Particles in the New Testament.* NTTS 3. Leiden: Brill, 1962.

Thurston, Bonnie Bowman. *The Widows: A Women's Ministry in the Early Church.* Minneapolis: Fortress Press, 1989.

Torjesen, Karen J. "In Praise of Noble Women: Gender and Honor in Ascetic Texts." *Semeia* 57 (1992) 41–64.

Trible, Phyllis. "Bringing Miriam Out of the Shadows." *BibRev* 5 (1989) 14–25, 34.

————. "God the Father." *TToday* 37 (1980) 116–118.

————. *Texts of Terror.* Philadelphia: Fortress Press, 1984.

Turner, M. B. "Jesus and the Spirit in Lucan Perspective." *TynB* 32 (1981) 3–42.

Tyson, J. B. "The Birth Narratives and the Beginning of Luke's Gospel." *Semeia* 52 (1990) 103–120.

Van Cangh, J.-M. "La femme dans l'Évangile de Luc. Comparaison des passages narratifs propres à Luc avec la situation de la femme dans le judaïsme." *RTL* 24 (1993) 297–324.

Via, E. Jane. "Women in the Gospel of Luke." *Women in the World's Religions, Past and Present,* edited by Ursula King. God in the Contemporary Discussion Series. 38–55. New York: Paragon, 1987.

————. "Women, the Discipleship of Service, and the Early Christian Ritual Meal in the Gospel of Luke." *SLJT* 29 (1985) 37–60.

von Kellenbach, Katharina. *Anti-Judaism in Feminist Religious Writings.* AAR Cultural Criticism Series 1. Atlanta: Scholars Press, 1994.

Wahlberg, Rachel Conrad. *Jesus According to a Woman*. New York: Paulist, 1976.

Wainwright, Elaine. "In Search of the Lost Coin: Toward A Feminist Biblical Hermeneutic." *Pacifica* 2 (1989) 135–150.

————. *Towards a Feminist Critical Reading of the Gospel According to Matthew*. Berlin/New York: de Gruyter, 1991.

Walker, W. O. "1 Corinthians and Paul's Views Regarding Women." *JBL* 94 (1975) 94–110.

Wall, R. W. "Martha and Mary (Luke 10:38-42) in the Context of a Christian Deuteronomy." *JSNT* 35 (1989) 19–35.

Waller, Elizabeth. "The Parable of the Leaven: A Sectarian Teaching and the Inclusion of Women." *USQR* 35 (1979–80) 99–109.

Wilcox, Max. "Luke 2,36-38 'Anna bat Phanuel, of the tribe of Asher, a Prophetess. . . .'" BETL 2. 1571–1579. Leuven: University Press, 1992.

Wilkinson, J. "The Case of the Bent Woman in Luke 13:10-17." *EvQ* 49 (1977) 195–205.

Wire, Antoinette Clark. *The Corinthian Women Prophets: A Reconstruction Through Paul's Rhetoric*. Minneapolis: Fortress Press, 1990.

Witherington, Ben. "On the Road With Mary Magdalen, Joanna, Susanna, and Other Disciples—Luke 8:1-3." *ZNW* 70 (1979) 243–248.

————. *Women and the Genesis of Christianity*. New York: Cambridge University Press, 1990. Pp. 65–68.

————. *Women in the Earliest Churches*. New York: Crossroad, 1988.

————. *Women in the Ministry of Jesus: A Study of Jesus' Attitudes to Women and their Roles as Reflected in His Earthly Life*. SNTSMS 51. Cambridge: Cambridge University Press, 1984.

Wood, H. G. "The Use of *agapaō* in Luke 7:42, 47." *ExpTim* 66 (1954) 319.

Wright, A. G. "The Widow's Mites: Praise or Lament?—A Matter of Context." *CBQ* 44 (1982) 256–265.

Index of Scripture Quotations

Index of Authors

CPSIA information can be obtained
at www.ICGtesting.com
Printed in the USA
FSHW020648020221
78068FS